MORE PRAISE FOR
BUT WHICH MUTUAL FUNDS?

"Expert advice written for ordinary folk. . .Step-by-step instructions on many topics; straightforward explanations; numerous selections of funds worth more study."
HANK EZELL
Sunday Atlanta Journal-Constitution

"As a writer of a mutual funds column for *Kiplinger's Personal Finance* magazine, author Steven Goldberg is deluged with letters and e-mails with one question: With the thousands of funds for sale, which one is right for me? In response, he has written this book. It covers 12 groups of funds suited to people with specific needs, from parents saving for college for their children to retirees living on their income. The book is packed with useful information."
Knight-Ridder News Service

"Kiplinger and Steve Goldberg have done it again with their honest, direct and engaging style. They've taken what is often considered a complex subject and , without subtracting any vital points, have made it easy to understand. Newcomers to mutual funds will find this a pleasure to read and a financial lifesaver. Finance professionals will find it a refreshing glance at investing through the eyes of the investor."
MARK MOBIUS
Templeton Funds

"Solid advice from a financial writer who knows how to extract pearls of wisdom from the ocean of financial information available today."
SHELDON JACOBS
Editor and Publisher
The No Load Fund Investor

"Instead of searching for the next 'hot fund,' you're better off studying Steve's highly readable book. He provides the frame-

work for meeting your long-term investment objectives, while avoiding the pitfalls inherent in today's market environment."
ERIC KOBREN
President and Executive Editor
Fidelity & FundsNet Insight

"Stop, take a deep breath, and read this book. It asks the right questions to help you get to know yourself first—your goals, tolerance for risk, and time frame—and then guides you through a process to build a portfolio that meets your needs. Goldberg, associate editor of *Kiplinger's Personal Finance* magazine, suggests many funds by name and includes practical information for getting started."
Fidelity Focus

"While this is a down-and-dirty practical guide with charts and worksheets on how much to save and profiles of individual funds, there's also plenty of stock-market history to help neophyte investors to make sober decisions in bull or bear markets."
Publishers Weekly

"Goldberg compares most of the competition to cookbooks that describe how to build portfolios, pick funds, evaluate turnover, calculate standard deviation and alpha, beta and other technical measures. 'But most people don't want a recipe book; they just want to eat,' he said."
Milwaukee Journal-Sentinel

KIPLINGER'S

But Which Mutual Funds?

But *Which* Mutual Funds?

How to Pick
The Right Ones
to Achieve
Your Financial Dreams

BY STEVEN T. GOLDBERG

Kiplinger Books, Washington, D.C.

Published by
The Kiplinger Washington Editors, Inc.
1729 H Street, N.W.
Washington, D.C. 20006

Library of Congress Cataloging-in-Publication Data

Goldberg, Steven T., 1949–
     But which mutual funds? : how to pick the right
ones to achieve your financial dreams / Steven T.
Goldberg.
          p. cm.
     Includes index.
     ISBN 0–938721–79–8 (paperback : alk. paper)
     1. Mutual funds.   I. Title.
HG4530.G65 2000
332.63'27—dc21   00–063403

This publication is intended to provide guidance in regard to the subject matter covered. It is sold with the understanding that the author and publisher are not herein engaged in rendering legal, accounting, tax or other professional services. If such services are required, professional assistance should be sought.

9 8 7 6 5 4 3 2 1

First edition, paperback. Printed in the United States of America.

Kiplinger publishes books and videos on a wide variety of personal-finance and business-management subjects. Check our Web site (www.kiplinger.com) for a complete list of titles, additional information and excerpts. Or write:
          Cindy Greene
          Kiplinger Books & Tapes
          1729 H Street, N.W.
          Washington, DC 20006
          email: cgreene@kiplinger.com
To order, call 800-280-7165; for information about volume discounts, call 202-887-6431.

Book designed by Mary Pat Doherty

ACKNOWLEDGMENTS

SOMETIMES I HAVE GLANCED OVER THE ACKNOWLEDGments at the start of a nonfiction book and thought derisively, "Sure, I just bet all those people helped with that book." I never realized how much an author must rely on others' expertise.

I wish to thank colleagues at Kiplinger Books and coworkers at *Kiplinger's Personal Finance* magazine. This book would not have been possible without Pat Mertz Esswein's always-supportive editing, and Fred W. Frailey's editing and advice. Manuel Schiffres carefully read over the manuscript for errors. Robert Frick read an early draft and offered numerous helpful suggestions. Rosemary Beales Neff smoothed rough spots with her copy editing of the book, while Christine Pulfrey and Brian Knestout painstakingly checked facts. The magazine's art department lent their design expertise. David Harrison guided the book from inception. I also want to thank Theodore J. Miller, Kevin McCormally, Janet Bodnar and Kristin W. Davis. All of them made invaluable contributions.

Karen Kratzer assisted with retirement and tax matters, as well as the tables. Steve Norwitz and Judy Ward at T. Rowe Price produced tables and answered endless questions.

Finally, I wish to thank Laura Nelson Baernstein, Ellen Dye, Pearletha Hugee and Ron Kimball for being there when it counted.

Table of Contents

Chapter 6: Investing for College   77

Investing for college isn't as hard as many people fear • How much to save • Fund portfolios for college and for other goals (except retirement) that are more than ten years away

Chapter 7: Investing for the Short Term   89

Fund portfolios for goals (except retirement): Six to ten years away • Four to six years away • Two to four years • Less than two years

Chapter 8: How and Where to Buy Funds   95

Should you use an online broker? • Step by step through fund application forms • How to transfer an IRA or other retirement account • Looking up fund data

Chapter 9: Paying Uncle Sam   109

Keep careful records or use these shortcuts • Let your funds or online broker do the hard work • If you're selling shares of a fund, sell all of them • Don't write checks on bond funds • Don't buy a fund just before a dividend distribution

Chapter 10: 13 Investment Pitfalls   121

Timing the market is usually a mistake • Be wary of "hot funds" • Sell funds that underperform for several years • Ignore the stock market's short-term moves • You only need a handful of funds • Stay away from "bear-market" funds

Chapter 11: Want Someone to Do It for You?   135

Do it yourself in about the same time for less money • Help getting started • Leads from friends and relatives, and other ways to find skilled financial advisers • What to ask a prospective adviser • Assistance from fund companies: good, free advice from some of them

PART THREE: How to Pick Good Stock Funds   **149**

Chapter 12: A Look at the Long Term   151

Why it makes so much sense to invest as much of your long-term money in the stock market as your time horizon and tolerance for risk will allow • Accounting for inflation • Performance snapshots: stocks versus bonds versus cash, 1926–1999. What they mean if you're investing for periods of one year, five years, or ten years or more • Average after-inflation returns of stocks since 1802 are strikingly similar to those since 1926 • Two bad bear markets municipal bond and money-market funds • Individual bonds instead of bond funds?

After a few years of investing, Paul and Nancy DiBenedetto look back on what they've learned, offer advice to new investors and discuss their plans for the future.

Introduction

EAR INVESTOR,
This book is for you. As an associate editor of *Kiplinger's Personal Finance* magazine, I receive queries every day about mutual funds from readers, friends, relatives and even coworkers. While they use different words, many of these people essentially ask the same thing: "With thousands of funds for sale, which ones are right for me?" The question usually comes from people who know little about funds or who are overwhelmed by the flood tide of fund information available, or both. I've dubbed this condition "Financial Decision Making Paralysis." If you suffer from it, this book supplies the cure.

If I'm getting hundreds of letters and e-mails like this every year from people confused about funds, there must be hundreds of thousands, if not millions of other people with the same question. These people know investing is important, but they aren't sure how to go about it. They've turned to mutual funds partly because they've heard or believe correctly that funds are the simplest—and often the best—way to invest.

From that seed, the first edition of this book, which was published in hardback in late 1998, began to germinate. While dozens of mutual fund books are for sale, none of them answer the question that bedevils so many investors and prospective investors: "But *which* mutual funds?" The first edition sought to fill that void. It offered investors solid portfolios of funds suited to their individual needs. That it was so well received by experts and ordinary readers alike shows how eager people are for the information it provides.

Since each investor's situation is different, no one fund or group of funds is appropriate for everyone. Instead, this book provides 12 solid groups of funds that are suited to your specific needs—whether you are a parent saving for college for your young children, a middle-aged person saving for retirement, a retiree living off your income or a couple saving for a down payment on your first home.

But Which Mutual Funds? offers good funds and more. It uses simple language and a straightforward approach so you can determine how much you need to invest each month to accomplish your life's financial goals—whether they are far in the future or just around the corner. After you take a short, self-scoring test that measures your tolerance for stock-market declines, you'll know how much of your money should be invested in stock funds, bond funds and money-market funds—the most important decision any investor makes. Finally, you'll find specific groups of funds that can fulfill your goals.

The book also gives you the nuts and bolts of how and where to buy funds, covers the details of mutual fund taxes (and offers some shortcuts), and tells you how to avoid common investment pitfalls. Most important: All this information is contained in the first 147 pages of the book. If you're a beginning investor, you need only read these pages to assemble a top-notch financial plan.

And who better to edit and publish such a book than Kiplinger's, which has such a widespread reputation as a reliable, canny and objective source of information about funds? For 50-plus years the most trusted name in individual investing, the magazine has more than one million subscribers because of its down-to-earth guidance and lack of fluff.

The Second Time Around

THIS IS THE SECOND EDITION OF *BUT WHICH MUTUAL FUNDS?*, and the first time it's being published in paperback. I've updated it throughout to reflect the changes in the investment climate, in the tax laws and in the best funds available to investors. To save you time, I've shortened the book and further simplified the language wherever possible. I've changed a number of the funds recommended in Chapter 17—largely because better funds have come along, but also, alas, because a few of the funds I picked for the first edition turned out to be clunkers.

Lots has changed in the investing world since the first edition of this book was published. "Because there is so much competition," I wrote then, "you can reach many discount brokers in the evenings and on weekends." How quaint that sounds now, when many investors have become accustomed to buying and selling funds and stocks online around the clock, and when a cornucopia of information (and misinformation) is instantly available on the Internet. A new edition of the book was needed, if only to explain how you can use the time-saving tools of the Internet—without becoming overwhelmed by the vast quantities of financial data in cyberspace.

The Internet sparked a boom in stock trading and an unprecedented surged in technology stocks. Many beginners may wonder whether funds make sense anymore. Surprisingly, while financial information travels at warp speed nowadays, investing hasn't fundamentally changed, and mutual funds are as worthwhile as ever.

To show that investing in mutual funds isn't nearly as hard as it's made out to be, I decided when I wrote the first edition, to work with a couple, Paul and Nancy DiBenedetto, who knew nothing about mutual funds. You'll follow their progress throughout the book. I've left intact almost all of what they said from the first edition, because the questions they raised are the ones that beginning investors most often have. You'll follow their steps forward throughout this book, and a brief Afterword updates their progress.

If You Want to Take It a Step Further

INVESTMENT NEOPHYTES MAY CHOOSE TO INVEST IN ONE OF THE 12 fund portfolios that I've provided in the book. That's certainly the easiest course, and you won't go wrong with them. But there's nothing magic about these fund portfolios. None of them contain your only choices—nor will they necessarily be the top performers. Each portfolio is a solid group of funds designed to work together—delivering healthy returns, while limiting overall fluctuations in your overall investments.

Let me make a confession. I like mutual funds. They are,

in addition to my work, a hobby. I enjoy learning about obscure funds, and about arcane terms of art such as Sharpe ratios, alpha and r-squared. That's why I work at Kiplinger's.

If you want to understand more about mutual funds, Parts Three and Four are for you. They will show you how to pick winning funds yourself and how to combine them into well-diversified portfolios. They will also provide insight into how I selected the fund portfolios recommended in the earlier chapters.

Just as some folks take pleasure in tinkering with cars, or in lawn care or in home improvements—rather than treating them merely as chores that have to be done as quickly and painlessly as possible—other people enjoy tracking mutual funds, or feel they haven't done a thorough job until they understand the "whys" of their investment choices. And just as people who cut their own grass tend to have greener lawns, so mutual fund do-it-yourselfers often end up earning slightly higher returns on their investments.

Understanding more about how funds work is likely to make you a better investor if only because you're more apt to stick with an investment plan when you fully understand it. If you already know a fair amount about funds, these sections of the book can help you where you're weak. Even fund aficionados will find things they didn't know.

But Parts Three and Four are strictly optional. This book was written primarily with the beginning investor in mind—the investor who wants to put together a good investment plan as quickly and painlessly as possible, and then get on to other things.

Whatever path you choose, I wish you many happy returns.

STEVEN T. GOLDBERG

KIPLINGER'S

But Which Mutual Funds?

PART ONE

The First
(and Most Important)
Steps

This section explains why investing in mutual funds is such a good way to achieve your financial dreams. You'll establish your investment goals and learn your tolerance for risk—that is, prolonged market declines. Finally, you'll determine what percentage of your money to put into stock funds, bond funds and money-market funds—the most important decision any investor makes. You'll also meet Paul and Nancy DiBenedetto, neophyte investors who are learning alongside you.

Getting Started

How this book will help you with mutual funds

P AUL AND NANCY DIBENEDETTO ARE INTELLIGENT, well-educated people. But when it comes to investing, they're all thumbs. They've never taken the time to learn about it. "We're illiterate in this area," Paul says ruefully. "We know we need to do something, but we never seem to get around to it." Adds Nancy, "What's held us back is the time I've spent at work, and with our 2½-year old son, Paul Jr. But we know we need to start saving for his college."

The trim, athletic couple are like millions of Americans who know they need to learn something about investing but have yet to start—or, if they have started, lack an overall investment plan. With the government and employers picking up an ever-smaller proportion of the retirement tab, the DiBenedettos know they need to become proficient investors. They've skimmed financial articles in the newspaper and even picked up a magazine or two. But the sheer number of investment choices overwhelms them.

If you see a little bit of yourself in Nancy and Paul DiBenedetto, you're reading the right book. It will take you, quickly and easily, through the process of determining:
- **your financial goals,**
- **how much you need to invest** to meet them, and
- **how to invest in top-performing mutual funds** that work together so that you can attain those goals.

If you don't want to learn all the ins and outs of mutual fund investing, but simply want to assemble a good mix of funds, all you need to read are the first 147 pages of the book. You can read the rest of the book when and if you are ready to learn the fine points of investing. If you're a more experienced investor, however, you'll find plenty in this book to improve your investing skills, particularly in Parts Three and Four. Don't be fooled by the easy-to-understand language. I'll discuss the topics that top financial advisers address. The only difference is that I'll leave out useless jargon so that any investor—beginner or veteran—can use

Funds bring the skills of first-rate money managers to any investor who can come up with the $2,000 or so it takes to open a fund account.

advanced concepts to increase his or her wealth. Like so many other subjects, mutual funds have a language all their own. While some of the arcane language is necessary, much of it seems designed mainly to make the simple appear complex. One of the more vexing things about mutual funds—and investing in general—is that disagreements crop up over what the terminology means. It's enough to make you want to stick your money under the mattress and forget about it. But, rest easy. You can skip most of the jargon and still become a first-class investor.

In the course of reading this book, you'll meet the DiBenedettos several times. I enlisted them because many of the questions they have are likely to be ones that other beginning investors have, too. Paul, who was 39 when this book was written, teaches third grade; Nancy, 31, is a hospital recreation therapist. They live in Fairfax, Va.

What Are Mutual Funds?

THE DIBENEDETTOS ARE REFRESHINGLY CANDID ABOUT THEIR lack of knowledge about investing and mutual funds. "What is a mutual fund?" is Nancy's first question. "Aren't there other ways to invest?" Sure. Plenty of people invest in real estate or individual stocks and bonds. But these take much more time to master, and they usually won't yield better results than funds will. Mutual funds remain the best investment choice for those who want to spend as little time as possible monitoring their investments. They're also often the best investment medium for stock-market aficionados because they give you access to top investment managers.

To answer Nancy's first question: Funds simply pool money from investors like you to buy stocks and bonds (and sometimes other investments). The investors own the fund and share in its profits (or losses) and the expenses of running it. Funds employ highly paid professional managers who decide what stocks and

How Funds Pay You

FUNDS EARN YOU money in the four ways listed below:

Dividends

The stocks or bonds a fund owns pay dividends or interest. The fund distributes this money to you as dividends. You pay taxes on that income at your ordinary income-tax rate.

Increase in net asset value

The stocks or bonds a fund buys increase in value, and the fund's manager holds on to them. When this happens, the fund's *net asset value* (the price at which you can sell a share of the fund) increases. You don't pay any taxes on your gains in this instance until you sell the fund.

Distribution of capital gains

A fund manager buys stocks or bonds and sells them at a higher price. The fund distributes your share of the gains to you at least annually as capital gains. Under the tax code:

Short-term capital gains (gains made on stocks or bonds the fund held one year or less) are taxed at your ordinary income-tax rate.

Long-term capital gains (gains made on stocks or bonds the fund held for more than 12 months) are almost always taxed at a 20% rate. The exception: If you are in the 15% tax bracket, long-term capital gains are taxed at only 10%.

When you sell fund shares

What if you buy a fund for a low price and sell it for a higher price? You pay taxes in exactly the same way as in the example immediately above. For instance, if you held the shares 12 months or less, your gain would be taxed as ordinary income, while if you held shares of the fund more than 12 months, your gain is taxed at a 20% rate.

---

bonds to buy and sell. The funds' boards of directors are charged with looking out for shareholders' interests. The shareholders elect the directors. Sometimes directors seem to worry more about increasing the profits of the company that sponsors the fund than they do about maximizing shareholders' gains. However, scandals involving mutual funds have been rare.

THE PLUSES OF FUNDS

What's so great about mutual funds? Funds bring the skills of first-rate money managers to any investor who can come up with the $2,000 or so it takes to open a fund account. Most of these managers were formerly available only to the wealthy. Moreover, funds provide one of the lowest-cost ways of investing. Odds are, you'll pay much less in fees to a well-run mutual fund than you would to a broker to pick stocks for you. And it's a lot easier to select good funds than it is to find a good broker, because funds have public track records that anyone can examine. Another advantage: Funds offer instant diversification among a variety of stocks or bonds—almost all funds contain at least 20 securities, and most contain 50 or more. That's enough to keep your nest egg from being wiped out if one company's stock thuds to earth. And, if you're dissatisfied with a fund or if you need your money, you can simply pick up the phone and have your money transferred to another fund—or mailed to you. These pluses explain why Americans have invested more than $7 trillion in funds—more than the total in the nation's savings and loans.

Americans have invested more than $7 trillion in funds—more than the total in savings and loans.

LOADS AND NO-LOADS

Here's a rule of thumb you can *forget* when it comes to mutual funds: *You get what you pay for.* What you pay to buy a fund is called a "load." A load is a sales commission paid to someone who helps you pick a fund. Load stock funds typically charge 5% of what you invest in the fund. So if you're investing $1,000, you'll pay $50 to the salesperson and only $950 will go to work for you. Here's the key thing about loads: Whether a fund is a load fund or a no-load fund has everything to do with how it is sold and nothing to do with how it performs. Study after study has shown that sales charges don't make funds perform better. On average, funds that levy sales charges underperform funds without them—by approximately the amount of the sales charge.

So What If the Sky Is Falling?

HERE ARE SOME of the things you can stop worrying about if you invest in funds: the direction of the economy, the rise or fall of interest rates, the rate of inflation, and the daily ebb and flow of the stock and bond markets. Just tune out this "noise" from the daily news, and leave the driving to the professionals who manage your funds. After all, when you buy shares in mutual funds, you're hiring other people to do the worrying for you.

Make them earn their money.

That's not to say you should overlook changes in your personal situation or your funds' performance. But you don't need to worry over the news from Wall Street. You can also ignore anything you hear about more esoteric investments, such as options, index futures, commodities, and the like. Never heard of any of these? Good, you don't ever need to learn about them.

Sound Familiar?

HERE ARE SOME common reasons that people delay investing:
- "I don't have enough money."
- "I don't have enough time to learn about funds."
- "I want to stick to something safe, like a bank certificate of deposit."
- "It's hard to choose among all the different funds."
- "I'm afraid. I don't want to make mistakes and lose my money."
- "I just never seem to get around to it."

No-load funds usually sell directly to investors. Investors call toll-free numbers or visit Web sites to get applications, and send them back with their initial investment. No-load funds aren't free, of course. All funds charge annual expenses—say, 1.5% of the money invested in the fund, or $15 of every $1,000 that you invest in it. I'll discuss the advantages of lower-expense funds later on.

Drawbacks? The biggest one, ironically, is that there are so many funds— close to 13,000 mutual funds now.

Load funds are sold through brokers, financial planners, insurance agents and banks. They come in an extraordinary variety. Some charge sales commissions when you buy shares of a fund. Some charge commissions when you sell your shares. Others assess commissions *every year* you own the fund. And still others impose combinations of these different sales charges. Since you're reading this book and learning to invest on your own, you'll never want to buy a load fund— unless there is a truly exceptional fund for which there is no comparable no-load fund. Besides saving you money up front, sticking with no-loads will also make life simpler—you can automatically eliminate about half of all funds from consideration.

THE DOWNSIDE

The biggest drawback of funds, ironically, is that there are so many—close to 13,000 mutual funds now—more than four times the number of stocks listed on the New York Stock Exchange. No wonder the DiBenedettos don't know where to start. "If there are so many of them, how do we choose?" Nancy asks. "There are so many commercials for mutual funds, they just confuse me."

The number of choices is paralyzing to the DiBenedettos—and to many other investors. One article talks about how great one fund is, and the next article criticizes the first and recommends a second. It's not that there's not enough information on funds; it's that there's too much, and most of it fails to address the question the DiBenedettos—and you—need answered: "Which mutual funds are right for me?"

The Advantage of Starting Early

THE TABLE ON THESE pages illustrates the power of compounding. When you earn money from investments, you can reinvest it. What you earn in subsequent years on that reinvested money is compounded wealth. For instance, suppose you invest $100 in stocks annually. The first year you earn 11%—the long-term average for stocks. You then have $111. The next year you earn 11% again. At the end of the second year, you have $223.21, rather than $222 ($111 plus $111), because your money has compounded in value. Over just a few

Account Value of IRA Investor Who:

| | STARTS EARLY | | STARTS LATE | |
AGE	AMOUNT INVESTED	END OF YEAR BALANCE	AMOUNT INVESTED	END OF YEAR BALANCE
30	$2,000	$2,220		
31	2,000	4,684		
32	2,000	7,419		
33	2,000	10,456		
34	2,000	13,826		
35	2,000	17,567		
36	2,000	21,719		
37	2,000	26,328		
38	2,000	31,444		
39	2,000	37,123		
40		41,206	$2,000	$2,220
41		45,739	2,000	4,684
42		50,770	2,000	7,419
43		56,355	2,000	10,456
44		62,554	2,000	13,826
45		69,435	2,000	17,567
46		77,073	2,000	21,719
47		85,551	2,000	26,328

Why You Should Start Now

ANY PEOPLE HAVE ANOTHER REASON THEY DON'T START investing: Something always crops up to spend money on. No matter how much you earn, it still can be hard to get ahead of the monthly bills and focus on your long-term goals. The best way to save for the future is to "pay yourself first"—that is, decide how much you will save each month, and

years, compounding doesn't do much to add to your returns. But over the long haul, it makes an enormous difference.

The table shows how two investors will do—one who starts early and has plenty of time for his or her investment money to compound, and one who starts late.

As you can see, investing just $2,000 annually from age 30 to age 39 will leave you in a better position at age 65 than investing $2,000 from age 40 to age 25. The investor who begins early invests just $20,000 altogether, while the late-comer invests a total of $52,000.

AGE	STARTS EARLY		STARTS LATE	
	AMOUNT INVESTED	END OF YEAR BALANCE	AMOUNT INVESTED	END OF YEAR BALANCE
48		$ 94,962	$2,000	$ 31,444
49		105,407	2,000	37,123
50		117,002	2,000	43,426
51		129,872	2,000	50,423
52		144,158	2,000	58,190
53		160,016	2,000	66,811
54		177,618	2,000	76,380
55		197,156	2,000	87,002
56		218,843	2,000	98,792
57		242,915	2,000	111,879
58		269,636	2,000	126,406
59		299,296	2,000	142,530
60		332,219	2,000	160,429
61		368,763	2,000	180,296
62		409,327	2,000	202,348
63		454,352	2,000	226,827
64		504,331	2,000	253,998
65		559,808	2,000	284,157

SOURCE: T. ROWE PRICE ASSOCIATES INC.

then invest that money *before* you pay your other bills. The DiBenedettos already do this. In the last year or two, as they have finished paying off student loans and watched their salaries rise to a combined total of $80,000, they've saved more. When they stopped making the $347 monthly payment on Paul's car, they began stashing that money in a credit union savings account. A little later, when they paid off Nancy's car, they began putting that $237 monthly into the credit union. Now, they need to set their goals for the future and begin investing to meet them.

Like the DiBenedettos, you may have put off getting start-

What You Need to Save Per Month

HERE'S HOW TO FIGURE how much you need to save each month to accumulate $10,000 by your dead-line for any goal. Say that you have 15 years to retirement. In the table below, find where 11% (the average

	RATE OF RETURN				
YEARS	3%	4%	5%	6%	7%
1	$820	$815	$811	$807	$802
2	404	400	395	391	387
3	265	261	257	253	249
4	196	192	188	184	180
5	154	150	146	143	139
6	127	123	119	115	112
7	107	103	99	96	92
8	92	88	85	81	78
9	81	77	73	70	66
10	71	68	64	61	57
11	64	60	57	53	50
12	58	54	51	47	44
13	52	49	45	42	39
14	48	44	41	38	35
15	44	41	37	34	31
16	41	37	34	31	28
17	38	34	31	28	25
18	35	32	29	26	23
19	33	29	26	24	21
20	30	27	24	22	19
21	29	25	22	20	17

ed in investing. But if you finish just the first two parts of this book, your reasons for procrastinating will evaporate. Here's the most important reason to get started now: The sooner you begin investing, the less money you'll need to invest to reach your goals, and the more money you can spend on things you want now. How can that be? Through the financial miracle known as compounding. Compounding means simply that you will earn money on the money you have already earned. The impact of this simple phenomenon is enormous. Consider this example of two investors:

historical rate of return for stocks) and 15 years intersect. The result, $22, is about how much you need to save monthly. To save $100,000 would require ten times as much—in this case, $220.

RATE OF RETURN				
8%	9%	10%	11%	12%
$798	$794	$789	$785	$781
383	379	375	371	367
245	241	237	234	230
176	173	169	165	162
135	132	128	125	121
108	104	101	98	95
89	85	82	79	76
74	71	68	65	62
63	60	57	54	51
54	51	48	46	43
47	44	42	39	36
41	39	36	33	31
36	34	31	29	27
32	30	27	25	23
29	26	24	22	20
26	23	21	19	17
23	21	19	17	15
21	19	17	15	13
19	17	15	13	11
17	15	13	12	10
15	13	12	10	8

One is a youngster who puts $2,000 into an individual retirement account (IRA) every year from age 16 to age 25, and then stops investing. Assuming stocks continue to earn 11% annually, as they have on average since 1926, he or she will have more than $2 million ($2,173,890, to be exact) by age 65. This example needn't be hypothetical. If your children earn money from baby-sitting or lawn mowing, you can open an IRA for them. And the money that goes into their IRAs doesn't have to be the same money they earn, so, if you like, you can invest an equivalent amount in IRAs for them and let them spend what they earn. (I'll discuss IRAs in more detail in Chapter 5.)

The other investor starts putting $2,000 annually into an IRA at age 40. He or she can contribute $2,000 *every year* through age 65 and still wind up with just $284,157—a pittance com-

The Magic of Compounding

COMPOUNDING IS A powerful force in building wealth. This table shows you, rounded to the nearest $10, how fast $100 a month will grow at different rates of return, assuming you invest at the beginning of each month. If you save more than $100 a month, say, $500 a month, sim-

How $100 a Month Will Grow

| YEAR | RATE OF RETURN | | | | |
	3%	4%	5%	6%	7%
1	$1,220	$1,230	$1,230	$1,240	$1,250
2	2,480	2,500	2,530	2,560	2,580
3	3,770	3,830	3,890	3,950	4,020
4	5,110	5,210	5,320	5,440	5,550
5	6,480	6,650	6,830	7,010	7,200
6	7,900	8,150	8,410	8,680	8,970
7	9,360	9,710	10,080	10,460	10,860
8	10,860	11,330	11,820	12,340	12,890
9	12,410	13,020	13,660	14,350	15,070
10	14,010	14,770	15,590	16,470	17,410
15	22,750	24,690	26,840	29,230	31,880
20	32,910	36,800	41,280	46,440	52,400
25	44,710	51,580	59,800	69,650	81,480
30	58,420	69,640	83,570	100,950	122,710

pared with what the early investor has. To put it another way, the late-starter invests two-and-a-half times what the early investor does, yet ends up with slightly more than one-eighth of what the early investor has when they both reach age 65. On each dollar invested, the early investor earns 20 times what the late-starter does! (For a similar example, see pages 8–9.)

So even if you have just a little money—say, $50 a month—*now* is the time to start investing. As you begin investing and watch your nest egg grow, you'll find it will become easier to save even more for your goals.

COMPOUNDING FOR YOURSELF

Want to compute the effects of compounding for yourself? It's simple, thanks to the "rule of 72." To find out how many years it

ply divide the amount you invest monthly by $100—and multiply it by the appropriate number in the table to get your total return. In this instance, $500 divided by $100 equals 5. Assuming you're earning an 8% return and are investing for eight years, you'll have 5 times $13,480 or $67,400 at the end of those years.

RATE OF RETURN				
8%	9%	10%	11%	12%
$1,250	$1,260	$1,270	$1,270	$1,280
2,610	2,640	2,670	2,700	2,720
4,080	4,150	4,210	4,280	4,350
5,670	5,800	5,920	6,050	6,180
7,400	7,600	7,810	8,020	8,250
9,260	9,570	9,890	10,230	10,580
11,290	11,730	12,200	12,680	13,200
13,480	14,090	14,740	15,430	16,150
15,850	16,670	17,550	18,490	19,480
18,420	19,500	20,660	21,900	23,230
34,830	38,120	41,790	45,890	50,460
59,290	67,290	76,570	87,360	99,910
95,740	112,950	133,790	159,060	189,760
150,030	184,450	227,930	283,020	352,990

will take your money to double, just take the annual percentage gain you expect to make on an investment, expressed as a whole number, and divide the result into 72. For instance, if you're making 7% annually on an investment, it will take you 10.3 years to double your money (72 ÷ 7 = 10.3). If you're earning 9% annually, it will take you eight years to double your money (72 ÷ 9 = 8).

An easy way to think about stock-market investments, which historically have earned more than 10% annually, is that they should, *on average*, double every seven years. Contrast this with bank rates of return, say 5%, which would take almost 15 years to double. Of course, a bank account is federally insured, and you can't *lose* money. Another way to look at how fast your money grows is to consult the table on pages 10–11, which shows how much you need to save each month at varying rates of return to earn $10,000 by the time you need it. A second table, on pages 12–13, shows how a $100 monthly investment will grow at different rates of return.

Building a Solid Portfolio

THERE ARE A FEW GREAT FUNDS, A FEW AWFUL FUNDS AND A LOT of so-so funds. This book will steer you away from the mediocre funds and toward the best ones, and it will teach you how to size up funds yourself.

But this book goes beyond simply picking funds. Imagine bringing your car into your mechanic and, before telling him what's wrong, asking him, "Mike, what's the best part you have?

Well, whatever it is, install it on my car." No one would say that. You might end up with a new transmission when you need brake shoes. But many beginning investors want to know: "What's the best mutual fund?" The answer, just as with your car, depends on what you need it for.

Even then, it usually isn't enough to pick one good fund, or even two or three good funds. Much of the advice about mutual funds badly fails investors because it doesn't get around to what's most important: how to put together a good portfolio of funds that suits their needs. *A portfolio is a group of funds that work in sync in all kinds of investing environments.* In any particular investment climate, one fund may do badly while another soars. The important thing is that your overall holdings don't get decimated. Only by building a portfolio of funds will you reduce risk and increase your odds of earning big profits. In the first half of this book, you'll learn how to use top-flight funds to build bulletproof portfolios for different goals. The DiBenedettos, for instance, will need very different funds to invest for retirement some 30 years from now than they will to buy their dream house in a year or so.

Before choosing funds, you need to establish your goals. After determining how long you plan let your money grow and how much tolerance you have for gut-wrenching market declines, you can construct an entire investment plan of first-class mutual funds from the portfolios in Part Two. If you plan to use one of these ready-made sets of funds, you can skip Parts Three and Four, which I've written for investors who want to go beyond the basics. (Later, if you want to learn more, you can return to those chapters.) Or, you can complete the entire book and be prepared to confidently and knowledgeably assemble your own portfolio.

Introducing Your Guide

ONE LAST QUESTION: WHO AM I TO TELL YOU HOW TO invest? I'm in my early fifties and have been a journalist, as well as an investor, for more than 25 years. What's more important, I have the resources of *Kiplinger's Personal Finance* magazine, my employer for the past seven years, behind me. *Kiplinger's* invented the personal-finance genre; it's been publishing the magazine since 1947. It has become the most trusted name in investing because it provides straightforward, no-nonsense information, and because it doesn't pretend to predict the unpredictable—such as what will happen to the stock market over the short term.

Key Points

- *Even if you know little about funds, this book will help you become a savvy investor.*
- *Mutual funds are the easiest and best way for most people to reach their investment goals.*
- *The time to start investing is now.*
- *Picking good funds is just part of the job; assembling them into good portfolios is equally important.*

What Are Your Goals?

And a look at the returns of different investments

L IKE MOST PEOPLE, PAUL AND NANCY DIBENEDETTO have more than one dream. Sitting in a crowded living room amid Christmas decorations one winter afternoon, Nancy says: "This is absolutely the last year I'm living in this two-bedroom condo." Paul, keeping a watchful eye on Paul Jr., nods in agreement. The couple have taped a photograph of their dream house from a magazine to the refrigerator. It's a four-bedroom colonial—Paul and Nancy plan to have another child or two—with a wraparound porch, garage, finished basement, family room, living room and "big, big kitchen, because everybody lives in their kitchen," Paul says.

"What other goals do you have?" I ask Paul. "To be a millionaire by age 40," he says, laughing. "No, a billionaire. To win the Publishers' Clearinghouse sweepstakes." Assuming they don't win, the DiBenedettos want to save enough to pay for roughly half, if not all, of their children's college educations. Although the DiBenedettos both went to state universities, they'd like to give their children the option of attending more expensive private colleges.

Then there's retirement. That's three decades away, and Paul and Nancy haven't given it a great deal of thought. But they are both outdoors people. They like skiing, tennis, hiking and camping. Nancy also Rollerblades, while Paul runs regularly. Besides continuing those activities, the DiBenedettos would like to travel in retirement—visit Europe, the Bahamas, perhaps Hawaii. "Taking vacations in retirement would be more important than having an 18-room house," says Paul. While a new house is important, they've decided that saving for college is their number-one priority right now, and retirement is number two.

You'll need to conduct a similar personal inventory before you can create an investment plan. Why? Because it won't do you much good to set a dollar goal—that is, an amount to shoot for—without first knowing what you want to spend it on. And knowing what you're aiming for and how long you have to achieve the goal largely determines the risks you should take and, therefore, the investments you should make. This is a crucial step, and one you need to give yourself plenty of time to ponder. Like the DiBenedettos, do you value traveling in retirement more than having a big house? Or do you want both? No matter; everyone will have different goals. Many people will find that their goals change over time. That's fine. Most times, you can easily readjust your savings and investment plans to meet your changing goals.

How Much?

NEXT, YOU NEED TO HAVE SOME IDEA OF HOW MUCH TO SAVE for each goal. While I'll provide worksheets on how much to put aside for retirement and college in Part Two, it's important to make a start now, with whatever amount you can afford.

The DiBenedettos already have amassed $14,000 in savings accounts, as well as $20,000 in Nancy's pension plan at work (which is funded entirely by her employer) and $27,000 in Paul's 403(b) tax-deferred retirement plan at school. The couple is saving more than $1,450 monthly, including $400 in Paul's 403(b). (While 403(b) plans are similar to the 401(k) plans in private industry, they are offered to employees of educational and other nonprofit organizations.)

Nancy and Paul have set the following goals for putting their money to work:

$269 a month toward Paul Jr.'s college

The average private college currently costs about $21,500 a year (that figure includes tuition, room and board, books and personal expenses) and costs are expected to rise about 5% annually. (Actually, since the first edition was published, current costs have risen to about $23,700 per year.) That means four years of college for Paul Jr. starting in 2013 is likely to cost a staggering $192,659. Figure half that money will come from financial aid, loans, and jobs Paul Jr. works to help foot the bills. To amass the other roughly $96,000, the DiBenedettos need to save roughly $3,200 per year—assuming they earn 9.5% annually on their money before taxes. (I'll get into more detail in Chapter 6 on how much you need to save for college.)

$700 a month toward their retirement

The DiBenedettos are currently saving that much in their retirement accounts because they figure their investments will have to

---

Your Goals

USE THIS WORKSHEET to map out your goals. Don't worry if you have to guess now at how much you need to save for some of these goals. You'll be able to refine your projections in Part Two. Use only those rows that apply to you.

Like the DiBenedettos, you need to assign priorities to these goals. These will vary from family to family, but most people will make their first priority an emergency fund—unless they already have one. Retirement and college are typically the next most important goals, respectively, and savings for other goals usually comes after that.

You may wish to consult the table "What You Need to Save Per Month" (pages 10–11) to figure your monthly investment amount for each goal.

Goal	TARGET AMOUNT	MONTHLY INVESTMENT	YEARS UNTIL YOU'LL SPEND THE MONEY
Emergency fund	$_____	$_____	_____
Retirement	_____	_____	_____
College fund #1	_____	_____	_____
College fund #2	_____	_____	_____
College fund #3	_____	_____	_____
Home down payment	_____	_____	_____
Vacation home	_____	_____	_____
Other	_____	_____	_____
TOTAL	$_____	$_____	_____

First Things First

BEFORE YOU START investing, make sure you've paid off all your credit cards and any other high-interest debt. (This does not include your home mortgage, because the interest is tax-deductible and probably a relatively low 6.5% to 9%. Over the long haul, you can expect to earn a higher return in the stock market, 10% or more, than you would by paying down your mortgage.) The dollar amount you pay in interest on credit cards may not seem like much each month, but paying off a debt bearing a 12% interest rate gives you an instant 12% return on your investment. So your wisest first investment is to pay off your balance every month. Also, make sure you have enough life and disability insurance, and three to six months' living expenses in a bank account, money-market fund or short-term bond fund. If you don't mind assuming more risk, you can live without that emergency fund, so long as you have an adequate home-equity line of credit.

generate $409,398 more than they have now to afford the things they want in retirement. This number doesn't include their pensions and estimated Social Security payments. To see how they reached this number, see the discussion and worksheet in Chapter 5. That chapter will help you figure out how to invest for retirement, including how much you'll need to save each month.

$500 a month toward their new house

They are planning to spend roughly $225,000 on a new house, and expect merely to break even on the sale of their condo. For a 10% down payment, they'll need $22,500. So far, they've saved $14,000, so they are on their way. (I'll talk more about saving for a house and other shorter-term goals in Chapter 7.)

Altogether, the DiBenedettos are saving $1,469 per month—$17,628 per year. If their savings program seems too ambitious for you, start with whatever you feel you can put aside.

How to Invest Your Money

NOW THAT YOU HAVE ESTABLISHED YOUR GOALS AND PRIORITIES, and set at least tentative dollar amounts that you need to put aside to meet them, it's time to begin looking at investing. With so many choices available among mutual funds, it's easy to miss the forest for the trees. Studies have shown that the most important decision you make is not which funds you invest in, but rather how you allocate your money—

Stocks, Bonds and Cash

SOME MUTUAL FUNDS OWN stocks and others own bonds; some own both.

A stock is an ownership share in a company. If the company's profits increase, over the long haul the value of your stock in the enterprise should also increase. If the company's profits fail to grow, however, your stock will likely decline in value.

A bond is an IOU. You, the bondholder, lend money to a corporation, a state, local or foreign government, or a government agency. You get your money paid back with interest—but you don't share in the growth of the company (or government, for that matter).

Cash is shorthand for very-short-term bonds, which usually pay your money back within six months or a year. Cash can be:

- money in a bank checking or savings account
- a short-term Treasury bill
- a *bank* money-market fund or a *mutual fund* money-market fund. A mutual fund money-market is much like a bank money-market, but bank money-markets are insured against loss by the federal government while mutual fund money-markets are not. Mutual fund money-market funds usually pay slightly higher interest rates than bank money-market funds.
- a short-term bank certificate of deposit
- an ultra-short-term bond fund.

Most investors put their cash into mutual fund money-market funds because they're simple, convenient and pay relatively high interest rates.

what percentage of your total investment goes into stocks, bonds and "cash." This section explains the relative risks and rewards of each type of investment (see the accompanying box for definitions). You'll get different rates of return from each type, and the higher the return, the greater the risk. Stocks usually return more than bonds, which usually return more than cash. By the same token, stocks are more volatile than bonds, which are more volatile than cash. By "more volatile," I mean that their returns fluctuate more from month to month and year to year, so that there is more risk of short-term loss.

Because deciding how to allocate your money is so crucial to your investing success, a lot of high-priced professionals—such as financial planners, stock brokers and the like—try to make people believe that determining the amount you should invest in each asset type is as hard as calculus. They use complex computer programs, long workbooks and interviews to generate

Bear and Bull Markets

A bear market is generally defined as a drop in stock prices of 20% from their previous high.

A correction refers to a decline of more than 10%, but less than 20%.

A new bull market is declared when the market recovers from a bear market and goes on to make new highs.

Understanding Bond Basics

BONDS CAN BE a little tricky to follow. To keep them straight, remember: When the interest rates on bonds fall, bond prices rise, and, conversely, when interest rates rise, prices fall. If a newscast says that bonds rose yesterday, that means their prices increased, while their yields (or interest rates) decreased.

That may seem counterintuitive. After all, when yields rise, you might expect your bonds to become more desirable and the price to rise, as well. Why are bonds so seemingly perverse?

Imagine you buy a bond that yields 6%. A year later other, similar bonds are being sold that yield 7%. Your bond is worth less than the 7% bonds for the simple reason that it doesn't pay as much interest, so it declines in value.

precise percentages for investors in particular circumstances. But the truth is that deciding how much to put into these different types of investments really isn't a science and needn't be all that difficult. It requires knowing only two things:

Your time horizon. How long will it be before you'll spend your money? The longer you have, the higher percentage you should put into high-returning stocks.

Your tolerance for risk. How much of a drop in the value of your portfolio can you handle without selling your investments in a panic or staying up at night worrying? The more you can tolerate the ups and downs of the stock market, the more you should invest in stocks.

By the time you've finished the next chapter, you'll know what percentages of your money to invest in stocks, bonds and cash. But first, here's an idea of what you can expect to earn from different types of investments. On average, since 1926 stocks have returned 11.3% annually, while five-year government bonds have returned 5.2% annually and cash has returned 3.8% annually. Meanwhile, inflation has averaged 3.1%. Over rolling five-year periods, stocks have outperformed bonds and cash more than three-quarters of the time. (By rolling five-year periods, I mean the first period started in January 1926 and ended in December 1930, the next period started in 1927 and ended in 1931, and so on.) And, after inflation, stocks actually have been *less likely* to lose money over rolling five-year periods than either bonds or cash.

But before you put all your money into stocks, bear in mind the following:

Stocks are far more volatile than bonds, meaning their returns bounce around more month to month and year to year. Cash is the least volatile investment.

In their worst year (1931), stocks plunged 43%, while five-year government bonds lost only 5.1% in their poorest year (1994), and the worst return on cash was a loss of 0.02% (in 1938).

Stocks have fallen by at least 20% about once every five years since 1926. On average, it has taken two years and five months for an investor who put money into stocks just before a 20% or greater decline to break even. After the 1929 crash (when stocks lost 86% of their value over three years), though, it took until 1944 to break even. And after the brutal 1973–74 bear market (when stocks fell 48%), it took more than three years to break even—and ten years to break even after inflation.

For a more detailed look at what you can expect to earn from stocks, bonds and cash, turn to Chapter 12, "A Look at the Long Term." But you get the idea: Stocks are great long-term investments; bonds and cash make more sense for shorter time periods. Think of stocks as a roller coaster, bonds as the bumper cars and cash as a carousel.

Key Points

- *Start by determining your investment goals.*
- *Pay off credit cards and other high-interest debt before investing.*
- *The most important investment decision you make is what percentage of your money to put into stocks, bonds and cash.*
- *While stocks offer a bumpy ride, they are the best long-term investment.*

Do You Like Fast Cars?

How much of your money to put into stock funds, bond funds and money-market funds

I T'S EASY TO LOOK AT THE NUMBERS AND CONCLUDE THAT you should put all your long-term money into stock funds. And many investors ought to do just that. But before you join them, you'll want to determine your tolerance for risk—that is, your ability to mentally withstand market crashes as well as long, dispiriting bear markets. After all, humans aren't machines; we aren't entirely rational. "What do you mean I'm not rational?" huffs Paul DiBenedetto. "Once you give me the information, I can make a rational decision." I asked Paul and his wife, Nancy, to take a simple, two-question test. Before you learn how they did, take it yourself:

1. Winning money
Which would you prefer?
a. You win $80,000.
b. You have an 80% chance of winning $100,000—and a 20% chance of winning nothing.

2. Losing money
Which would you prefer?
a. You lose $80,000.
b. You have an 80% chance of losing $100,000 (or a 20% chance of losing nothing).

Paul and Nancy answered "A" to question one and "B" to question two. Harold Evensky, a financial adviser in Coral Gables, Fla., who devised the test, says almost everyone chooses the same answers, even though there is no statistical advantage to A or B in either question. With A, you have a 100% chance of making or losing $80,000, and with B, a 20% chance of making or losing nothing. But you and I are not like *Star Trek*'s Mr. Spock, who makes decisions solely based on logic.

Paul now agrees that his decision making isn't totally rational. Offered a sure $80,000, most of us are unwilling to gamble it all for a chance to win just $20,000 more. Yet faced with the possibility of losing $80,000, most of us will grasp at even a fairly small chance of getting off scot-free. Evensky and psychologists say the test shows that most of us are less risk-averse than we are loss-averse; in other words, it's a lot harder for us to stomach losing money than to give up the opportunity to make more money. The test helps explain why some investors tend to sell stock funds too soon after they rise in price, and to hold on to stock funds that have fallen in price almost indefinitely, hoping to break even. More to the point, it demonstrates that there's an emotional side to investing. Ignoring its existence can be perilous to your financial health. (Those who want to learn more about how to sidestep emotional and other obstacles to successful investing should be sure to read Chapter 10, "13 Investment Pitfalls and How to Avoid Them.")

Declines That Make Your Teeth Grind

WATCHING YOUR MUTUAL FUNDS FALL IN VALUE IS NO FUN. But investing in stock funds guarantees that you'll watch them fall a good deal of the time. When your net worth starts shrinking, keeping your wits about you isn't easy. Evensky says: "We know that most of our clients have real time horizons of 20-plus years, but their psychological time horizons are often about ten seconds." Evensky isn't trying to insult investors' intelligence; he's speaking from long experience. He's learned that investors sometimes sell in panic when the stock market either plunges sharply or falls gradually in a protracted bear market. Many people find it tougher to hang on than they thought they would until they have experienced such a market. It's all too easy to throw in the towel and sell—often at just the wrong time. Peter Lynch, onetime manager of Fidelity Magellan fund, puts it this way: "The key organ for investing isn't the brain—it's the stomach." When stocks start to decline, will you have the stomach for market volatility and the broad-based pessimism that comes with it?

People who lived through the 1973–74 bear market, when the average stock lost nearly half its value and many stocks lost much more, know how hard it can be to hold tight. "It was two years of nothing but down," recalls Gerald Perritt, a Chicago money manager. "Things looked like a good deal, and you'd buy them, and they'd go down more." Inflation ate up much of what stocks were able to eke out in the remainder of the decade. In 1979, *Business Week* ran a famous cover story: "The Death of Equities." The story argued that the stock markets were never again going to offer the kind of appreciation they had in the past.

When stocks have fallen for a long period, it feels to many investors as though they will keep going down. Not long after the *Business Week* prediction, however, came the start of the biggest and longest bull market of the last century. The question for you to ponder is this: Would you be able to hold on to your stock-fund investments after the market had pummeled them for losses of 20%, 30% or even more? An old Wall Street adage notes: "The stock market is an expensive place to find out who you are."

Keep in mind, too, that the news media relish stories about stock-market declines. The inevitable crashes and bear markets in stocks often become front-page stories and breathless reports on television and radio—while a steadily rising stock market typically garners scant media attention. When the market goes down, reporters flock to interview those experts who have been bearish for years. These "perma-bears" often issue dire warnings: They may predict that stocks are doomed to have a bad couple of years—or a bad decade—and confide that "the smart money" has already been buying raw land, or German bonds, or gold, or some other investment that is equally inappropriate for most people.

Dollar-Cost Averaging

PROCRASTINATION IS THE ENEMY OF INVESTORS. YOU KNOW all the excuses: Either you don't have enough money, or you'd rather spend it on something else, or the market seems too risky just now, or you're already so far behind that starting would be pointless. "There's always a real solid reason to delay investing," says Jon Bull, a money manager with Starbuck, Tisdale and Associates in Santa Barbara, Cal. "It's natural to weigh both sides and put off plunging into uncertainty, which is what investing in the stock market is all about."

You'll feel better about making a move if instead of plunging you take a tentative step or two. The easiest way to accomplish this is *dollar-cost averaging*. That's just a fancy way of saying: invest the same amount regularly, whether the market goes up, down or sideways. Say you inherit a large sum that you don't plan to draw on for decades, and you put a small portion of it in stock funds each month until you've invested the full amount. Alas, big lump sums don't come around often for most of us. An equally valid application of dollar-cost averaging is to invest a modest but fixed amount from your salary in shares of stock funds every month. Funds typically allow a monthly (or quarterly) minimum of $50 or $100.

An almost mindlessly simple strategy, dollar-cost averaging nevertheless forces you to buy more shares when stocks are cheap and fewer shares when stocks are dear. Suppose your fund is selling for $10 a share. A $1,000 investment that month buys 100 shares. Then say the fund doubles in value to $20 a share the following month. Your $1,000 investment that month buys just 50 shares. So, you end up buying half as many shares when the price is higher. Dollar-cost averaging is a no-sweat way to implement the first half of Wall Street's most hallowed—but fiendishly hard to implement—strategy: "Buy low, sell high." It forces you to keep investing even when stocks are falling.

If you want to adorn this simple strategy, make your usual periodic purchase when the market rises and then step up your buying when the market declines—talk about going against the grain! You can set your own rules here. You could decide, for example, to invest $200 a month in stock funds, but to increase your monthly investment to $300 any time the market declines by at least 1% from the previous month.

Academic research has shown dollar-cost averaging isn't *statistically* the best way to invest a lump sum. Because the stock market has gone up more often then it has gone down, these studies show, you're usually better off just dumping the entire amount into stocks as soon as you can. The trouble with this approach is that it ignores human nature: It's extremely difficult to take a big sum and invest it all at once in stocks, particularly if prices are in decline. More often than not, people who plan to invest their money all at once end up delaying for months or even years while they wait in vain for the market to get cheaper or to seem "safer." Even worse, investors may invest a lump sum at a peak and then sell in a panic when the market dives. The beauty of dollar-cost averaging is that it is emotionally easy for people to implement.

Removing Temptation

INVESTING IS "LIKE ANYTHING ELSE THAT'S GOOD FOR YOU, LIKE your exercise program or your diet," says Kenneth Doyle, a financial psychologist who teaches at the University of Minnesota. "You're not going to convince me it's fun to sit down and think about my financial future." So have someone else swallow the medicine for you. If you're eligible for a 401(k) or 403(b) tax-deferred retirement plan at work, your employer will automatically deduct your contribution from your salary. And lots of mutual funds are more than willing to debit your checking account automatically for that $50 you've decided to invest each month. The DiBenedettos do all their investing this way. "After a while, you don't even think about it," says Paul. Funneling money into the market this way—in bull markets or bear— imposes a discipline that most investors need.

By automating your investing, you don't have to reconsider the decision to invest every month, and you thereby dodge a lot of emotional turmoil. Furthermore, you remove the temptation to spend earmarked money for a night on the town, new clothes, toys for your children—or any of a dozen other things that crop up every month and can sabotage the best-laid investment plan. You never see the money, so you never spend it, and you'll be pleased by how fast it grows.

Taking the Test

MOST PEOPLE SHOULDN'T PUT ALL THEIR INVESTMENT money in stocks—whether via dollar-cost averaging or all at once. The key to deciding what percentage of

How Much Risk Should You Take?

WHAT FOLLOWS IS A SIMPLE test designed to gauge your tolerance for risk. You can use it to determine how much of your money you should invest in stock funds versus less risky funds. There are no correct answers. As you become a more experienced and knowledgeable investor, you may want to retake the test. You'll probably then find you can comfortably invest a larger percentage of your assets in stocks. The test also accounts for the fact that people without a decent financial cushion may want to invest a little less aggressively. That's because a crash or a prolonged bear market could conceivably wipe out most of your savings if you don't have the wherewithal (either in savings or income) to avoid selling at the bottom.

1) The Dow Jones industrial average plunged 500 points today. Your reaction is to:
 a) consider selling some stock funds.
 b) be concerned, but sit tight because you figure the market is likely to go up over long time periods.
 c) consider investing more, because stock funds are cheaper now.

2) The news media is filled with stories quoting experts who predict stocks will lose money in the coming decade. Many suggest investing in real estate. You would:
 a) consider selling some stocks funds and buying real estate.
 b) be concerned, but stick to your long-term goals.
 c) dismiss the articles as a sign of unwarranted pessimism over stocks.

3) Which of the following statements best describes you:
 a) I often change my mind and have trouble sticking to a plan.
 b) I can stay with a strategy as long as it seems to be doing well.
 c) Once I make up my mind to do something, I tend to follow through with it regardless of the obstacles.

4) If you won $100,000 in the lottery, you would:
 a) pay off or pay down your mortgage.

your money to allocate to stocks is your time horizon, which we discussed briefly in the previous chapter, plus your tolerance for losses. The quiz, above, will help you judge your ability to withstand losses.

You probably already have a good idea of whether you're a conservative investor, who can barely stand to watch a fund you own decline by one penny per share, or whether you're a more aggressive investor, more willing to take risks. But what about your partner? Nancy DiBenedetto says she's pretty conservative. "One of the reasons we haven't invested is that we know that we're safe in the bank, and in investing there's always risk." But she adds, "It depends on how long I want my money to be tied up. If I'm interested in investing a certain amount of money for ten years, then I would be willing to take more risk." Paul is by nature more comfortable with risk. Before marrying, he and a

b) invest it safely in bank certificates of deposit and bond funds.

c) invest much of it in stock funds.

5) How much experience do you have investing in stocks or stock funds?

a) none.

b) a little.

c) a comfortable amount.

6) How would you react if your stock funds fell by 30% in one year?

a) I would sell some or all of them.

b) I would stop investing more money until the market came back.

c) I would invest more in stock funds.

7) At work, I am:

a) not covered by a retirement plan.

b) covered by a plan but tend to change jobs frequently.

c) covered by a generous plan and expect to stay with the company until I retire.

8) Equity in my home and probable inheritances will provide:

a) very little help financing retirement.

b) a decent amount, but not enough to fund a large part of my retirement.

c) a substantial amount of money.

9) If you can't sleep at night, you:

a) lie in bed worrying.

b) have both pleasant and unpleasant thoughts.

c) look forward to the next day.

10) If you had a financial reversal, you would:

a) take a long time to recover and be more cautious.

b) take some time to recover, but mostly get over it.

c) bounce back quickly.

(SOURCES: VALIC, JAMES GOTTFURCHT, OTHERS)

Scoring: For each *a*, give yourself 6 points; for each *b*, 7.5 points; and for each *c*, 10 points. If you score 60 to 70 points, you're a low-risk investor. A score between 71 and 85 points makes you a moderate-risk investor. And if you score 86 or more points, you're an aggressive investor.

buddy in Houston gambled on several "penny stocks"—extremely risky investments that typically lose money. That's just what Paul's stocks did. Nevertheless, he says, "I would be more of the risk taker than Nancy. I'm not really that conservative." It's important in investing to know not only your own risk tolerance but also that of your spouse. After all, when stocks are tumbling, it's best if you're both comfortable with the amount you have going along for the ride.

When Nancy and Paul took the test, she scored an 82 and he scored 94 out of a maximum 100 points. While the couple lacks investing experience, they are plainly pretty gutsy folks. Both of them love downhill skiing, and even Paul Jr., not yet three years old, has skied. Averaging their two scores, as a couple they get 88 points, which makes them aggressive investors. Accordingly, for their son's college money, which they won't need

How Much Money, Where?

AFTER YOU'VE IDENTIFIED your tolerance for risk, above, you can determine what percentage of your money to put into stocks, bonds and cash, based on how long it will be until you need your money.

Following are two tables: one for investing for retirement and the second for investing to meet all *other* goals. Find the column that matches your tolerance for risk (as determined in the preceding quiz) and the row that matches the amount of time you have until you'll start drawing on your money. The point at which they intersect tells you what percentage of your total investment you should put into stock funds. Invest the balance, if any, in bond funds.

Investing for retirement requires that you put a larger proportion of your money into stock funds than does investing for other goals. That's because you won't spend all your retirement money at once as you will for most other goals. (Chapter 5 is devoted to "Investing for Retirement.")

Table A:
How Much of Your Money to Invest in Stock Funds for Retirement

	TOLERANCE FOR RISK		
YEARS UNTIL RETIREMENT	LOW 60–70 POINTS	MODERATE 71–85 POINTS	HIGH 86–100 POINTS
More than 15	100%	100%	100%
10 to 15	70	80	100
6 to 10	60	70	100
0 to 6	40	50	85
Early retirement (65–75)	35	45	60
Late retirement (over 75)	30	40	50

Table B:
How Much to Invest in Stock Funds for All Goals *Except* Retirement

	TOLERANCE FOR RISK		
YEARS TO GOAL	LOW 60–70 POINTS	MODERATE 71–85 POINTS	HIGH 86–100 POINTS
More than 15	80%	100%	100%
10 to 15	60	80	100
6 to 10	55	65	80
4 to 6	30	40	60
2 to 4	10	25	35
0 to 2	0	0	0

for more than 15 years, they could put 100% of the investments into stock funds. But the money for their new house, which they plan to buy in a year or so, belongs in a bank CD or money-market fund.

Not long before taking this simple test, Paul and Nancy felt overwhelmed by the task of trying to invest sensibly. Now, after beginning their investment education, they have made the most important decisions about how they should invest their money. Picking good mutual funds is the next step.

Key Points

- *Don't let your emotions keep you from being a successful investor.*
- *It's hard to stay invested in stocks during bear markets.*
- *The most important investment decision you make is what percentage of your assets to put into stock, bond and money-market funds.*
- *To allocate your money among stocks, bonds and money-markets, all you need to know is your time horizon and your risk tolerance.*
- *Dollar-cost averaging—investing small amounts regularly—is the best way to invest in stock funds.*

Putting Together Your Investment Plan

N ow that you know what percentage of your money to invest in stock funds, bond funds and money-market funds, it's time to assemble a portfolio of funds to meet your needs. While I claim no ability to pick "the best funds," this section of the book offers you solid portfolios of funds that work together in concert—the kind of mix discussed at the end of the book's opening chapter. By the time you finish Part Two, just 147 pages into the book, you'll have all the information you need to successfully manage your fund investments. The remainder of the book is for those who want to understand funds in more depth.

Keeping It _Really_ Simple

Investing with index funds lets you save time, save money and match the market's performance

HILE YOU CAN LEARN A LOT ABOUT MUTUAL funds, you can also put together a solid portfolio of funds without knowing that much about funds. That's why this book is designed so that you don't have to master the art of picking mutual funds unless you want to.

In this chapter, moreover, I'll show you a way to invest that's even simpler than what's presented in the remainder of Part Two. Not only does this method take less time than the traditional way of selecting mutual funds, it requires almost no monitoring once you get it up and running. It employs just three funds: _Vanguard Total Stock Market Index_, _Vanguard Total International Stock Index_ and _Vanguard Total Bond Market Index_.

"Want to keep things _really_ simple?" I asked Nancy DiBenedetto. "That sounds awfully tempting to me," she replies, "but will I have to give up any returns?" Read on and make up your own mind whether you are willing to accept, perhaps, a slightly lower investment return in exchange for the time savings of putting your fund investing on autopilot. (If you're investing for college or retirement, however, even if you do use index funds, be sure to read the following two chapters for other tips on meeting those investment goals.)

Index Funds

THIS METHOD USES INDEX FUNDS, WHICH ARE DESIGNED TO mirror the market indexes, or averages. Indexes are used to take the temperature of the markets. They tell you how the stock or bond market as a whole has performed or how segments of the market have done. They also serve as the benchmarks against which fund performance is measured. So, rather than attempting to "beat the market," as most funds do, index funds aim to match the market's performance. They strive, in a sense, to be merely average.

The best-known index is the Dow Jones industrial average, which measures the performance of 30 of the largest U.S. companies. Even if you know nothing else about investing, you've probably seen news briefs relating the daily performance of the Dow Jones. A broader index, Standard & Poor's 500-stock index, provides a more accurate gauge of the stock market than the Dow, in part because it includes more stocks. The Wilshire 5000 is perhaps the most comprehensive index of the entire U.S. stock market. Specialized indexes include Nasdaq, which is dominated by technology stocks, the Russell 2000, which measures the performance of stocks of small U.S. companies, and the Morgan Stanley Europe Australasia and Far East index, which tells you how major foreign stock markets have done.

Indexes are used to take the temperature of the market and serve as benchmarks for fund performance.

ARE THEY BETTER?

Many academics believe investors are best off in index funds. Why? Because, they say, fund managers can't consistently pick stocks or bonds that will beat their market's index. As a result, most actively managed funds will trail index funds, simply because they charge higher expenses than index funds. Instead of beating your head against the wall trying to choose funds that beat the indexes, these experts argue, you're better off simply investing in index funds.

Burton Malkiel, a Princeton University economics professor, may best make that argument, in his classic book, *A Random Walk Down Wall Street*. The "random walk" theory argues that the market efficiently (or rationally and fairly) prices stocks because it has already factored all the information about each stock into its price, and day-to-day changes are unpredictable. So, a blind-folded monkey throwing darts at the stock listings will be able to select a portfolio that performs as well as those managed by professionals.

While almost all fund managers devote their energies to beating an index (because their bonuses and ultimately their continued employment may depend on their doing so), Malkiel says most are doomed to fail. Better, he says, just to match the index—which index funds do by buying all, or substantially all, the stocks in an index.

Perhaps it's no surprise that Malkiel ended up on the board of directors of the Vanguard family of mutual funds, which have become synonymous with stock-market indexing. In 1976, Vanguard launched the *Vanguard 500 Index* fund, which is designed to mirror Standard & Poor's 500-stock index, an index of stocks of mostly large companies. Indexing has been popular with some pension funds and other institutional investors for decades, but Vanguard was the first to offer these funds to individuals.

> **Instead of trying to choose funds that beat the indexes, these experts argue, you're better off investing in index funds.**

BEATING THE AVERAGES ISN'T EASY

In recent years, Vanguard 500 Index has been difficult to beat, primarily because it invests in larger companies than almost all fund managers buy. For the five years ending May 1, 2000, only 18.9% of actively managed U.S. stock funds were able to best the S&P. It has likewise been difficult to outdo the S&P in other periods when big companies were the market leaders. Even in more normal times, when stocks of small- and medium-size companies outperform or match their big brothers, the S&P tends to beat the average fund. It's no secret why: Fund managers and other money managers, along with individual investors, *are* the stock market. It's unrealistic to expect more than half of them to beat a broadly based market index like the S&P.

Think of it in baseball terms. All baseball players try to get the highest batting percentage they can each season. But no more than half will surpass the median batting percentage for all baseball players. After all, the median *is* the batting percentage that half the players exceed and the other half fall short of. Similarly, Garrison Keillor's Lake Wobegon, where "all the children are above average" can exist only in fantasy. Since the S&P

and other stock indexes are stock-market averages, you can't expect more than about half of all fund managers to beat these indexes.

THE ADVANTAGE OF LOW EXPENSES

Expenses are the other reason more fund managers don't out-perform the averages. The average stock fund charges 1.26% of assets annually in expenses to cover its costs and to earn a prof-it. (In other words, it has an *expense ratio* of 1.26%. That means $1.26 of every $100 invested in the fund goes annually to the fund company.) The S&P 500—and all other stock indexes, for that matter—have no expenses to subtract from their gain. Index funds do have some expenses, but these can be very low. After all, while it takes some computer muscle to track an index, there are no research analysts to hire, no companies to visit, no brokerage research reports to buy. Wisely, when Vanguard set up its Index 500 fund, it chose to assess very low expenses. Here's the bottom line: Vanguard Index 500 charges investors a mere 0.18% of assets annually, or 18 cents for every $100 invested.

Index funds do have some expenses, but these can be very low.

THE S&P 500: A VERY EFFICIENT MARKET

Swarms of analysts follow every hiccup of most of the companies in the S&P 500. When companies announce their earnings every three months, most of them hold conference calls with analysts and money managers. Investors often execute a blizzard of pur-chases or sales *during* these conference calls—propelling a stock up or down in moments. If ever there were a group of stocks that's thoroughly researched, it's those in the S&P 500. To use Malkiel's phrase, it is a very efficient market.

For that reason, any investor—not just those in search of simplicity—could do a lot worse than to buy Vanguard 500 Index or a similar low-cost index fund instead of an actively managed large-company fund. Over the long haul, the S&P 500 has beaten roughly two-thirds of all stock funds (even after subtracting Vanguard's 0.18% in expenses). I think an investor who takes the time to thoroughly research funds, or who uses a good source of information, like this book, may well select large-company funds that will consistently outperform the index. But almost no one is going to beat the index by much over the long term, and the average fund will likely continue to trail the index.

Expand Your Universe

I T'S NOT A GOOD IDEA, HOWEVER, TO PUT ALL YOUR MONEY IN AN S&P index fund. Here's one reason: Since 1926, stocks of small companies have outperformed large-company stocks by more than one percentage point annually, according to Ibbotson Associates, a Chicago-based research firm. Small companies, on the other hand, are inherently riskier than bigger companies; many have only a couple of products and lack the money to stay afloat through hard times. You wouldn't want to invest _all_ your money in small stocks, but most investors should put 20% or so of their stock money into small stock funds.

But the S&P contains hardly any small stocks, and furthermore it's composed almost exclusively of domestic stocks. Nearly half the world's stock-market value is outside the U.S. Why limit your choices? "We like to think of investing abroad as doubling our shopping aisles," says John Spears, co-manager of Tweedy Browne Global Value. Moreover, the ebbs and flows of the U.S. stock market often occur at different times than the ebbs and flows of overseas stock markets. By owning both foreign and domestic stocks, you'll smooth out some of the ups and downs in your overall investment portfolio. Investors with time horizons of ten years or longer could put 20% to 25% of their stock money abroad, depending upon their risk tolerance and preference.

Most actively managed small-company and almost half of international funds have beaten their indexes.

Most actively managed small-company funds have beaten the Russell 2000, a small-company index. Similarly, almost half of actively managed foreign funds have beaten the Morgan Stanley Europe, Australasia and Far East index of foreign stocks. Why? These stocks are not as carefully researched as are large U.S. stocks, so it's easier for savvy managers to uncover bargains.

As a consequence, you can probably do better with actively managed funds in these markets. But if you use actively managed funds, you need to spend some time monitoring them. They can't simply be bought and forgotten. Index funds can. Moreover, if your choice is between hiring an investment adviser to build a portfolio for you and buying index funds, you'll almost certainly do far better with index funds because your costs will be much lower. (Many investment advisers themselves employ index funds.) With index funds, there is only one thing you need to keep in mind:

Mind Your Costs

T HERE'S NO EXCUSE FOR PAYING A SALES FEE (OFTEN CALLED A load) for an index fund. A commission is payment for an investment professional's advice, and no broker or financial planner can provide much useful advice or insight about future performance of an index fund. (More on load and no-load funds can be found in Chapter 1.)

When comparing funds that follow the same or similar indexes, go with the one that has the lowest expense ratio. The average index fund that follows the S&P 500 has an annual expense ratio of 0.45%—less than one-third that of the typical U.S. stock fund. This difference, when compounded over time,

For index funds unlikely to raise their costs, you might do best with Vanguard and USAA, which have long been low-cost providers.

gives index funds a sizable performance advantage over managed funds. Say $1,000 investments made by two funds earn 10% annually for ten years. The fund charging annual expenses of 0.45% will end up being worth $2,490, while the one charging 1.26% will be worth only $2,267. (You can find the expense ratio in the prospectus or by visiting the fund's Web site or calling its toll-free number.)

Occasionally, companies launch low-cost index funds, or lower the expense ratios on funds they already have, to attract more investor dollars. It's fine to buy one of these, but be sure to keep an eye on it. Some of these funds may later up the ante. When your semiannual reports arrive in the mail, look up the "annual expense ratio." If it has risen, consider swapping into a cheaper index fund. For index funds unlikely to raise their costs, you might do best with Vanguard and USAA, which have long been low-cost providers.

Which Funds to Buy

You can build a fine stock portfolio with just two funds:

Vanguard Total Stock Market Index (800-635-1511; VTSMX; www.vanguard.com) seeks to track the Wilshire 5000 index, a broad U.S. stock-market index. While the fund emphasizes large stocks, it also holds many small stocks among its 1,900 issues. Expenses are 0.2% annually. If your account balance is less than $10,000, you also pay a $10 annual fee.

Vanguard Total International Stock Index (VGTSX) gives you the rest of the world by investing in other Vanguard index funds. Ninety percent of the fund seeks to replicate the Morgan Stanley Europe, Australasia and Pacific index by investing in Vanguard's Europe and Pacific index funds. The final 10% is in Vanguard's emerging-markets index fund, which invests in developing nations in Asia, Latin America, Eastern Europe and Africa. Total expenses of the underlying funds are about 0.34% annually, plus a $10 annual fee for accounts under $10,000.

How Much, Where?

Depending on your investment goal, your score on the risk-tolerance test on pages 30-31 and your time horizon (when you will need your money), you'll put all or part of your money in stock funds and the balance, if any, in more-conservative bond funds. The tables on page 32—one for retirement and one for all other goals—will help you determine what the breakdown of your investment should be.

Investing for Goals Other Than Retirement

For goals more than six years away, about three-quarters of the money you invest in stock funds should go into *Vanguard Total Stock Market Index* and the remainder into *Vanguard Total International Stock Index.* For example, say you're going to invest $200 a month and Table B (on page 32) tells you that you should invest 70% of your money in stock funds, or $140 (.70 x $200). Of that, you would put $105 (.75 x $140) in Vanguard Total Stock Market Index and $35 (.25 x $140) in Vanguard Total International Stock Index. (You may notice that the portfolios in this chapter offer slightly different proportions of funds that invest in stocks of large companies, small companies and foreign companies than do the portfolios for actively managed funds enumerated in the following three chapters. That's largely because of differences in risk among the recommended index funds and actively managed funds. All the portfolios, are designed to help you reach the same goals with roughly the same risk.)

Bond alternatives
If the table says you need to put some of your money in bonds—which are less volatile but also less rewarding than stocks—invest that portion in *Vanguard Total Bond Market Index*, which holds a representative sampling of all types of bonds. (In the example above, you would invest $60 (.30 x $200). Expenses are 0.2% annually plus a $10 annual fee for accounts under $10,000.

If you are in the 28% tax bracket or higher, and are investing outside of a tax-deferred account, use *Vanguard High-Yield Tax-Exempt* instead of the bond index fund. The dividends from this fund are tax-exempt, and taxpayers in the 28% bracket or higher will end up with more money in their pockets with this fund instead of Total Bond Market Index.

With four to six years to go
For goals four to six years in the future, other than retirement, you'll want to limit risk by reducing your holdings in *Vanguard Total International Stock Index* from 25% of your stock funds to about 10%.

With two to four years to go
For goals two to four years in the future, other than retirement, divide your bond money evenly between *Vanguard Total Bond Market Index* and *Vanguard Short-Term Bond Index*. However, if you're investing outside a tax-deferred account and are in the 28% tax bracket or higher, split your money instead between *Vanguard Intermediate-Term Tax-Exempt* and *Vanguard Limited-Term Tax-Exempt*. All your stock money should be placed in *Vanguard Total Stock Market Index*.

With less than two years to go
Invest your money as follows:
Vanguard Short-Term Bond Index (50%), or if you're in the 28% tax bracket or higher, *Vanguard Limited-Term Tax-Exempt*.
Vanguard Prime Money Market (50%), or if you're in the 36% tax bracket or higher, *Vanguard Tax-Exempt Money Market*.

INVESTING FOR RETIREMENT
Portfolio for six or more years from retirement
Allocate your money between stocks and bonds as shown in Table A on page 32. Put 75% of your stock money in *Vanguard Total Stock Market Index* and 25% in *Vanguard Total International Stock Index.* Any bond money should go into *Vanguard Total Bond Market Index,* or if you're in the 28% tax bracket or higher, into *Vanguard High-Yield Tax-Exempt.* (*Note:* never buy a municipal bond fund inside a retirement account, because retirement accounts are already tax-exempt.)

Portfolio for zero to six years from retirement
Depending on your risk tolerance, put between 15% and 60% of your money into bond funds, as Table A advises. If your tax bracket is lower than 28%, use *Vanguard Total Bond Market Index* for your bond money. Otherwise, divide your bond money between *Vanguard High-Yield Tax-Exempt* and *Vanguard Intermediate-Term Tax-Exempt.*

Early retirement (up to age 75)
Invest 40% to 65% of your money in bond funds as indicated in the table. Invest your bond money as in the previous portfolio. Of your stock money, invest 85% in *Vanguard Total Stock Market Index* and 15% in *Vanguard Total International Stock Index.*

Late retirement (over 75)
Put all of your stock money into *Vanguard Total Stock Market Index.* Invest between 30% and 50% of your portfolio in stocks as the table on page 32 advises. Put half your bond money into *Vanguard Short-Term Bond Index,* leaving the remainder in *Vanguard Total Bond Market Index*—unless you are in the 28% tax bracket or higher, in which case you'll want to divide your bond money between *Vanguard Intermediate-Term Tax-Exempt* and *Vanguard Limited-Term Tax-Exempt.*

EASY MAINTENANCE
Once you've invested in your funds, you need only make sure they stay in proper proportions. In other words, if foreign stocks rally for several years, don't let them grow from the recommended 25% to, say, 50% of your portfolio. If your funds get way

out of kilter, simply sell off some of the soaring fund and spread the proceeds among the laggards.

For instance, suppose you start out with $15,000 in Vanguard Total Stock Market Index, and $5,000 in Vanguard Total International Stock Index, giving you 25% in foreign stocks. The U.S. stock market doesn't budge for two years, so your $15,000 remains unchanged in value. But foreign stocks double during those same years, giving you a total of $10,000 in Vanguard Total International Stock Index. Instead of having 25% in foreign stocks, you now have 40% in foreign stocks ($10,000 divided by $25,000 equals 40%). In this instance, if you sell $3,750 of your foreign stocks and move that money into U.S. stocks, you will again have 20% of your money in foreign stocks (25% of $25,000 equals $6,250; $10,000 - $6,250 = $3,750).

Alternatively, instead of selling off part of your foreign stock fund, direct all your new investments to the U.S. stock index fund until your portfolio is rebalanced. This will minimize your taxes.

Another Approach

YOU DON'T HAVE TO USE INDEX FUNDS TO MAKE YOUR MUTUAL fund investing simple. *T. Rowe Price Spectrum* (800-638-5660; www.troweprice.com) funds and *Fidelity Asset Manager* and *Fidelity Asset Manager Aggressive* (800-544-8888; www.fidelity.com) funds offer equally good methods for making things really easy. While the future is impossible to predict, both Fidelity and T. Rowe Price have long histories of providing solid results. (All of these funds are no-load.)

T. Rowe Price Spectrum funds

The Price Spectrum funds are "funds of funds." Funds of funds invest in other funds, and most provide only anemic performance while charging an extra layer of expenses. But Spectrum funds charge nothing except the expenses of the underlying funds, and have produced decent results.

Spectrum Growth invests in eight T. Rowe Price stock funds, including a small-company fund and a foreign fund. At times the fund even puts some assets in a money-market fund.

Spectrum Income invests in five bond funds and often places a little money in a conservative stock fund.

To invest using the Spectrum funds, turn back to the "How Much to Invest in Stocks" tables on page 32. Use Spectrum Growth in place of stocks and Spectrum Income in place of bonds. For example, if you're investing for retirement between six and ten years away, and you're a risk-averse investor (who scored between 60 and 70 points on the risk-tolerance test), you'll want to put 60% of your money in Spectrum Growth and the other 40% in Spectrum Income.

Fidelity Asset Manager funds

Fidelity Asset Manager Aggressive normally keeps about 85% of its assets in stocks, 10% in bonds and 5% in short-term investments. The managers adjust the mix depending on their view of market conditions. Fidelity's stock selection is usually good, and you'll likely do better in this fund over the long haul than you would

Taxable Versus Tax-free Accounts

USING A BOND INDEX fund is all well and good if you're investing your money in a tax-sheltered retirement account, such as an IRA. But what if you're investing your money in an account that's subject to income taxes? In that case, a tax-exempt bond fund—whose dividends are free from federal taxes—is often a better bet than a taxable bond index fund.

That's because most ordinary mutual fund accounts are fully taxable. You'll pay 15% to 39.6% of your taxable bond-fund dividend income to the federal government in taxes.

Bond-fund investors who are in the 28% tax bracket or higher (single investors earning at least $25,751 annually or couples earning at least $43,051 in 2001) will generally do better in tax-exempt bond funds. These funds invest in municipal bonds. Their yields are lower than those of taxable bond funds, but after taxes you'll wind up ahead.

Tax-exempt accounts—such as IRAs, 401(k)s, 403(b)s and variable annuities—are a different story. If you're invested in these, you pay no taxes on earnings until you start to withdraw your money. In the case of Roth IRAs, earnings are generally tax-*free* if withdrawn after age 59½.

Here it's best to use taxable bonds so you can get the higher return within this already tax-sheltered environment. Usually, you'll want to keep stock funds in your retirement accounts whenever you can, because stock funds tend to have higher returns (which would be taxed in a taxable account) than do bonds funds.

One caveat: Tax-exempt money-market funds tend not to give as good an after-tax deal to investors. As a result, unless you're in the 36% bracket or higher, you should probably stick with taxable money-market funds rather than tax-exempt ones.

paying an adviser. It's ideal for long-term investors.

Fidelity Asset Manager normally holds 55% in stocks, 35% in bonds and 10% in short-term investments. It's well suited for investors with four to six years before they'll need their money.

Key Points

- *Index funds are the easiest way to invest, because you don't have to monitor the funds once you've selected them.*
- *Many academics believe low-cost index investing is likely to beat all other methods.*
- *You can put together an index portfolio with as few as two funds, or three if you need to invest in bonds as well as stocks.*
- *Fidelity and T. Rowe Price offer alternatives to index investing that also require little monitoring.*

Investing for (and in) Retirement

How to make sure your money will be ready when you are

T HE SOCIAL SECURITY TRUST FUND WILL BE BANKRUPT in about three decades unless Congress fixes it. Most people aren't saving nearly enough for retirement. And fewer wage earners can expect monthly pension checks from their employers. Such discouraging news may tempt you to forget about retiring altogether and plan to work until you drop. Fight that pessimistic impulse. Yes, you'll need to save a lot more than your parents did to afford a comfortable retirement, but you have more tools than ever before. You just need to learn how to use them—and this chapter will give you that knowledge.

Mutual funds have become *the* way Americans are saving for retirement. A third or more of the assets at many fund companies are invested in retirement accounts. Moreover, the fund industry has made it easy and cheap for investors to set up different types of retirement accounts.

That's not to say you don't have a challenge ahead of you. Retirement is probably the main reason for investing, and it's also the trickiest goal to invest for. Unlike investing for shorter-term goals—such as a new car, a new house or even college for your children (discussed in the following chapters)—it's difficult to get a handle on how much money you'll need to afford a comfortable retirement. To invest for retirement, you need to figure out how much to put aside each year for decades—and how to invest it so that you will achieve the returns you want. Investing for retirement is kind of like launching a rocket; it has to fly straight and true for a long, long time—and you can't afford to undershoot your target by too much. But investing for retirement needn't be hard. We'll take you through the process step by step. And if you've already mapped out a retirement investing plan, this chapter will help you determine whether you're headed in the right direction and assist you in making any necessary midcourse corrections.

In an hour or two, you'll have everything you need to know about investing for retirement.

Once you've read this chapter, completed the worksheet on pages 56–57 (which was prepared with the help of Karen Kratzer, a financial planner at PriceWaterhouseCoopers), and consulted Table A on page 32, you'll know how much you need to save each year for retirement and what percentages of it to invest in stocks and in bonds. You'll find sample mutual fund portfolios appropriate for investors with different amounts of time left until retirement (see pages 67–72). In an hour or two, you'll have everything you need to know about investing for retirement—from soup to nuts. Here are the steps you need to take.

Get Serious

EVEN THOUGH THEY'RE STILL IN THEIR THIRTIES, PAUL AND Nancy DiBenedetto have been saving for retirement for several years. Paul has $27,000 in a 403(b) plan through the school system where he teaches. Nancy has saved up another $20,000 in a retirement plan at the hospital where she works as a recreation therapist. Still, after talking with me over several months, Paul says, "You've opened our eyes about what we really need to do for ourselves." In truth, the couple needed only to invest more aggressively because their investments were too conservative for people their age.

As a rough rule of thumb, you'll be in fine shape for retirement if you:

• **you have a 401(k) or 403(b) tax-deferred retirement plan** at work that lets you put aside at least 10% of your income annually,

• **you contribute the maximum,** and

• **you put it into stock funds** starting in your twenties or early to mid thirties.

Starting in your early forties? You'll likely be all right if you contribute 10% annually to your 401(k) or 403(b) and also make the maximum $2,000 annual contribution to individual retirement accounts (IRAs). Whatever your age, if you're married be sure your spouse makes the same contributions you do, so far as he or she is allowed to. Of course, you're better off if you don't wait until your forties before you start putting money away for retirement. But even starting in your late forties or your fifties, your money will grow surprisingly fast if you invest regularly.

Set Your Goals

ONCE YOU'VE MADE THE DECISION TO INVEST FOR RETIRE-ment, it's time to set your income goal (see page 56; line 1 of the worksheet in today's dollars and line 2 in inflation-adjusted dollars). The traditional guideline is that you'll need 70% to 80% of your preretirement income to live comfortably in retirement. That's a good benchmark for some people, but not for others. I've given you a broader range of 70% to 100%, because some people find they spend as much in retirement as they did when they were working.

If you're relatively close to retirement—say, within five to ten years—you'll have a better idea of what you'll *actually* spend in retirement, so you're best off using that estimate. Use your current income as a starting point, and add to or subtract from it based on these big-ticket items:

Your mortgage. Will you still be making mortgage payments after you retire?

College. Will the brain drain on your finances have ended?

Health insurance. If you retire before medicare kicks in (which is now at age 65, but in the future will likely be later), health insurance could cost $500 a month or more.

Work. Do you plan to work even part-time in retirement?

Taxes. Using government data, Stephen King, a retirement expert with Aon Consulting, found that a couple with one 65-year-old wage earner earning $80,000 annually pays an average of $21,000 in social security and income taxes. After retirement, the same couple pays only about $5,000 in taxes, on average, due to a drop in both income and taxes. While this is just one example, your taxes are likely to drop dramatically in retirement, mostly because your taxable income will decline markedly.

Lifestyle. How expensive a lifestyle do you want in retirement? Many people live parsimoniously in retirement, while others spend as much as or more than they did while working.

Paul and Nancy picked 80% of their pre-retirement income without much hesitation. Despite their relatively young ages, they're pretty clear about their priorities for retirement: to continue enjoying sports and outdoor recreation, to travel, and not to be too concerned about "a big house or a fancy car," as Paul puts it. They are also toying with buying some lake-front property at some point. "I'd love to live on a lake when I retire," Paul says.

Many people find that they spend more than they had anticipated in the early years of retirement.

Unlike the DiBenedettos, you may not be sure how much you want to spend in retirement. If you're like many people—particularly if you're decades from retirement—you may not have any idea how much you plan on spending, other than a vague notion that more will probably be better. As with other questions on the worksheet, if you aren't sure what to answer, make an educated guess. Later, you can always refine your answers and complete it again. Or try doing the worksheet twice—say, figuring 90% of your pre-retirement income the first time and 75% the second time. It's a good idea to make several photocopies of the worksheet beforehand so you can try out different scenarios.

Many people find that they spend more than they had anticipated in the early years of retirement. In the later years, people's spending tends to decline, at least until their health fails and medical bills increase.

Add Up Your Pensions

START WITH SOCIAL SECURITY. YOU CAN APPROXIMATE YOUR social security benefits using the numbers provided with line 3 of the worksheet. For this exercise, I have assumed a retirement age of 65. Beginning with workers born in 1938, however, the retirement age for full benefits will gradually increase, eventually reaching 67 for people born in 1960 and later. Paul and Nancy hope to retire by the time they are 65 but are aware they may have to work longer to get full retirement benefits.

Reform proposals could push normal retirement age to 70.

While social security is not going to be eliminated, some cut-backs are inevitable. The worksheet assumes wage earners who are now around age 55 will get the full benefits at retirement that they are entitled to under current law. For workers around age 45, however, I have assumed a reduction of 15% from current law. And for wage earners around age 35, I have assumed a 30% reduction. These adjustments were made after consulting with numerous social security experts about how much benefits are likely to be reduced.

Direct from Social Security

You can obtain an official social security calculation by calling the Social Security Administration at 800-772-1213 and asking for the "Personal Earnings and Benefit Estimate Statement" (or by visiting www.ssa.gov on the Internet). After you fill out the form and mail it back, the Social Security Administration will tell you what benefits you will have earned if you work until full retirement age (65 to 67, depending on your current age). Be aware that the numbers you get from the Social Security Administration may be higher than what the worksheet shows because the agency doesn't assume any changes in current law. (The Social Security Administration automatically mails annual statements. Be sure to check yours over. If you have worked jobs that you have not received credit for from Social Security, you'll want to have your records corrected.)

> **Remember that if you change jobs you may end up with a lower pension than if you stay put.**

YOUR PENSION

Next, estimate your pension benefits (line 4 on the worksheet). Your employee benefits office can provide this number. Most employers will give you the number in today's dollars. If yours does, be sure to use the appropriate inflation factor (from line 2 on the worksheet) to determine what your pension will likely be when you retire. Remember that if you change jobs you may end up with a lower pension than if you stay put. Also, many employers are skimping on pensions and leaving most of the work of saving for retirement to employees through 401(k) and 403(b) retirement plans.

Add Up the Years

ARE YOU PLANNING TO RETIRE EARLY? IF SO, YOU WILL HAVE to make do with smaller social security checks—or do without them entirely until you reach the age at which you can receive full benefits. The same may go for your pension, depending on your employer. Plus, your savings will have to support you longer if you retire early. In doing the worksheet, you may find you have to readjust your retirement target age.

To figure how long you'll need to support yourself in retirement, you also need to estimate how long you'll live. No one, of course, can predict this with much accuracy. Lynn Hopewell of the Monitor Group, a financial planning firm in Fairfax, Va., says, only half in jest, "The objective of retirement planning is to run out of breath and money at the same time."

"The objective of retirement planning is to run out of breath and money at the same time."

The table associated with line 7 of the worksheet shows how long the average man or woman can expect to live based on his or her current age. Remember that median life expectancy means that half the people live longer. And with advances in medicine, life expectancies will likely be greater by the time you retire. So you may want to plan for an extra five years in retirement beyond what the table suggests. If your health is particularly good and your relatives lived to ripe old ages, you might add even more. Paul and Nancy are both trim, active athletically and in good health. To be on the safe side, they estimate that at least one of them will live to be 95.

Count Your Savings

TOTAL UP WHAT YOU'VE ALREADY SAVED. THAT MEANS EVERY-thing you have in IRAs, 401(k) plans and other tax-deferred retirement accounts, other savings or investments earmarked for retirement, and any inheritances you're confident you'll receive. Be sure to include the *current* value of assets—such as the equity in your home, investment real estate or business—if you plan to sell those assets to help fund your retirement. Revise their value downward a bit if you think they won't appreciate at least 11% annually, which is the rate the worksheet assumes aggressive investors will earn (see line 8). The easiest way to do this is to use the worksheet's conservative invest-ment assumption even if you plan to invest aggressively, that is, assume your total investments will earn 8% rather than 11%. If you already invest conservatively, reduce the *current* value of any low-returning assets by, say, 20% or 25%.

CONSIDER THE LIMITS OF THE EXERCISE

Please don't look on the worksheet as anything more than a good estimate of your retirement savings. An increase—or decrease—of one percentage point in inflation between now and when you retire could alter your bottom line considerably, as could a change of one or two percentage points in your investment return. Look at the DiBenedettos. Assuming they earn 11% annually (as the worksheet projects aggressive investors will) they need save just $3,685 annually to age 65 for a comfortable retirement. However, suppose stocks return only 8% annually (as we assume in the worksheet for conservative investors who own stocks and bonds in their retirement accounts). In that event, the DiBenedettos would need to save $13,778 annually—or almost four times the $3,685. The moral is clear: This worksheet can be a valuable planning tool, but it's

Nancy and Paul's Results

NANCY AND PAUL DIBENEDETTO found filling out the table a simple matter. They want an annual income in today's dollars of 80% of their current income, or $63,200 *(line 1)* and would like to retire in 25 years.

Their desired income, when adjusted for future inflation, will need to be $149,152 *(line 2)*.

Social Security should pay them $40,361 in future dollars *(line 3)* and their pension should pay $43,487 in future dollars *(line 4)*, or a total of $83,848 *(line 5)*.

They'll need another $65,304 in future dollars from their investments *(line 6)*.

Since they are budgeting to live 40 years in retirement, they will need $1,048,128 at retirement from what they invest *(line 7)*.

But their current $47,000 in retirement savings should grow to $638,730 *(line 8)*.

That means they'll need to amass another $409,398 *(line 9)*.

To accomplish that, they need to save $3,685 annually *(line 10)*—or $307 per month. They're already saving $700 a month, or more than twice what they'll need. As I've emphasized, the earlier you start saving, the less you'll need to save later on.

(continued on page 58)

How Much You Need to Save

THIS WORKSHEET will show you how much you need to save each year to retire in style. It assumes that you are saving in tax-deferred accounts, that inflation will average 3.5% annually and that, prior to retirement, conservative investors will earn 8% annually, while aggressive investors will make 11%. During retirement, conservative investors are assumed to earn 7% and aggressive investors, 9%.

1. Annual income in current dollars desired during retirement
Usually you'll need 70% to 100% of your current income. .... $ _____

2. Inflation-adjusted income desired
Multiply line 1 by the factor in the following table that corresponds most closely to the number of years you plan to work until retirement. ....$ _____

Years until retirement	5	10	15	20	25	30	35	40	45
Inflation factor	1.19	1.41	1.68	1.99	2.36	2.81	3.33	3.96	4.70

3. Annual social security benefits
Multiply the appropriate number from this table by the inflation factor from step 2 to get your approximate benefit in future dollars. If your spouse works, figure his or her benefits separately, and add both benefits together. Couples with a nonworking spouse should add the benefits for the nonworking spouse to that of the wage earner. .... $ _____

Current income	$36,000	$48,000	$76,200+
Current age, 55			
Worker benefits	$13,092	$14,556	$16,260
Nonworking spouse	6,444	7,164	8,004
Current age, 45			
Worker benefits	$11,087	$12,475	$14,423
Nonworking spouse	5,447	6,120	7,079
Current age, 35			
Worker benefits	$8,551	$9,635	$11,214
Nonworking spouse	4,108	4,629	5,384

4. Annual employer-paid pension benefits
Ask your employee benefits office for this number. If it isn't adjusted for future inflation, multiply it by the proper factor from step 2. .... $ _____

5. Income from pension and social security
Add lines 3 and 4. .... $ _____

6. Retirement income needed from your investments
Subtract line 5 from line 2. .... $ _____

7. Assets needed to generate required investment income during retirement

Multiply line 6 by the number in the table below that corresponds to how long a retirement you need to finance, based on your age now and your life expectancy. Choose the conservative or aggressive multiplier, depending on how you plan to invest. .... $ _____

How long in retirement?		Life expectancy							
This table offers a clue to how many years you can expect to live in retirement by showing average life expectancies. Subtract your planned retirement age from your life expectancy to estimate the length of your retirement.	AGE NOW	30	35	40	45	50	55	60	65
	MEN	78	78	79	79	79	80	81	82
	WOMEN	84	84	85	85	85	85	86	86

Years in retirement	15	20	25	30	35	40	45
Conservative	11.52	14.21	16.48	18.39	20.00	21.36	22.50
Aggressive	10.04	11.95	13.41	14.53	15.39	16.05	16.55

8. Total nest egg for retirement

Add present tax-deferred and taxable retirement savings (including any real estate or business that will be sold to fund your retirement) and multiply by the appropriate number from this table. As in line 7, choose either conservative or aggressive investments. .... $ _____

Years to retirement	5	10	15	20	25	30	35	40	45
Conservative	1.47	2.16	3.17	4.66	6.85	10.06	14.79	21.72	31.92
Aggressive	1.69	2.84	4.78	8.06	13.59	22.89	38.57	65.00	109.53

9. Additional capital needed

Subtract line 8 from line 7. .... $ _____

10. Annual savings needed to meet your goal

Multiply line 9 by the appropriate number from this table, based on how you plan to invest. .... $ _____

Years to retirement	5	10	15	20	25	30	35	40	45
Conservative	0.170	0.069	0.037	0.022	0.014	0.009	0.006	0.004	0.003
Aggressive	0.161	0.060	0.029	0.016	0.009	0.005	0.003	0.002	0.001

SOURCE: KAREN KRATZER, PRICEWATERHOUSECOOPERS

only as good as its assumptions. You'll need to be flexible as you get closer to retirement, so that you can adjust your goals to reflect changes in inflation and your investment returns—and in your own personal situation. Even during retirement you may have to do some fine-tuning.

Because the worksheet—or any retirement-planning worksheet or software—can't do more than provide an estimate, I've deliberately chosen to make this one easy to complete—even at the expense of precision in a few places. Most important, I have assumed that you've invested almost all your retirement assets in tax-deferred vehicles, such as 401(k)s, variable annuities or tax-managed funds (more on these last two in a minute). If you're 20 or more years from retirement and you've invested a large portion of your retirement money in ordinary taxable accounts, consider adding an extra five years onto your years in retirement to counterbalance the taxes you'll pay along the way.

And other retirement-planning tools

If you want a worksheet that takes a more exacting look at retirement planning, T. Rowe Price (800-638-5660; www.troweprice.com) offers one of the most comprehensive, at no charge. A version can also be found on their Web site, at www.troweprice.com. Kiplinger.com, the Web site of *Kiplinger's Personal Finance* magazine, also features a free, retirement-savings calculator. Don't be fooled, though. Staying up half the night completing a worksheet or working with a computer program doesn't necessarily make the numbers you come up with any more meaningful. I've tested the Internet retirement programs from several companies, including Kiplinger's. All give you significantly different results, simply because they make different assumptions about such things as inflation, social security and your future investment return. For most investors, I think the worksheet here provides all the information you need.

Just Do It

THE WORKSHEET GIVES YOU A GOOD IDEA OF HOW MUCH YOU need to save each year. All you have to do now is start investing. In saving for retirement, several tax-deferred options are available.

TAX-DEFERRED SAVINGS AND INVESTING

All of the plans described below let your money compound tax-free until you take it out in retirement (or, in the case of a Roth IRA, you pay no taxes when you withdraw your money). Here are brief descriptions of these different retirement-savings vehicles, and whom they suit best.

401(k)s

401(k)s are the most ubiquitous retirement accounts. They are available to employees of most for-profit corporations. 401(k)s allow you to invest only in the funds or other investment choices your employer offers. Generally, employers (and federal restrictions) limit your annual contributions to 10% or 15% of your salary—with a maximum annual contribution for 2001 of $10,500, which increases with inflation. (As this book goes to press, Congress is considering increasing the annual contribution limits.) Often the company provides some match of, say, the first 6% of your salary that you contribute. 401(k) plans may

The Power of Tax-Deferred Compounding

LEARN HERE HOW quickly your money grows in a tax-deferred account without the drag of paying taxes every year. This table compares returns in a tax-deferred account versus a taxable account. The table assumes a $2,000 annual investment, a 9% annual rate of return and a 28% tax rate. (The final column actually understates the true value of tax deferral, because it assumes withdrawal of the entire amount at once. In reality, you'll withdraw money from tax-deferred retirement accounts gradually over many years during retirement.)

YEARS	VALUE OF TAXABLE ACCOUNT	VALUE OF TAX-DEFERRED ACCOUNT BEFORE TAXES	VALUE OF TAX-DEFERRED ACCOUNT AFTER PAYING TAXES UPON WITHDRAWAL
15 years	$51,400	$64,000	$54,500
20 years	82,500	111,500	91,500
25 years	125,100	184,600	146,900
30 years	183,300	297,200	230,800

SOURCE: T. Rowe Price Associates Inc.

allow you to borrow money. When you repay the loan, with interest, all the money goes right back into your account. When you borrow money from a plan, however, you don't earn any investment return on that sum until you repay it. It's best not to dip into your 401(k) unless you have no better choice.

403(b)s

403(b)s are like 401(k)s except they are offered to employees of public school systems and other nonprofit enterprises. In most cases, the 403(b) is offered by an insurance company the employer has selected. That adds a needless layer of expenses. For details on switching your 403(b) investment to any mutual fund you would like, see the discussion beginning on page 73.

IRAs and Roth IRAs

IRAs, short for individual retirement accounts, allow you and your spouse each to save $2,000 annually in pretax income (if you qualify to make deductible contributions) with whatever mutual fund company, brokerage, insurance company or bank you choose. The money is taxed as ordinary income when you withdraw it during retirement.

Contributions to Roth IRAs are not deductible, but the long-term tax benefits are enormous.

If you are covered by a pension plan, you can make a fully deductible contribution so long as your adjusted gross income is below a certain level. For 2001, the threshold is $33,000 for a single person or $53,000 for a couple. If you're married and are not covered by a pension plan but your spouse is, you can make a fully deductible contribution if your combined income is less than $150,000. If neither you or your spouse (if you're married) are covered by a pension plan, you can make a deductible contribution regardless of your income.

Roth IRAs, like regular IRAs, allow an individual to contribute $2,000 annually if his or her adjusted gross income is under $95,000; the maximum contribution phases out gradually as income rises to $110,000. Married couples who file joint returns can each invest up to $2,000, so long as their combined adjusted gross income is less than $150,000; their maximum contribution phases out gradually as income rises to $160,000. For example, if the adjusted gross income on a joint return is $155,000, that's halfway through the phaseout zone, so each partner's maximum contribution would be cut in half, to $1,000. (Married taxpayers who file separate returns may not open Roth IRAs.)

The Roth advantage. While contributions to these accounts are not tax-deductible, the long-term tax benefits are enormous: You don't pay any taxes when you take the money out. For nearly all investors, Roth IRAs are a much better deal than regular IRAs. (The main exception is investors who plan to leave their money invested for less than about ten years and who, therefore, may benefit more from the initial tax break—the deductibility of contributions—to a regular IRA.) That's because the money you withdraw in retirement from regular IRAs is taxed as ordinary income in your usual tax bracket, so you lose a big chunk of your IRA to Uncle Sam. By contrast, Roth IRAs will never be taxed, no matter how much your money grows before and during retirement.

Moreover, Roth IRAs allow you to decide when to withdraw money in retirement, while strict and complicated rules govern retirement withdrawals from traditional IRAs. Be sure to make the full $2,000-per-individual contribution to a Roth IRA even if you have to cut back a bit on your other retirement savings, including 401(k) or 403(b) plans for which you are not receiving an employer match.

Convert to a Roth? Another option worth considering is to convert your current IRAs to Roth IRAs. This option is available only to individuals *or* married couples whose adjusted gross income is $100,000 or less. You'll have to pay taxes now on your existing IRAs, but you'll never have to pay taxes on future earnings. If you can afford to pay those taxes with money from outside your IRAs, and you're roughly 20 years or more away from retirement, you'll probably be better off converting to Roth IRAs.

Early withdrawals. In most circumstances, you may take money out of IRAs at any age to pay for college expenses, a first home or certain other expenses without paying the usual 10% early-withdrawal tax penalties. Use these provisions only if absolutely necessary, though. Why? You'll still have to pay taxes on the contributions and earnings you withdraw from a deductible IRA and on the earnings you withdraw from a nondeductible IRA or Roth IRA. (*Note:* Withdrawals from a Roth for a first home can be tax-free.) And the money won't be there to fund your retirement—which was the whole point of funding an IRA in the first place.

(continued on page 63)

If You Need to Save More

TAX-MANAGED INDEX FUNDS are one of the best ways to save money for retirement. These funds track stock-market indexes, such as Standard & Poor's 500-stock index (see the previous chapter for more on index funds), but through various accounting gimmicks they manage to pay little or no capital gains to their shareholders. That means no (or very small) capital gains taxes for investors—so long as you hold onto the funds.

Unfortunately, there's a lot of hype about the advantages of tax efficiency and tax-managed funds. The fact is that tax-managed funds make little, if any, sense unless you're a very long-term investor. Suppose you're in the 31% tax bracket and have a choice between two funds, each of which earns 11% annually including 2% in dividends. One is perfectly tax-efficient—that is, it never pays out any capital gains. The other is a typical stock fund, paying out half its gains every year, 1.5 percentage points in short-term gains and 3 percentage points in long-term gains.

Over three years, a $10,000 investment in the tax-efficient fund nets you $12,850, versus $12,767 for an ordinary fund, assuming you sell both funds at the end of that period, according to Vanguard, which computed these numbers.

Over five years, the tax-efficient fund nets you $15,278, versus $15,068 for the ordinary fund, an annualized difference of just 0.3 percentage point.

Over ten years, the tax-efficient fund nets you $23,926, versus $22,979 for the ordinary fund, which is an annual-

ized difference of 0.44%.

But over longer-time periods, tax-managed funds can work miracles. Over 20 years, the tax-efficient fund would net you $61,314, versus $54,603 for the ordinary fund. And over 30 years, the tax-efficient fund nets you $161,691, versus $131,663. Unlike a variable annuity (see pages 74–75) or an IRA, moreover, almost all your income taxes on a tax-managed fund will be long-term capital gains, which are never higher than 20%. Plus, if you end up leaving the fund to your heirs, they pay no taxes whatever on the unrealized capital gains attained during your lifetime.

It's hard enough picking an actively managed fund that will do well over the next couple of years. It's virtually impossible to pick one that will do well over 20 or more years. That's why tax-managed index funds make the most sense.

Among the best are the tax-managed funds offered by Vanguard (800-635-1511, www.vanguard.com), including *Tax-Managed Growth & Income* (VTGIX), which tracks the S&P 500; *Tax Managed International* (VTMGX), which mirrors the Morgan Stanley Europe Australasia and Far East index; and *Tax-Managed Small Cap* (VTMSX), which tacks Standard & Poor's Small Cap 600 index.

Just a hair more expensive are the Schwab index funds (www.schwab.com; 800-435-4000), including *Schwab 1000* (symbol SNXFX), *International Index* (SWINX), *Small Cap Index* (SWSMX) and *S&P 500* (SWPIX). All but the last of these track Schwab's homemade indexes.

SEP-IRAs

SEP-IRAs are similar to IRAs, but they're for people who are self-employed or who own very small businesses. They allow self-employed people to deduct about 15% of their earnings and put it into a SEP-IRA. The advantage of SEP-IRAs is that they generally let you put away far more tax-deductible income in a tax-sheltered account than do ordinary IRAs.

Keogh plans

Keogh plans are also for people who are self-employed or in partnerships. They allow you to contribute up to 20% of your earnings to a tax-deferred plan. But Keoghs involve more paperwork than SEP-IRAs.

SIMPLE IRAs

SIMPLE IRA plans are for businesses of up to 100 employees that want to offer a 401(k)-like plan without some of the administrative costs. They allow employee contributions of up to $6,000 and employer matches of up to 3% of contributions. They can be a good option for self-employed people.

GETTING STARTED

Start by contributing the maximum to your 401(k) or 403(b) that your employer will match.

Next, fully fund Roth IRAs for yourself and your spouse, if you are eligible.

If you can afford to, contribute the maximum allowed to your 401(k) or 403(b), or to a SEP-IRA, SIMPLE or Keogh plan if you're self-employed. All except the Roth IRAs allow you to stash pretax money in retirement plans. If your combined federal and state tax rates total 35%, by investing pretax money you can put $1,000 into your retirement account for every $650 in after-tax income you forgo. Moreover, the employer match of at least a portion of your contributions to 401(k) and 403(b) plans is too good to pass up. If your company offers a 50% match, based on the preceding example, you could squirrel away $1,500 in your retirement plan for every $650 in after-tax income you forgo. You've more than doubled your money even before your investment starts growing.

Next, if you're not eligible for a Roth IRA, consider a nondeductible

Funds' Investment Objectives and Styles

YOU'LL SMOOTH THE volatility of your overall portfolio if you choose funds for your retirement from a variety of investment objectives and, in the case of stock funds, from a cross section of investment styles (see also Part Three, Chapters 13, 14 and 15). An investment objective tells you *what* the fund tries to do; its style tells you *how* it aims to accomplish that objective. Following are thumbnail descriptions of the major investment objectives and styles of stock funds.

Major investment objectives

Aggressive-growth funds try to achieve maximum growth and are usually extremely volatile (meaning their investment results bounce around a lot from month to month and year to year).

Long-term-growth funds also aim for growth, but are less volatile.

International stock funds invest overseas.

Sector funds invest in just one industry or a group of industries. High-yielding real estate funds, which invest in commercial real estate, make sense for many investors.

Growth-and-income funds seek both growth and income, and are among the least-volatile stock funds. They may contain bonds as well as stocks.

Balanced funds are the most conservative funds with any stocks in them. Their managers try to earn high yields and decent returns—but take special care to try to avoid big losses.

High-quality bond funds invest in taxable bonds with high credit ratings. They differ from one another primarily based on how long it will be until the average bond in their portfolio reaches maturity and pays back to the fund all the money it originally borrowed. The longer a fund's average maturity (the more long-term it is), the more risky it is.

High-yielding bond funds invest in high-yielding, low-quality "junk" bonds. These funds can be nearly as risky as stock funds, but in reasonable quantities they provide diversification and high income.

Municipal bond funds earn tax-exempt income by investing in bonds issued by states and municipalities and their agencies. Most invest in high-quality bonds, but some invest in high-yield bonds. As with taxable bonds, funds with longer average maturities tend to be more risky.

Investing styles of stock funds

Large-company value funds buy stocks of large companies (often household names such as Sears, Ford and Caterpillar) that are selling at low prices relative to their current earnings or assets and are unpopular among most investors, usually because of fears that earnings won't grow rapidly.

Large-company growth funds invest in stocks of large companies with rapidly increasing earnings (such as Cisco, Intel and Pfizer). These stocks are often glamour issues and sell at high prices relative to their current earnings.

Small-company value funds invest in stocks of small companies that sell at low prices relative to their earnings or assets. Bad news about these neglected companies, such as forecasts of slow earnings growth, is often already reflected in their stock price.

Small-company growth funds invest in stocks of small companies with rapidly growing earnings. These stocks tend to sell at the highest prices relative to their current earnings. They are among the riskiest of all stocks.

IRA. While you don't get the initial tax break, your money still compounds tax-deferred.

Put It on Automatic

B Y NOW, YOU MAY BE SAYING: ALL THESE IDEAS SOUND wonderful, but where in the world am I going to find the extra money to invest for retirement? Especially if you're already saving for college for your children, extra money is a scarce commodity. No one would suggest that you give up activities you love, such as travel and hobbies. After all, life is short, and there's no point depriving yourself.

How much you can afford to invest in stock funds as you near retirement will depend, in part, on how financially secure you are.

We can't help you find extra cash, but we can suggest a way to make saving less painful. As discussed in Chapter 1, many investors have found that the key to investing for retirement is to have money automatically withdrawn from their paychecks. Most mutual funds will debit your checking account for monthly investments in IRAs, SEP-IRAs or taxable accounts.

Choose Your Funds

Y OU'LL LIKELY LIVE MANY YEARS IN RETIREMENT, SO YOU'LL tap your money gradually instead of all at once. Because the rate of return on your money must at least keep up with the rate of inflation before and during retirement. you'll want to keep a large portion of it in stock funds. Table A on page 32 indicates what percentage of your retirement assets to put in stock funds based on your risk-tolerance score. But you'll notice that when investing for retirement, I encourage you to put much more money into stock funds than when investing to meet all other goals.

How much you can afford to invest in stock funds as you near retirement and during retirement, however, will also depend in part on how financially secure you are—rather than solely on your time horizon. If you have a generous pension, or a more-than-adequate amount of savings socked away already, you can afford to put more of your money into stocks and keep less in bonds and other lower-risk investments. Even if the stock market suffers a prolonged decline, you'll be able to ride it out comfortably. But if your pension and other retirement savings are meager and you'll be more dependent on income from your investments, invest more conservatively.

If you aren't financially secure as you near or live in retirement, you may want to reduce by 10% the amount of stock funds the table recommends (see page 32) and invest that money in bond funds instead. Otherwise, a bear market could depress the value of your savings, leaving you in a precarious situation. Conversely, if you are financially quite well off—as you get close to retirement and while living in retirement—I'd suggest you increase the percentage of assets you invested in stocks by 10% over the table's recommendation.

Regardless of your financial wherewithal as you get within a couple of years of retirement and after you retire, be sure to keep enough money in a money-market fund or a low-risk bond fund (such as *Vanguard Limited-Term Tax-Exempt*) so that—combined with your other sources of income—you can support yourself for two or three years. Do this even if you need to sell some stocks. Such a cushion can help prevent you from having to sell stocks when the market is depressed.

SOME SUGGESTED PORTFOLIOS OF FUNDS

I have devised portfolios that embody these principles of diversification among objectives and styles. The portfolios vary among each other in their aggressiveness. Keep in mind that they are merely suggestions for how to deploy your money. You can build equally good investment plans by choosing other funds that use the same objectives and investment styles (such as those described in Part 4) or by selecting your own funds based on performance, costs, consistency and other factors (to learn how to pick your own funds, see Chapter 15).

In truth, the particular fund you choose is rarely paramount. What *is* important is to pick funds that invest in different types of stocks—small companies, large companies, growth companies, value companies and foreign companies. For that reason, if one of the funds I recommend is closed to new investors by the time you read this book, simply turn to Chapter 17, "Great Stock Funds," and substitute any fund that has the same investment objective and invests in the same type of stocks. For instance, if

TCW Galileo Select Equity were closed, you could instead use *Harbor Capital Appreciation,* which is also a long-term growth fund that specializes in stocks of large companies with fast-growing earnings.

Moreover, if you are investing for more than one goal at once—say, for retirement and college—you don't have to invest in all the funds listed in the retirement portfolio *and* all the funds listed in the college portfolio. While there's nothing wrong with doing that, you'll have to keep track of a lot of funds. Instead, you might use funds from one of the portfolios, say the retirement portfolio, for both college and retirement. Just earmark the proper proportion of your money for each goal. Also, be sure that for each goal, your percentage of stock funds, bond funds and money-market funds is appropriate given your time horizon and tolerance for risk (see pages 30–31). If you can, aim to build one overall portfolio that suits all your needs.

However you put together your retirement portfolio, don't let the proportions of fund types get too out of whack over time. If one fund does so well that it becomes a much bigger part of your portfolio than you had intended, sell some of it and put the proceeds into your lagging funds—or at least redirect your future contributions to the laggards until your allocations are back in line. (See the example of how this works on page 45.) Also, as you get closer to retirement, *gradually* move the appropriate portion of money from stock funds to bond funds; avoid doing it in one fell swoop.

All the funds are no-load, that is, they have no sales charges. (See Chapter 8 for details on purchasing funds through online brokers and directly from fund companies.) Decades from retirement, the DiBenedettos are putting all their money in stock funds. For more on their investment choices, see the Afterword, beginning on page 249.

Investing for Retirement

THE FOLLOWING PIE CHARTS illustrate how the portfolios outlined in this chapter divide your money between stock funds (by objective) and bond funds, depending on your time horizon and tolerance for risk.

More Than 15 Years From Retirement

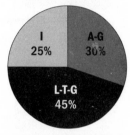

Aggressive-Growth = 30%
Long-Term-Growth = 45
International = 25
100%

More than 15 years from retirement

Janus Mercury (15% of your money; 800-525-8983; JAMRX; www.janus.com), is an aggressive-growth fund that invests in fast-growing companies, mainly large ones (for more information on this fund, see page 214).

Skyline Special Equities (15%; 800-458-5222; SKSEX) is an aggressive-growth fund that invests in stocks of small, undervalued companies (page 217).

Legg Mason Opportunity (20%; 800-577-8589; www.leggmason.com; LMOPX) is a long-term-growth fund that invests in stocks of undervalued, mostly mid-size companies (page 221).

TCW Galileo Select Equity (25%; 800-386-3829; www.tcwgroup.com; TGCNX) is a long-term-growth fund that hunts for large companies that are growing rapidly (page 223).

Artisan International (25%; 800-344-1770; www.artisanfunds.com; ARTIX) invests in foreign stocks (page 230).

10 to 15 years from retirement

If you had a score of 86 or higher on Table A, "How Much to Invest in Stocks for Retirement," on page 32, your funds and their allocations will remain unchanged from those in the portfolio just discussed. But if you had a lower score, put 20% to 30%

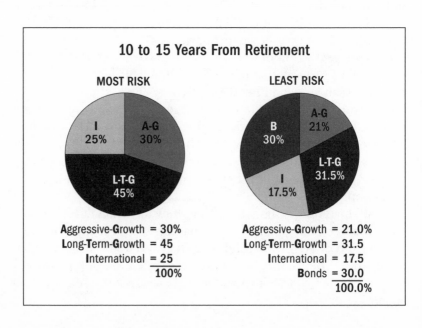

10 to 15 Years From Retirement

MOST RISK

I 25%
A-G 30%
L-T-G 45%

Aggressive-Growth = 30%
Long-Term-Growth = 45
International = 25
100%

LEAST RISK

A-G 21%
B 30%
L-T-G 31.5%
I 17.5%

Aggressive-Growth = 21.0%
Long-Term-Growth = 31.5
International = 17.5
Bonds = 30.0
100.0%

of your total portfolio—a little from each of your funds—in *Loomis Sayles Bond*, which holds long-term bonds (the riskier side of bond investing, but more conservative than stocks; 800-633-3330; www.loomissayles.com; LSBRX; see page 239).

If you're investing the bond money outside of a retirement account, use *Vanguard High-Yield Tax-Exempt* (800-635-1511; www.vanguard.com; VWAHX; page 247), a tax-exempt fund that invests in long-term bonds, instead of Loomis Sayles.

Whether in a tax-deferred or taxable account, keep your holdings in the stock funds in the same proportions as before.

Six to ten years from retirement
Invest your stock money as follows:

Janus Mercury (10% of your money; 800-525-8983; www.janus.com; JAMRX) is an aggressive-growth fund that buys stocks of fast-growing companies, mainly large ones (for more information on this fund, see page 214).

Skyline Special Equities (15%; 800-458-5222; SKSEX) is an aggressive-growth fund that invests in stocks of small, undervalued companies (page 217).

Legg Mason Opportunity (25%; 800-577-8589; www.leggmason.com; LMOPX), is a long-term-growth fund that invests in mostly mid-

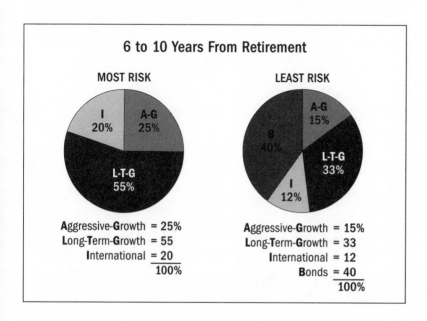

6 to 10 Years From Retirement

MOST RISK

I 20%
A-G 25%
L-T-G 55%

Aggressive-Growth = 25%
Long-Term-Growth = 55
International = 20
100%

LEAST RISK

A-G 15%
B 40%
L-T-G 33%
I 12%

Aggressive-Growth = 15%
Long-Term-Growth = 33
International = 12
Bonds = 40
100%

size, undervalued companies (page 221).

TCW Galileo Select Equity (30%; 800-386-3829; www.tcwgroup.com; TGCNX), is a long-term-growth fund that hunts for large, fast-growing companies (page 223).

Deutsche International Equity (20%; 800-730-1313; BTEQX; www.deam-us.com;), invests in foreign stocks (page 239).

If you had a high score on the risk-tolerance test, continue to invest all your money in stock funds. But if you had a lower score, put 30% to 40% of your total portfolio in *Loomis Sayles Bond* (800-633-3330; www.loomissayles.com; LSBRX; page 239) which invests in long-term bonds.

If you're investing in a taxable account, use tax-exempt *Vanguard High-Yield Tax-Exempt* (800-635-1511; VWAHX; www.vanguard.com; page 247) instead.

Zero to six years from retirement

Use the same stock funds as in the previous portfolio (for investors who are six to ten years from retirement). Depending on your tolerance for risk (see Table A on page 32), put between 15% and 60% of your money into bond funds, split evenly between *Loomis Sayles Bond* (800-633-3330; LSBRX; www.loomissayles.com; see page 239), and *Harbor Bond*

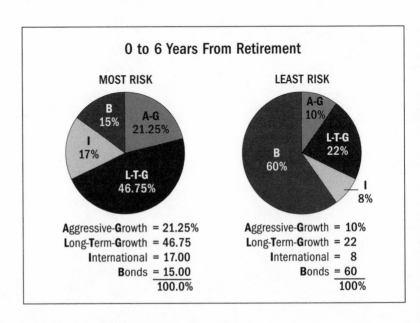

0 to 6 Years From Retirement

MOST RISK

B 15%
A-G 21.25%
I 17%
L-T-G 46.75%

Aggressive-Growth = 21.25%
Long-Term-Growth = 46.75
International = 17.00
Bonds = 15.00
100.0%

LEAST RISK

A-G 10%
L-T-G 22%
B 60%
I 8%

Aggressive-Growth = 10%
Long-Term-Growth = 22
International = 8
Bonds = 60
100%

(800-422-1050; www.harborfunds.com; HABDX; page 236), a fund that holds bonds with medium-term maturities. If you're investing in a taxable account, instead of using Loomis Sayles and Harbor, divide your bond money between *Vanguard High-Yield Tax-Exempt* (800-635-1511; www.vanguard.com; VWAHX; page 247) and *Vanguard Intermediate-Term Tax-Exempt*.

Early retirement (up to age 75)

Invest 40% to 65% of your money in bonds, depending on your results from the "How Much to Invest in Stocks" table (see page 32). Invest your bond money in the same proportions as in the previous portfolio. Invest your stock money as follows:

Delphi Value (20%; 800-895-9936; www.kobren.com; KDVRX), a low-risk, long-term growth fund that invests in small- and medium-size undervalued stocks (see page 218).

Selected American Shares (50%; 800-243-1575; SLASX; www.selectedfunds.com), a growth-and-income fund that invests in large, undervalued companies with potential for growth (page 224).

Tweedy Browne Global Value (20%; 800-432-4789; TBGVX; www.tweedy.com), a low-risk fund that invests in foreign companies (page 231).

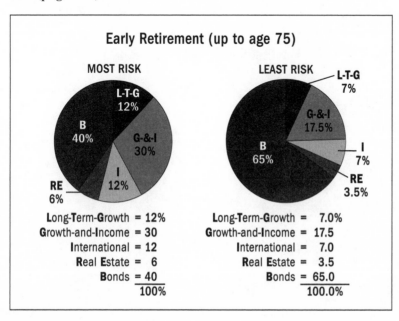

Columbia Real Estate Equity (10%; 800-547-1707; CREEX; www.columbiafunds.com), a fund that invests in high-yielding real estate investment trusts, which, in turn, invest in commercial property (page 226).

Late retirement (generally ages 75 and older)

Invest 50% to 70% in bonds. Divide your bond money as follows:
Harbor Bond (50%; 800-422-1050; www.harborfunds.com; HABDX), a fund that invests in bonds with medium-term maturities (see page 236).
Vanguard Short-Term Corporate (25%; 800-662-7447; VFSTX; www.vanguard.com), a fund that invests in short-maturity bonds (page 241).
Northeast Investors Trust (25%; 800-225-6704; NTHEX; www.northeastinvestors.com), a high-yielding "junk bond" fund (page 239).

If your bond money is in a taxable account and your tax bracket is 28% or higher, use the following in place of the first two funds: *Vanguard Intermediate-Term Tax-Exempt,* which invests in medium-term tax-exempt bonds (800-635-1511; VWITX; www.vanguard.com; page 247), and *Vanguard Limited-Term Tax-Exempt* (VMLTX; page 247), which invests in short-term tax-

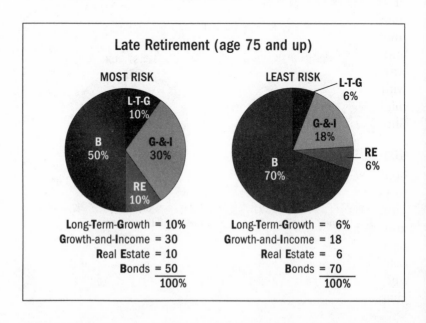

Late Retirement (age 75 and up)

MOST RISK

- L-T-G 10%
- B 50%
- G-&-I 30%
- RE 10%

Long-Term-Growth = 10%
Growth-and-Income = 30
Real Estate = 10
Bonds = 50
100%

LEAST RISK

- L-T-G 6%
- G-&-I 18%
- B 70%
- RE 6%

Long-Term-Growth = 6%
Growth-and-Income = 18
Real Estate = 6
Bonds = 70
100%

exempt bonds. Hold on to *Northeast Investors Trust* for the income it produces.

Invest your stock money as follows:

Delphi Value (20%; 800-895-9936; www.kobren.com; KDVRX), a low-risk, long-term growth fund that invests in low-risk, under-valued small companies (page 218).

Selected American Shares (60%; 800-243-1575; SLASX; www.selectedfunds.com), a growth-and-income fund that invests in undervalued large companies with potential for growth (page 224).

Columbia Real Estate Equity (20%; 800-547-1707; CREEX; www.columbiafunds.com), a fund that invests in real estate companies (page 226).

IF YOUR RETIREMENT PLAN DOESN'T OFFER THESE FUNDS

This chapter gives you a simple way to put together an investment plan for retirement. If your employer-sponsored retirement plan doesn't offer the funds in the suggested portfolios, though, you'll have to do a little more work. Start by looking at the funds listed in Chapters 17 and 18 to see whether they match funds offered in your retirement plan. If they do, you may be able to construct at least part of your portfolio from them, substituting funds that match the investment objectives and styles of those you must replace. Otherwise, you'll want to read Parts Three and Four to learn the ins and outs of picking funds. That way you'll be able to construct a portfolio on your own within the limits of what your 401(k) program offers. You might also ask your employer to add more and better funds. Show your benefits department this chapter if you'd like.

If your 401(k) plan doesn't offer the funds in the suggested portfolios, you will have to do a little more work.

403(B)S: HOW TO GET OUT OF MEDIOCRE ONES

403(b)s are similar to 401(k) plans, though they are offered only to people who work for nonprofit and educational institutions. Unfortunately, insurance companies dominate the 403(b) market, and most charge high fees—often one percentage point annually more than a mutual fund charges. That's because these insurance companies generally sell variable annuities rather than plain mutual funds to 403(b) members. Over a long period, those extra charges can put a big dent in your retirement savings. A notable exception: *TIAA-CREF* (800-223-1200; www.tiaa-cref.org), which sells very low-cost annuities with good long-term records.

Paul DiBenedetto bought into one of the high-priced plans without even knowing it. There were virtually no other options. "I had no idea how much I was paying for the annuity," he says. Fortunately, a list of approved 403(b) vendors for the Arlington, Va., school system included USAA, a solid, low-cost fund company. So he switched his 403(b) savings into USAA funds, and he puts his new 403(b) investments directly into USAA funds. That saves Paul a bushel of money because the funds are not in an annuity and because USAA charges low expenses on its funds.

Insurance companies dominate the 403(b) market. Most charge high fees. Those can put a big dent in your retirement savings.

If you're investing in an annuity in your 403(b) plan, call your benefits department to see if any no-load (no-sales-charge) mutual fund companies are approved vendors at your place of work. Or call a few of the big fund companies, which offer low-cost annuities and good funds, to see if they are approved vendors with your employer. Try *Fidelity* (800-544-8888; www.fidelity.com), *T. Rowe Price* (800-638-5660; troweprice.com) or *Vanguard* (800-635-1511; www.vanguard.com). If that fails, ask your employee benefits department if it will add one of these fund companies to its list of approved vendors.

Still no luck? There is one more way, though it's a little more cumbersome and some employers forbid it. Contribute to your employer's plan (if you can, to avoid fees, choose a money-market option) and then transfer the money to a 403(b)(7) custodial account that you set up with a fund. That strategy will keep your money out of an annuity. But be careful to avoid surrender charges; your old company may bill you when you take your money out. Also, find out whether your plan will impose any restrictions. Some plans won't match 403(b) contributions made to an outside mutual fund, and it's not worth transferring your money if you lose a match. If you follow this course, you'll have to arrange the transfers yourself. But it might be well worth the effort. Contact the above-named fund companies to begin the process. Be persistent. Ask specifically for a phone representative who handles 403(b) accounts. Even some 403(b) telephone representatives don't know it's possible. But if you find a good rep, he or she will steer you through the process.

If You've Maxed Out on Tax-Deferred Saving: Variable Annuities?

IF YOU HAVE PUT THE MAXIMUM IN ALL YOUR TAX-DEFERRED retirement accounts (including 401(k)s, 403(b)s, IRAs, Roth IRAs, SEP-IRAs, Keoghs and SIMPLE plans) and you still need to save more for retirement, a variable annuity may be an option. Variable annuities work a lot like nondeductible IRAs. Your contributions are not tax-exempt, but your money compounds tax-deferred until you withdraw it, at which time it is taxed in your top tax bracket. There are important differences, however. One plus of variable annuities is that you can invest as much as you want in them. But there are several minuses:

Expensive insurance you don't need. Variable annuities gain their tax deferral by having a thin layer of insurance wrapped around them. All it insures is that your heirs will get at least as much back as you invested if you die before making withdrawals. Since the stock market tends to go up over time, this is not usually worthwhile insurance. But the insurance costs money, raising the costs of your investment.

Higher taxes. Variable annuities convert capital-gains income, which is taxed at a lower level, into ordinary income, which is taxed at a higher level. If you pay taxes as you go in an ordinary taxable account, most of your earnings are capital gains, which are taxed at a maximum 20% rate for assets held more than 12 months. When you withdraw money from a variable annuity (or an IRA, for that matter), all of it is taxed as ordinary income, which for higher-income taxpayers means the tax rate can be as high as 39.6%.

A high cost at death. Variable annuities are a lousy way to leave money to your heirs. They are heavily taxed upon your death or, depending on how your contract is written, upon the death of both you and your spouse. For that reason, make sure to take your money out of a variable annuity in a stream of income payments that will last throughout your lifetime(s). That's the only way to get their full benefit assuming you don't die too soon— payments stop when you die. Don't use a variable annuity as emergency cash to tap when you need it. And don't plan to leave money in a variable annuity to your children.

All that said, if you are young enough and are already contributing the maximum to all other available retirement plans, variable annuities can be a decent choice for saving more. (You may not have time to overcome the expenses and tax disadvantages unless you start early, before, say, age 45.) Be sure you want a variable annuity before you buy, though. Buying one is a little like getting married: Changing your mind later can be an expensive proposition.

The plans offered by Fidelity, T. Rowe Price and Vanguard are all reasonably priced. Plans sold by insurance agents are almost all too expensive. (If you're already in a poorly performing, overpriced variable annuity, call Fidelity, T. Rowe Price or Vanguard to inquire about a tax-free exchange.)

Unfortunately, most variable annuities are sold rather than bought. Want proof? Half the money in variable annuities is inside tax-deferred retirement accounts, which is a little like wearing a raincoat indoors.

Key Points

- *Get started now.*
- *The worksheet on pages 56–57 will help you determine how much you need to save each month.*
- *Use tax-sheltered retirement plans whenever possible.*
- *Roth IRAs are almost always better than regular IRAs.*
- *Consider tax-managed funds.*
- *Choose a solid mix of funds, like those listed here.*
- *Get out of bad 403(b) plans if you can.*
- *Be wary of variable annuities.*

Investing for College

Or other goals (except for retirement) more than ten years in the future

EW THINGS CAN BE SCARIER TO A PARENT THAN THE thought of simultaneously saving for retirement and trying to salt away enough money to pay the sky-high costs of college one reads about. But here's a secret: Investing for college isn't as difficult as it's made out to be. This chapter will show you how to do it. (The fund mixes on pages 85–87 are also appropriate for any other savings goals *more* than ten years in the future—except for retirement, which was covered in Chapter 5.) If your son or daughter will be going to college in less then ten years—or you'll need money that soon for any reason other than retirement—consult the next chapter, "Investing for the Short-Term." Here's why the hype about college is worse than the reality:

College doesn't cost as much as you might think.

The *average* private college costs about $23,700 annually, and the average state college costs about $10,900 once you include tuition and fees, room and board, books and supplies, transportation, and personal expenses, including visits home. That's not cheap, but it's less than the $35,000 figure bandied about so much, which is the sticker price of the most expensive private colleges.

College-cost increases are slowing.

For years, college costs rose at annual rates of about 7% to 9%. The main reason: Colleges had too few students, so they made up the difference by charging the students they had higher prices. With many baby-boomers' children now of college age, enrollment is climbing and will continue to increase for years to come. As a result, college-cost increases have dropped to about 5% annually and will likely keep rising at no more than that rate.

Education savings plans may help.
So-called education IRAs allow parents earning less than $150,000 (or $95,000 for a single parent) to contribute $500 per child. Other relatives may also make contributions—but annual contributions per child from all sources can't total more than $500. While contributions aren't tax-deductible, the earnings on the money are tax-free if used for education.

Even better than education IRAs are state college savings plans. These are offered by many states, but you usually don't have to be a resident of that state, nor does your child have to attend a college in that state to benefit from one of these pro-

What College Will Cost

THE TABLE BELOW gives you an idea of what total college costs will be (tuition and fees, room and board, books and supplies, and personal expenses) assuming costs rise 5% annually. It also takes into account increases during college years. If your child begins school in ten years, for instance, add the annual costs for years ten through 13 to get the total cost. If you think a child will attend an elite private college, use the $35,000 figure. For a state college, use the $10,900 figure. Use the $23,700 number if you're not sure.

TODAY	1 YEAR	2 YEARS	3 YEARS	4 YEARS	5 YEARS	6 YEARS	7 YEARS
$35,000	$36,750	$38,588	$40,517	$42,543	$44,670	$46,903	$49,249
$23,700	24,885	26,129	27,436	28,807	30,248	31,760	33,348
$10,900	11,445	12,017	12,618	13,249	13,911	14,607	15,337

TODAY	8 YEARS	9 YEARS	10 YEARS	11 YEARS	12 YEARS	13 YEARS	14 YEARS
$35,000	$51,711	$54,296	$57,011	$59,862	$62,855	$65,998	$69,298
$23,700	35,016	36,766	38,605	40,535	42,562	44,690	46,924
$10,900	16,104	16,909	17,755	18,643	19,575	20,554	21,581

TODAY	15 YEARS	16 YEARS	17 YEARS	18 YEARS	19 YEARS	20 YEARS	21 YEARS
$35,000	$72,762	$76,401	$80,221	$84,232	$88,443	$92,865	$97,509
$23,700	49,271	51,734	54,321	57,037	59,889	62,883	66,027
$10,900	22,660	23,793	24,983	26,232	27,544	28,921	30,367

grams. Earnings on the account are tax free until the money is taken out, and taxes on the earnings are usually paid at the student's rate—typically 15%. What makes these plans so attractive is that they allow you to contribute far more than education IRAs, with essentially the same tax benefits.

For instance, the New Hampshire Unique College Investing Plan (800-544-1722), one of the nation's best, allows you to sock away up to $50,000 annually. The money is invested in an age-based portfolio of Fidelity funds that's 88% in stocks for preschoolers; bonds don't overtake stocks until a child is about 15. Annual expenses on the funds are just 1%.

Another first-rate plan, the Utah Education Savings Plan Trust (800-418-2551; www.uesp.org), employs Vanguard index funds, and allows you to choose how aggressively to invest.

These state college plans are almost always superior to prepaid-tuition plans offered in many states. Prepaid-tuition plans are, at best, suitable only for conservative, short-term savers—say, if your son or daughter is just three or four years from college. The best move: avoid them altogether. They don't earn high enough returns, they can cost you if your son or daughter decides not to go to college, and in many instances, there's no guarantee the plans will really pay for the full cost of college.

Note: You can't contribute to both an education IRA and a college savings plan in the same year.

You don't have to pay the full sticker price.

More than half of families receive a discount on college costs based on their ability to pay—and you needn't be poor to qualify. A family with a $50,000 income will almost certainly qualify for generous assistance for a child attending an expensive private college—even with significant assets, such as $150,000 in home equity and $50,000 in mutual funds. And a family with two children at such a college should qualify for aid even with a $100,000 income. "Many families tend to think they won't qualify for student aid without even checking," says John Joyce of the College Board. "A lot of times if a family completes a financial aid application, they find they're eligible for more than they would have guessed."

Non-need-based aid is available from colleges, too. A study by the National Association of College and University Business

What You Should Save Each Month

THE TABLE ON page 78 gives you a good idea of total college costs for one child anywhere from one to 21 years from now. After you've found your estimated costs on the table, complete the following worksheet to get an idea of how much to save monthly.

A. Savings goal

Multiply your anticipated college costs from the table on page 78 by the percentage of costs you want to have saved in advance. If you don't know, pick a number between 50% and 100%. Say you pick 50% and your daughter will start college in 15 years. Adding the costs for that year and the following three years—$49,271 plus $51,734 plus $54,321 plus $57,037—means her total college will be $212,363.

Your expected college cost x _____ % = $_____

B. Estimate your investment return

If most or all of your money is in stocks (based on Table B, "How Much to Invest in Stocks for All Goals *Except* Retirement," on page 32) you can expect to earn about 10% annually. If you're investing more conservatively, with 55% to 70% in stocks, figure a return of 7.5% annually. But let's say that you'll have all your college money in stocks, and you're estimating an annual return of 9.5%.

Your estimated investment return_____%

C. Figure your after-tax return

Multiply your pretax return by 1 minus your highest tax rate. For instance, if you are in the 28% federal tax bracket and pay a 6% state income tax, your after-tax return on a 9.5% investment is: $1 - 0.34 = 0.66 \times 0.095 = 0.0627$, or 6.3%.

1 – _____ your federal tax bracket –_____ your state income tax
x _____% (from Step B) =_____%

D. Count what you've already saved

Take any money you've already accumulated for college and find out what it will be worth by the time your son or daughter is halfway through college (see the table on page 82–83). Subtract this number from your "Savings Goal" (Step A) to determine what you still need to save.

$_____your savings goal (from Step A) – $_____ your savings to date
= $_____what you still need to save

E. Determine your monthly savings

Say your daughter will be halfway through college some 17 years from now. On the table on pages 10–11 (Chapter 1), find where 17 years intersects with 6% (the closest whole percentage point to 6.3%; see Step C, above). The result is $28—what you need to save monthly to end up with $10,000. By dividing $10,000 into $106,182, the total amount you want to save, and multiplying the result by 28, you know you need to save $297 monthly for college.

$_____total amount you want to save ÷ $10,000 x
$_____monthly amount needed to save $10,000 (from table on pages 10–11) =
$_____amount you need to save monthly to achieve your goal

Officers found that the majority of freshmen were receiving some sort of institutional grant that reduced tuition by a quarter to a third. Many of those grants were not based on need, but rather targeted students who might otherwise not have enrolled.

You don't have to save everything in advance.
A typical student can borrow more than $17,000 over four years, sometimes with no interest payments on the loan during college years. Larger loans are available to parents to cover the balance. Plus, many students work part-time during college.

How Much Should You Save?

WHILE THERE'S NO ONE-SIZE-FITS-ALL ANSWER TO THE question of how much to save, you'll likely be in great shape if you save 75% of what you'll need for college— and in good shape if you save 50%—by the time your son or daughter is halfway through college. You don't need all your child's college money saved by freshman year. Once you've completed the worksheet below, you'll have a better idea of how much to save.

The key to investing for college, as for other goals, is to automate your investing: Have money withdrawn monthly from your checking account and sent directly to a mutual fund.

Also take a minute to flip to the table on pages 10–11 (in Chapter 1) showing how long it takes to save $10,000 at different rates of return. You can see the importance of earning a high return, sure, but the table also vividly shows how much it helps to start saving and investing early. If you have 20 years to save $10,000 and assume you'll earn an 11% return, you have to invest only $12 per month. But you won't be able to invest wholly in stock funds for the entire time you're saving for college. As you get closer to the time you'll need the money, you'll want to put more and more into safer, but lower-returning, bonds and money-market funds. So your return over 20 years—even if you start by investing aggressively—is likely to be about 10%. Conservative investors will likely earn closer to 7.5%.

If you have only ten years, you'll have to invest nearly four times as much—$46 per month at 11%, but you might want to assume a return of 8.5% if you're an aggressive investor with ten or fewer years to go, and a return of 6% if you're a conservative investor. That's because by the time you are two or three years from needing your money, you shouldn't expect to earn more than 5% or so annually.

Nancy and Paul DiBenedetto aren't overly concerned about the costs of college for their children, Paul Jr., age 2½, and a second child they're expecting. Nancy finished getting her master's degree in health administration from the

What You've Saved Already

HAVE YOU ALREADY put some money aside for your children's college? If so, you have a big head start. The table below illustrates how much $1,000 will grow to at different rates of return, depending on how many years you have until you'll need the money.

(For an idea of what return you can expect to earn on your money, see the discussion in the text on pages 81–82.)

Saved more than $1,000? Find the number at the intersection of the rate of return you expect and the number of years you

	RATES OF RETURN						
YEARS	5%	5.5%	6%	6.5%	7%	7.5%	8%
1	$1,050	$1,055	$1,060	$1,065	$1,070	$1,075	$1,080
2	1,103	1,113	1,124	1,134	1,145	1,156	1,166
3	1,158	1,174	1,191	1,208	1,225	1,242	1,260
4	1,216	1,239	1,262	1,286	1,311	1,335	1,360
5	1,276	1,307	1,338	1,370	1,403	1,436	1,469
6	1,340	1,379	1,419	1,459	1,501	1,543	1,587
7	1,407	1,455	1,504	1,554	1,606	1,659	1,714
8	1,477	1,535	1,594	1,655	1,718	1,783	1,851
9	1,551	1,619	1,689	1,763	1,838	1,917	1,999
10	1,629	1,708	1,791	1,877	1,967	2,061	2,159
11	1,710	1,802	1,898	1,999	2,105	2,216	2,332
12	1,796	1,901	2,012	2,129	2,252	2,382	2,518
13	1,886	2,006	2,133	2,267	2,410	2,560	2,720
14	1,980	2,116	2,261	2,415	2,579	2,752	2,937
15	2,079	2,232	2,397	2,572	2,759	2,959	3,172
16	2,183	2,355	2,540	2,739	2,952	3,181	3,426
17	2,292	2,485	2,693	2,917	3,159	3,419	3,700
18	2,407	2,621	2,854	3,107	3,380	3,676	3,996
19	2,527	2,766	3,026	3,309	3,617	3,951	4,316
20	2,653	2,918	3,207	3,524	3,870	4,248	4,661
21	2,786	3,078	3,400	3,753	4,141	4,566	5,034

University of Maryland in 1997, so she knows the ins and outs of paying for education. She was lucky, too. Her employer paid $2,000 per year of her tuition—more than half of what it cost her, so she graduated without taking out any loans.

As for the children, Nancy says, "The bottom line is, we want them to go where they want to go. That's why it's so important to save as much money as possible. But I'm not worried about it. Whatever money we have, we'll be able to offer to them.

have to invest. Then multiply that number by the multiple of $1,000 that you've saved. For instance, if you've saved $15,000 already and anticipate earning 8% on that money over 20 years, find the point where 8% and 20 years intersect, and multiply the result ($4,661) by 15 ($15,000 divided by $1,000), which equals $69,915. When you've finished, insert the result in line D of the worksheet on page 80.

RATES OF RETURN							
8.5%	**9%**	**9.5%**	**10%**	**10.5%**	**11%**	**11.5%**	**12%**
$1,085	$1,090	$1,095	$1,100	$1,105	$1,110	$1,115	$1,120
1,177	1,188	1,199	1,210	1,221	1,232	1,243	1,254
1,277	1,295	1,313	1,331	1,349	1,368	1,386	1,405
1,386	1,412	1,438	1,464	1,491	1,518	1,546	1,574
1,504	1,539	1,574	1,611	1,647	1,685	1,723	1,762
1,631	1,677	1,724	1,772	1,820	1,870	1,922	1,974
1,770	1,828	1,888	1,949	2,012	2,076	2,143	2,211
1,921	1,993	2,067	2,144	2,223	2,305	2,389	2,476
2,084	2,172	2,263	2,358	2,456	2,558	2,664	2,773
2,261	2,367	2,478	2,594	2,714	2,839	2,970	3,106
2,453	2,580	2,714	2,853	2,999	3,152	3,311	3,479
2,662	2,813	2,971	3,138	3,314	3,498	3,692	3,896
2,888	3,066	3,254	3,452	3,662	3,883	4,117	4,363
3,133	3,342	3,563	3,797	4,046	4,310	4,590	4,887
3,400	3,642	3,901	4,177	4,471	4,785	5,118	5,474
3,689	3,970	4,272	4,595	4,941	5,311	5,707	6,130
4,002	4,328	4,678	5,054	5,460	5,895	6,363	6,866
4,342	4,717	5,122	5,560	6,033	6,544	7,095	7,690
4,712	5,142	5,609	6,116	6,666	7,263	7,911	8,613
5,112	5,604	6,142	6,727	7,366	8,062	8,821	9,646
5,547	6,109	6,725	7,400	8,140	8,949	9,835	10,804

SOURCE: KAREN KRATZER, PRICEWATERHOUSECOOPERS

But it still may mean taking out loans depending on what colleges they want to go to."

Nancy and Paul are saving $269 per month for college. They aim to save $96,000 for Paul Jr.'s college, which would pay roughly half the four-year bill at an average private college starting in 2013. Nor do they worry about saving "too much" for college. Unfortunately, there's a dangerous notion afoot that parents are penalized for saving for college. In fact, college-aid formulas place much more weight on your annual income than they do on your assets. Of your taxable savings, roughly the first $20,000 (for a young single parent) to the first $70,000 (for a two-parent family where one parent is 65 or older) isn't even considered in calculating what share you should pay of your children's college education. Amounts above those are tapped at a maximum of 5.6% annually so long as assets are held in a parent's name, although there is a move afoot to increase that percentage. There is also legislative pressure to decrease the 35% annual rate at which assets in a student's name may be utilized.

Investing for College and Other Long-Term Goals Except Retirement

THESE PIE CHARTS illustrate how the portfolios outlined in this chapter (beginning on page 85) divide your money between stock funds (by objective) and bond funds, depending on your time horizon and tolerance for risk.

15 or More Years From the Goal

MOST RISK

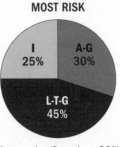

I 25%
A-G 30%
L-T-G 45%

Aggressive-**G**rowth = 30%
Long-Term-**G**rowth = 45
International = 25
100%

LEAST RISK

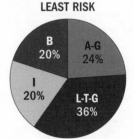

B 20%
A-G 24%
I 20%
L-T-G 36%

Aggressive-**G**rowth = 24%
Long-Term-**G**rowth = 36
International = 20
Bonds = 20
100%

The Portfolios

FOLLOWING ARE TWO PORTFOLIOS—ONE FOR PEOPLE SUCH AS the DiBenedettos whose son is more than 15 years from college, and the other for people with children ten to 15 years from college. I've designed these portfolios for children who will be *halfway* through college in more than 15 years or ten to 15 years, respectively. These two portfolios are also suited for any other goals more than 15 years in the future or ten to 15 years in the future, respectively. (Fund mixes for college and other goals less than ten years away are in Chapter 7). The portfolios in these chapters are only ideas; you can do as well by picking a variety of funds from Chapter 17, or by using other top-performing funds.

Also keep in mind, if you are investing for more than one goal at once—say, college and retirement—you don't need to buy each fund in each portfolio. Instead, you can use funds from one of the portfolios, say the retirement portfolio, for both college and retirement. Just be sure that for your college savings, your percentage of stock funds, bond funds and money-market funds is appropriate given your time horizon and tolerance for risk.

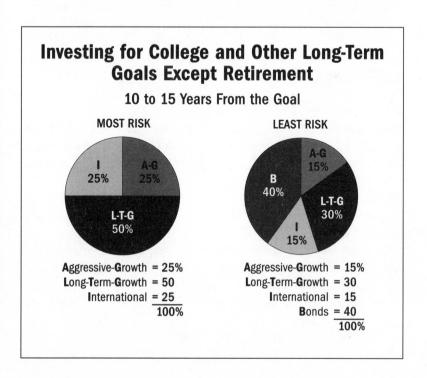

Investing for College and Other Long-Term Goals Except Retirement

10 to 15 Years From the Goal

MOST RISK

I 25%
A-G 25%
L-T-G 50%

Aggressive-Growth = 25%
Long-Term-Growth = 50
International = 25
100%

LEAST RISK

A-G 15%
B 40%
L-T-G 30%
I 15%

Aggressive-Growth = 15%
Long-Term-Growth = 30
International = 15
Bonds = 40
100%

More Than 15 Years From the Goal

Janus Mercury (15% of your money; 800-525-8983; www.janus.com; JAMRX) is an aggressive-growth fund that invests in fast-growing companies, mainly large ones (for more information on this fund, see page 214).

Skyline Special Equities (15%; 800-458-5222; SKSEX) is an aggressive-growth fund that invests in stocks of small, undervalued companies (page 217).

Legg Mason Opportunity (20%; 800-577-8589; www.leggmason.com; LMOPX) is a long-term growth fund that invests in stocks of undervalued companies, mainly mid-size ones (page 221).

TCW Galileo Select Equity (25%; 800-386-3829; www.tcwgroup.com; TGCNX) is a long-term-growth fund that hunts for large companies with rapidly growing earnings (page 223).

Artisan International (25%; 800-344-1770; www.artisanfunds.com; ARTIX) invests in foreign stocks (page 230).

If Table B, "How Much to Invest in Stocks for All Goals Except Retirement," on page 32 indicates you should own some bond funds, keep the above stock funds in the same proportions, but use *Loomis Sayles Bond* (800-633-3330; www.loomissayles.com; LSBRX; page 239)—or, if you're investing in a taxable account and your tax bracket is 28% or higher, *Vanguard High-Yield Tax-Exempt* (800-662-7447; www.vanguard.com; WVAHX; page 247)—for the bond portion of your investment plan.

10 to 15 Years From the Goal

Janus Mercury (15% of your money; 800-525-8983; JAMRX; www.janus.com) is an aggressive-growth fund that buys stocks of fast-growing companies, mainly large ones (for more information on this fund, see page 214).

Skyline Special Equities (10%; 800-458-5222; SKSEX) is an aggressive-growth fund that invests in undervalued small companies (page 217).

Legg Mason Opportunity (25%; 800-577-8589; www.leggmason.com; LMOPX) is a long-term growth fund that invests in mainly mid-size, undervalued companies (page 221).

TCW Galileo Select Equity (25%; 800-386-3829; www.tcwgroup.com; TGCNX) is a long-term-growth fund that hunts for large, fast-growing companies (page 223).

Artisan International (25%; 800-344-1770; www.artisanfunds.com;

ARTIX) invests in foreign stocks (page 230).

If Table B on page 32 indicates you should own some bond funds, keep the above stock funds in the same proportions, but use *Loomis Sayles Bond* (800-633-3330; www.loomissayles.com; LSBRX; page 239)—or, if you're investing in a taxable account and your tax bracket is 28% or higher, *Vanguard High-Yield Tax-Exempt* (800-635-1511; www.vanguard.com; VWAHX; page 247)—for the bond portion of your investment plan.

Whose Name Should You Save In?

THE TAX CODE GIVES YOU A BREAK FOR SAVING IN YOUR children's names. In 2001, the first $750 of investment income earned in a child's name each year is tax-free. Assuming your child is in the 15% tax bracket, as most are, the next $750 is taxed at 15% (just 10% if it's a long-term capital gain). Anything more than that first $1,500 is taxed at your rate when your child is under 14. After your child turns 14, moreover, everything after the first tax-free $750 is taxed at his or her rate, so you may save even more on taxes.

To save in your child's name, check the box on a fund application form that indicates you want to open a custodial account, and then fill in the box that says you want to open a Uniform Gift to Minors Act (UGMA)/Uniform Transfer to Minors Act (UTMA) account. Then fill in the box that tells what state the child lives in. Be aware, though, that some states allow children to do as they please with the money as soon as they turn 18; others make them wait until they're 21. If given the option, always choose 21. This will help avoid the dreaded Ferrari scenario, in which your child gets his or her hands on tens of thousands of dollars and instead of college—well, you get the idea. For assistance in completing the form, see Chapter 8 or call the fund's toll-free number.

The other drawback to putting money in your child's name is that college-aid formulas consider as much as 35% of a student's savings to be available each year to pay for college. If you save in your name, no more than 5.6% of your assets will be considered available annually to pay for college—unless changes in current law, which some are lobbying for, shrink the difference between how parent's and children's assets are counted.

Money in a college savings plan is considered an asset of the owner, usually the parent, for aid purposes. That's the good news. The bad news is that once the student begins using the money, the annual earnings from the plan (but not the principal) show up as income on the student's tax return, and thus plays a role in aid calculations in subsequent years. (Half of student income, after an allowance, is tapped for the family contribution.) Overall, the treatment is still better than having the money in a custodial account, but it will have some impact on aid eligibility.

Here's How to Decide

If your taxable income is $100,000 or more, you'll probably be better off saving in your child's name. That's because you're unlikely to qualify for much financial aid in any event.

If you're in the 15% tax bracket, you'll get little tax break from saving in your children's name(s), so you might as well keep the money in your name.

Anywhere in between is a tougher call. Consider how responsible your child is likely to be at age 18 or 21, and guesstimate what your income and tax bracket will be when your child reaches college age. Then use your best judgment.

Key Points

- *Investing for college is not as hard as it's made out to be because you may not have to pay full price, your child's college will likely cost less than the highest-cost schools, college-cost increases are slowing, and you don't need to save everything before your child's freshman year.*
- *College savings plans can be a big help in saving for college.*
- *Invest in solid portfolios of funds, like those listed above. The fund mixes in this chapter are also useful for other long-term goals.*
- *Use the worksheets to help you figure out how much you need to save each month for college.*
- *Whether you should save in your name or your child's name depends largely on your income.*

Investing for the Short Term

Portfolios for intermediate- and short-term goals other than retirement

ITH TEN YEARS OR LESS TO INVEST TOWARD A goal, you'll want to be more conservative than when investing for longer periods. That means you'll need a mix of stock funds and bond funds. And the stock funds you buy should be more conservative than the ones listed in the previous two chapters for longer-term goals. If the overall market crashes, your stock funds will still go down, but probably not nearly as far as the market averages.

Following are portfolios for goals up to ten years away. If you're investing for longer periods or for retirement, you'll want to read Chapters 5 and 6. The portfolios in this chapter are ideal for saving for college, a new house, a car—in fact, any relatively short-term goal except retirement.

Note that if you're now ten years from your goal, you'll want to readjust your portfolio every few years. For instance, when you have only six years to go, switch to the appropriate portfolio provided below. Another adjustment makes sense when you are two to four years from your goal. Better still, make the adjustments gradually as your goal becomes closer and closer. These shorter-term portfolios emphasize bond funds and low-risk stock funds. While they are less risky, they probably won't earn the high returns that an all-stock portfolio can.

The funds listed in this chapter are only suggestions. You

can construct equally solid portfolios by choosing other funds that use the same objectives and investment styles (see Chapters (17 and 18) or by identifying your own funds (see Chapter 15).

For goals six to ten years in the future
Depending on your tolerance for risk and Table B, "How Much to Invest in Stocks for All Goals *Except* Retirement," on page 32, invest 20% to 45% of your money in bonds. Put half your bond money in *Loomis Sayles Bond* (800-633-3330; LSBRX; www.loomissayles.com; for more information on this fund, see page 239) and the rest in *Harbor Bond* (800-422-1050; HABDX; www.harborfunds.com; page 238).

If you're investing in a taxable account and are in the 28% tax bracket or higher, split your bond money instead between *Vanguard High-Yield Tax-Exempt* (800-635-1511; WVAHX; www.vanguard.com; page 247) and *Vanguard Intermediate-Term Tax-Exempt* (VWITX).

Allocate any stock-fund money as follows:

Investing for Intermediate and Short-Term Goals Other Than Retirement

THESE PIE CHARTS illustrate how the portfolios outlined in this chapter divide your money between stock funds (by fund objective) bond funds and money-market funds, depending on your time horizon and tolerance for risk.

Goals 6 to 10 Years in the Future

MOST RISK

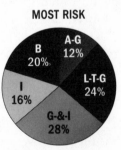

Aggressive-Growth =	12%
Long-Term-Growth =	24
Growth-and-Income =	28
International =	16
Bonds =	20
	100.0%

LEAST RISK

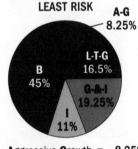

Aggressive-Growth =	8.25%
Long-Term-Growth =	16.50
Growth-and-Income =	19.25
International =	11.00
Bonds =	45.00
	100.00%

Skyline Special Equities (15%; 800-458-5222; SKSEX), an aggressive growth fund that buys stocks of small, undervalued companies (page 217).

Harbor Capital Appreciation (30%; 800-422-1050; HACAX; www.harborfunds.com), a long-term-growth fund, which invests in stocks of large companies with rapidly growing earnings (page 220).

Selected American Shares (35%; 800-243-1575; SLASX; www.selectedfunds.com), a growth-and-income fund that buys stocks of large, undervalued companies with good growth prospects (page 224).

Tweedy Browne Global Value (20%; 800-432-4789; TBGVX; www.tweedy.com), a relatively low-risk fund, which invests mainly in foreign stocks (page 231).

For goals four to six years in the future
Bond funds should make up 40% to 70% of your total investments, depending on where you fit in the "How Much to Invest in Stocks" table on page 32. Put one-quarter of your bond money

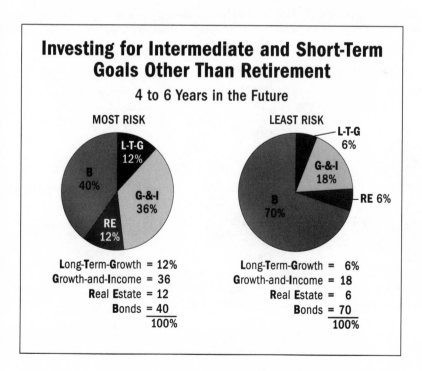

Investing for Intermediate and Short-Term Goals Other Than Retirement
4 to 6 Years in the Future

MOST RISK

L-T-G 12%
B 40%
G-&-I 36%
RE 12%

Long-Term-Growth = 12%
Growth-and-Income = 36
Real Estate = 12
Bonds = 40
100%

LEAST RISK

L-T-G 6%
G-&-I 18%
B 70%
RE 6%

Long-Term-Growth = 6%
Growth-and-Income = 18
Real Estate = 6
Bonds = 70
100%

in high-yielding *Northeast Investors Trust* (800-225-6704; www.northeastinvestors.com; NTHEX; for more information on this fund, see page 241). Invest the remainder in *Harbor Bond* (800-422-1050; www.harborfunds.com; HABDX; page 238) or, if you're investing in a taxable account and are in the 28% tax bracket or higher, in *Vanguard Intermediate-Term Tax-Exempt* (800-635-1511; www.vanguard.com; VWITX; page 247).

Allocate your stock money as follows:

Delphi Value (20%; 800-895-9936; www.kobren.com; KDVRX), a low-risk, long-term-growth fund that invests in undervalued small and mid-size companies (page 218).

Selected American Shares (60%; 800-243-1575; SLASX; www.selectedfunds.com), a growth-and-income fund that invests in large, undervalued companies that have good growth prospects (page 224).

Columbia Real Estate Equity (20%; 800-547-1707; CREEX; www.columbiafunds.com), which invests in real estate companies, which are fairly low risk (page 226).

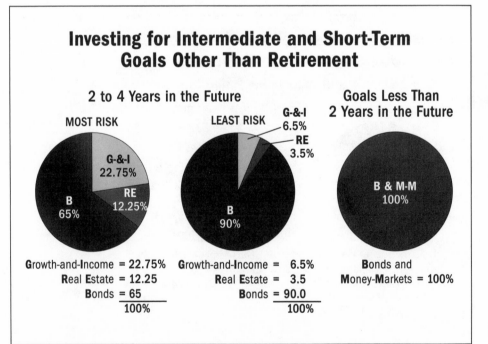

Investing for Intermediate and Short-Term Goals Other Than Retirement

2 to 4 Years in the Future

MOST RISK

G-&-I 22.75%
RE 12.25%
B 65%

LEAST RISK

G-&-I 6.5%
RE 3.5%
B 90%

Growth-and-Income = 22.75%
Real Estate = 12.25
Bonds = 65
100%

Growth-and-Income = 6.5%
Real Estate = 3.5
Bonds = 90.0
100%

Goals Less Than 2 Years in the Future

B & M-M 100%

Bonds and Money-Markets = 100%

For goals two to four years in the future

Divide your bond money—between 65% and 90% of your investments—evenly among *Harbor Bond* (800-422-1050; HABDX; www.harborfunds.com; for more information on this fund, see page 238), *Northeast Investors Trust* (800-225-6704; NTHEX; www.northeastinvestors.com; page 241), and *Vanguard Short-Term Corporate* (800-635-1511; www.vanguard.com; VFSTX; page 243).

If you're investing in a taxable account and your tax bracket is 28% or higher, use *Northeast Investors Trust,* but substitute *Vanguard Intermediate-Term Tax-Exempt* (800-662-7447; VWITX; www.vanguard.com; page 247) and *Vanguard Limited-Term Tax-Exempt* (VMLTX; page 247) for the other two funds.

Divide your stock money as follows:

Selected American Shares (65%; 800-243-1575; SLASX; www.selectedfunds.com), a low-risk growth-and-income fund that invests in stocks of large, undervalued companies with good growth prospects (page 224).

Columbia Real Estate Equity (35%; 800-547-1707; CREEX; www.columbiafunds.com), which invests in real estate companies, which are fairly low risk (page 226).

For goals less than two years in the future

Invest your money as follows:

Strong Advantage (50%; 800-368-1030; www.strongfunds.com; STADX), an ultra-short-term bond fund (for more information on this fund, see page 242). If you're in the 28% tax bracket or higher, substitute *Vanguard Limited-Term Tax-Exempt* (800-635-1511; www.vanguard.com; VMLTX; page 247).

Vanguard Prime Money Market (50%; 800-635-1511; www.vanguard .com), a money-market fund. If you are in the 39.6% tax bracket, substitute *Vanguard Tax-Exempt Money Market.* (For more on money-market funds, pages 244–245.)

Key Points

- *These portfolios are appropriate for shorter-term goals than those listed in the previous two chapters.*
- *The closer you are to needing your money, the more conservative you'll want to be. That means putting less in stock funds and more in bond funds and money-market funds.*

How and Where to Buy Funds

Filling out fund application forms, tracking your funds' progress, using an online broker, and transferring retirement accounts to funds

HEN I DROPPED BY THE DIBENEDETTOS IN LATE spring, their condominium looked surprisingly spacious. Nancy explained that it was on the market and the real estate agent had suggested rearranging some furniture to make it look bigger. The couple had decided that the two-bedroom condo was just too small.

Over in a corner of the living room, Paul had neatly stacked a growing pile of investment literature—prospectuses, annual reports and account applications—they had received from funds, based on my suggestion of investment choices for Paul Jr.'s college and for their retirement. (For details on the funds, see Chapters 5 and 6.) It wouldn't be a neat stack for long, though. On this Saturday afternoon, Paul Jr., not yet 3, found playing with the forms more interesting than watching Barney on television. With Paul Jr. "helping," Nancy and Paul began to fill out the forms.

Almost immediately, Nancy complained about the growing quantity of junk mail they had been receiving since they called the fund companies' toll-free numbers to request applications. "They send us this all the time," Nancy says. "It's just more and more paper in the mail. Who has time to go through all this? I just want to invest quickly and get it over with.

I am beginning to feel a little uneasy. Here I am on a mission to show how easy it is for beginners to invest in funds, and Paul and Nancy are finding it harder than I thought they would. "Well," I tell them, "there is an even simpler way. Let's see if you can buy your funds through an online broker."

Buying Through an Online Broker

ONE OF THE NICE THINGS ABOUT THE FINANCIAL-SERVICES industry is that, because there is so much competition, you can reach most online brokers by telephone 24 hours a day, seven days a week. And, at least theoretically, their Web sites are always there to help you.

When you buy and sell funds through an online broker, you'll usually use fund ticker symbols to identify the funds. That's why I've included ticker symbols with the data for funds throughout the book. If you forget a ticker symbol, the online-brokerage screen will let you type in a fund name to retrieve the symbol.

Charles Schwab

For starters, I visited the Web site of Charles Schwab (800-435-4000; www.schwab.com), which runs the biggest "mutual fund supermarket" in terms of total client dollars invested. (All transaction fees listed in the following discussion are for buying or selling online unless otherwise noted. It's usually more expen-

---

Sales Charges and Transaction Fees

ONLINE BROKERS sell mostly funds that have no sales charges, although you can buy load funds (as well as stocks and bonds) from them if you wish. On many funds without sales charges, an online broker charges you nothing: The fund pays the broker to sell the fund. On some other no-load funds, however, online brokers assess investors a small transaction fee—less than 1.0% of the amount you invest except on very small purchases. The difference between a sales charge and a transaction fee may seem like a distinction without a difference—either way you're paying money to buy a fund. But keep this in mind: Sales charges tend to be much, much higher than transaction fees.

sive to buy and sell over the phone.)

The Schwab program gives you access to some 2,480 funds, most without any sales charges or transaction fees. The other funds are available for relatively low transaction fees—a minimum of $39. As long as you don't plan to buy or sell often, that's not much to pay for the convenience of getting one consolidated monthly statement for all your funds and being spared an avalanche of mail from fund companies.

Another big plus: Schwab provides a free annual tax summary for all funds you've sold in the previous year. This can save a lot of time and aggravation when doing your taxes (see Chapter 9 for details on doing your fund taxes).

And, more
Fidelity Investments Brokerage (800-434-3548; www.fidelity.com) offers Fidelity funds without transaction fees—something you can't find anywhere else. Overall, the brokerage offers 2,107 no-load funds, just over half of them without a transaction fee. Fidelity's service is fairly good. It charges a flat fee of $75 for online trades—cheaper than Schwab for large trades. Fidelity also provides its customers with a free yearly tax summary.
Muriel Siebert (800-872-0711; www.siebertnet.com) offers 2,436 no-load funds, almost half of them without transaction fees. Its transaction fees are $35, a little lower than Schwab's and Fidelity, plus it also offers a free yearly tax summary.

A number of other online brokers offer numerous funds without transaction fees. Most charge even lower transaction fees than Schwab, Fidelity and Siebert for those funds that have transaction fees. But they don't offer year-end tax summaries, which can be a big inconvenience if you aren't investing in an IRA or other tax-deferred account (see the discussion under "What Your Fund Sends You," as well as chapter 9). They include:
TD Waterhouse (800-839-2837; www.tdwaterhouse.com; 2,342 no-load funds; 1,386 without transaction fees; transaction fees, $24)
DLJ Direct (800-825-5723; www.dljdirect.com; 1,835 no-load funds; 981 without transaction fees; transaction fees, $35)

While they don't offer year-end summaries and do charge transaction fees, the following firms offer a great variety of funds:
Ameritrade (800-263-7487; www.ameritrade.com; 2,596 no-load funds; $18 transaction fees)

Helpful Web Sites

MANY FUND COMPANIES offer helpful education and financial-planning materials at their Web sites, and you usually don't have to be an investor in the fund to explore the site. Some of the best include www.estrong.com, www.fidelity.com, www.troweprice.com, www.vanguard.com. You'll also find good information at www.kiplinger.com and www.morningstar.com. For a listing of other good Web sites, turn to pages 194–195 in Chapter 15.

Brown and Company (800-822-2021; www.brownco.com; 2,596 no-load funds; $19 transaction fees)

SHOPPING STRATEGY

Prices, selections and services change so frequently that you'll find it worthwhile to visit several Web sites. Find out which one has the best deals and offers more of the funds you want without high fees.

Whether you use the Internet or the telephone to buy and sell funds, be sure *not* to limit yourself to no-transaction-fee funds. Funds that charge a low transaction fee are sometimes better than their no-fee competitors—and very often cheaper (in terms of annual expenses), because they don't pay online brokers to hawk them. If you are buying and holding for a long period, as all savvy investors should, the small transaction fee will make very little difference.

Generally, the convenience of buying and selling through online brokers is well worth the occasional transaction fees—particularly if you get a free, year-end cost-basis summary. If you decide to sell a fund, you don't have to wait for a check from your old fund company before you can reinvest the money in a new fund. Typically, you can sell one day and buy the next; some firms will let you sell and buy the same day. The only drawback to trading online is that it is so easy that you can be beguiled into trading funds more than you should. Remember the advice in the rest of this book: Don't give up on a fund unless it does badly against its peers for a good, long time. (See especially Chapter 16.)

Unfortunately for Nancy and Paul, Schwab and its lower-cost competitors levy transaction fees on several funds they want to invest in. While a small fee on a one-time or occasional basis is no big deal, such a fee charged every month on a purchase of only $50 to $200 *is* a big deal. If a fund charges you a $50 fee for investing $50,000, that equals just one-tenth of one percent. But if you pay a $25 fee on a $100 investment every month, you're paying a 25% transaction fee—a huge drag on your returns. So Paul and Nancy went back to filling in the forms from the fund companies. They made it through the forms for four funds in about 30 minutes. Once they had begun, they didn't find it all that difficult—even with Paul Jr.'s help.

Step by Step Through the Forms

APPLICATIONS FORMS, PARTICULARLY FOR REGULAR, TAXABLE accounts, usually aren't difficult to fill out—and you can always call the fund's toll-free number if you get stuck. Most application forms will be similar, and in this section, I discuss the elements that you can expect to find on any company's forms. Online brokerage forms are similar to those for fund accounts and are just as easy to fill out. They, too, offer toll-free numbers where you can find assistance.

STEP ONE: WHOSE ACCOUNT?

Step One asks you to fill in your name and social security number. If you're opening an individual account, or an account you'll own jointly with your spouse or someone else, that's easy. Nancy is investing for Paul Jr.'s college, however, which is a little trickier. The DiBenedettos have already decided to put the money in Paul Jr.'s name under the Uniform Gift to Minors Act/Uniform Transfer to Minors Act (UGMA/UTMA), as described on page 87–88. Nancy can't find a box to fill in her choice, and is flummoxed that she's stuck on Step One. "Instead of going through all this, I would rather have someone sit down with me and say, 'This is what this means. This is what that means,'" she says. I try to let her find her own way, and soon she figures out she needs to fill out the box for a custodial account. She lists herself as the custodian (the one who can move the money around until Paul Jr. comes of age). Paul Sr. could have listed himself as custodian if the couple had preferred, but only one adult can be listed as custodian. The form also requires Paul Jr.'s social security number and date of birth.

STEP TWO: WHERE ARE YOU?

Step Two requires your address and statement of citizenship. The fund company usually asks for your day and evening phone numbers. These are optional; leave them blank if you like. It's not a bad idea to list your work phone number, however. If you make a mistake on your application, the fund company can call and clear it up. I have never had a fund company call me for any other reason, much less to sell products.

STEP THREE: WHICH FUNDS?

Step Three asks you to select your funds. Make sure that you list each fund by its precise name. Many funds within the same fund family have very similar names. For instance, Vanguard has a fund called Windsor and another called Windsor II.

Be sure to write your personal check (no traveler's checks or third-party checks) and fill in the blank on the form for at least the minimum initial investment required. Minimum investments range from $100 to $100,000, but typically are between $1,000 and $3,000. If you can't afford the initial minimum, many funds will let you start with less so long as you join an automatic investment plan (see Step Five, below). Funds also usually have lower initial minimums for IRAs, generally $500 to $1,000.

STEP FOUR: TO RECEIVE OR REINVEST?

Step Four asks you how you want your capital gains and dividends handled. Unless you check one of the boxes indicating that you want your dividends or capital gains paid in cash, the fund will reinvest your dividends and capital gains in additional shares. I discuss reinvesting your dividends and capital gains on page 109.

STEP FIVE: FLIPPING THE SWITCH

Step Five contains instructions on how to set up an automatic investment plan, allowing the fund to automatically debit your checking account every month for an amount of money you specify, down to a minimum set by the fund company. You'll have to fill in bank information and attach a voided check.

Step Six: Check Writing

Step Six gives directions on how to set up check-writing if you are opening a money-market or bond-fund account. Check writing is a valuable convenience in a money-market fund, but to avoid tax headaches you may not want to use it for bond funds (see page 115 for details). If you need money from a bond fund, you may minimize tax headaches by transferring a relatively large amount, say $5,000, to a money-market fund in the same fund family, then writing checks on the money-market fund. That way you'll have only one taxable sale to report to the IRS, rather than the several you would have to report if you wrote checks on your bond fund. You usually can't write money-market checks for less than $250 or $500, though some funds are beginning to offer lower check-writing minimums.

Step Seven: Other Conveniences

Step Seven gives you the option to sell one fund and buy another one in the same fund family simply by calling the fund company's toll-free number. You can also redeem your shares in the fund with a phone call and have a check mailed to your home address. Some fund families allow you to redeem online (and all the online brokerages do). These are handy options.

Step Eight: Skip This Question

Step Eight is a request for information about your employer, occupation and work address. The fund company doesn't require you to answer these questions, and I see no benefit in answering them.

For regulatory reasons, the National Association of Securities Dealers requires fund companies to ask whether you work for a stock broker or related firm. But you don't have to answer them either.

Step Nine: Straight to and From the Bank?

Step Nine asks if you want to establish the ability to wire money from the fund company to your bank or vice versa. This can save you a little time when you want to redeem or purchase shares, but check first to see whether your bank will charge to send or receive money in this manner. If there is a charge, the service is probably not worth it. If your fund allows it, also check the box that will enable you to use electronic fund transfers (EFTs) between your fund and your bank. These transfers typically take a day or so, which is slower than wiring money, but they are almost always free.

STEP TEN: A FINAL FLOURISH

Step Ten is your signature. There's a lot of legal mumbo jumbo beforehand telling you that by signing you certify that the information on the form is correct and that you are not subject to IRS backup withholding (if you are, you know it). Just sign and date the application, enclose your check, and send off the application.

IRA Applications

FOR THE MOST PART, IRA APPLICATIONS ARE SIMILAR TO REGUlar account applications. I'll highlight the differences here and focus particularly on questions related to transfers.

WHAT KIND OF ACCOUNT AND HOW MUCH TO DEPOSIT?

Check "individual account" for yourself, if you're employed. Check "spousal account" for a spouse who is not employed. Each spouse can contribute up to $2,000 in earned income annually, so long as your combined earned income is at least $4,000. You can contribute for, say, calendar year 2001 from January 1, 2001, until the day you file your taxes in 2002, usually no later than April 15—or as a late as October 15 if you request two filing extensions. The earlier you contribute, the better; it gives your money that much more time to grow. Make sure to specify the correct year for your contribution. Otherwise, the IRS might think you didn't contribute anything for one year and contributed twice what's allowed the following year.

Also give your birth date, which will become important when you begin withdrawing money from your IRA, sometime between ages 59½ and 70½.

As with regular accounts, most IRAs give you the option of having your bank account debited every month until you hit the $2,000 mark. Don't contribute more than the $2,000 legal maximum. A monthly contribution of $166.66 will keep you under the $2,000 maximum.

ROTH IRAS

Opening one of the Roth IRAs is virtually the same as opening a regular IRA. The forms are essentially identical to the forms for the old IRAs, so they'll be no trouble to fill out. In many instances, the form simply asks you to check a box saying whether you want to open a Roth IRA or a regular IRA.

HOW TO HANDLE A TRANSFER

If your contribution to an IRA is annual, as most are, check that box on the form. But if you're moving your IRA from a bank or other custodian to the mutual fund, you'll want to check the box that indicates it's a transfer from an existing IRA. Be sure also to complete the "IRA Transfer Form," which you may have to specially request from the fund company. Print your name exactly as it was on the old IRA (including your middle name or an initial), and staple a copy of a recent statement to the transfer form.

Check with your current trustees to see whether they require a signature guarantee—a signature from a bank or a broker (not a notary public) verifying that you are who you say you are. Usually, you'll want the old trustees to convert all your assets to cash before transferring them to the new trustee. Otherwise, the mutual fund you're moving your IRA to might sell the securities and bill you for the brokerage transactions—or reject your application.

Other kinds of transfers

Whether you are transferring your account from another mutual fund, a bank, an insurance company or a brokerage, the process is pretty similar. The same goes for transfers into a new online brokerage account.

From multiple trustees. If you are transferring IRAs from more than one trustee, make sure to ask for enough forms to handle each transfer.

From a bank CD. If you are transferring from a bank CD, you will generally come out ahead by asking—in the appropriate space on the transfer-of-assets form—that the money be transferred upon maturity, thereby avoiding any early-withdrawal penalties.

From a former employer's 401(k) plan. If you want to transfer your retirement assets to an IRA, you're likewise best off having your previous employer send the check directly to the mutual fund company or mail you a check made out to the mutual fund company. The procedures and forms are quite similar to those for direct transfers from one trustee to another.

BENEFICIARIES

Make sure to designate your beneficiaries—the people you want to receive the proceeds when you die (usually your spouse or children). This is usually on the back of the IRA application or on a separate page. You can always change beneficiaries later.

FEES AND FINE PRINT

The information you get with the application from the fund company, or from an online broker, will include a lot of legalese about the IRA, most of which you can ignore. Be sure to

Keep each yearly statement for at least three years after you sell all your shares and file your tax return reporting the sale.

find out, however, what fees the sponsor charges for an IRA. You can find these in the small print, on the IRA application (sometimes), or by calling the fund. Some fund companies charge annual fees, sometimes for each fund account. Some charge a fee to open an account, and some even charge to close your account. Many funds don't charge anything anymore, because these fees irritate consumers. Don't stay away from a good fund company, however, simply because of a niggling $10 or $20 annual IRA fee. If the company has solid

funds with low annual overall expenses, you'll more than make up the difference.

What Your Fund Sends You

FUNDS AND ONLINE BROKERS SEND AN ACKNOWLEDGMENT OF every investment you make. Save each one at least until the next statement comes. Usually statements are cumulative, listing all transactions for the calendar year. At the end of each year, most funds send you statements summing up your activity. When these arrive, you can throw all the monthly and quarterly statements away for that year, but, make sure to keep each yearly statement for at least three years after you sell all your shares and file your tax return reporting the sale. So long as your account is open, keep yearly statements indefinitely.

If you have sold any funds in a taxable account during the

year, many fund compa-
nies will send you a separate annual tax state-
ment, which is a blessing
when you do your taxes.
Besides itemizing your
transactions, these sum-
maries show the tax basis
of any fund shares you
sold during the previous

Mutual Fund Mail

IF YOU DON'T WANT to receive a
bunch of mailings from the mutual
fund companies you contact, ask
them not to mail you anything
except the prospectus and application. Many fund companies will
honor such a request.

year—this is information the IRS demands on Schedule D of
your tax return. Again, keep these at least three years. Fund
companies also send you annual Form 1099-DIV statements,
showing dividends and other distributions that you must report
on your income tax.

The year-to-year paperwork is less onerous in IRAs and
other tax-exempt accounts. Once a year the fund company will
send you Form 5498 that tells you how much your IRA is worth
(a copy also goes to the IRS). Keep these forms in a folder against
the day you begin making withdrawals from your IRAs.

Look It Up

WANT TO SEE HOW YOUR FUND IS DOING? THE EASIEST WAY
is to look it up in the newspaper mutual fund tables or
on the Internet. Not all newspapers carry all funds, so
you may have to get a weekly *Barron's* or Friday *Wall Street
Journal* for complete fund information. You can usually find a
fair amount of information about most funds in any newspaper.
Internet listings, including those of online brokers,
Kiplinger.com and Morningstar.com, are usually more exten-
sive. A big plus of the Internet: Many Web sites allow users to
screen funds, so that you can identify, say, the ten aggressive-
growth funds with annual expenses under 1.5% that had the
best performance over the past five years.

Not all newspapers list the same data, nor do they list it the
same way. But following is a guide to the fund listings of many
newspapers. Even if yours is different, this guide should help you
navigate the fund tables. Most internet fund listings will provide
this data and more.

But *Which* Mutual Funds?

How to Read the Mutual Fund Listings

MOST DAILY NEWSPAPERS publish mutual fund tables in the business pages. Some have devised their own presentations. Here's a guide to the rest:

NAV is net asset value per share, that is, what a share of the fund is worth.

The **offering price** is what you pay per share.

NL in the pricing column means there is no sales load.

NAV Chg., daily chg or net chg is the change in the fund's NAV from the previous day.

YTD%ret is the year-to-date return.

p or b next to the fund's name means that it charges a yearly 12b-1 fee. Funds may be listed as NL even if they charge

this fee so long as it isn't more than 0.25% of assets.

r stands for redemption charge, which may be permanent or temporary. It may start as high as 6% and decline gradually. A fund can have a redemption fee but still be called no-load.

p and **r** mean that the fund levies both 12b-1 and redemption fees. In most cases, p and r listed together refer to a fund with a contingent deferred sales charge. Such a fund may not be listed as no-load.

Some newspapers substitute **t** for funds with both p and r charges.

x stands for "ex-dividend," meaning only current shareholders get the fund's next dividend payout, which is imminent. New buyers won't get it.

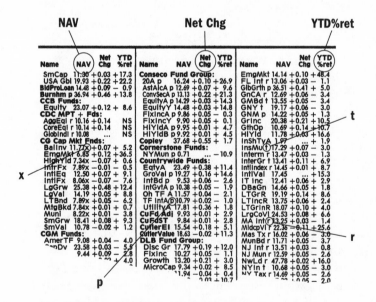

The fund name

First look for your fund alphabetically. Usually this is a straight-forward process, but not always. For instance, if you own EuroPacific fund, you'll have to know to look it up under the American family of funds—in the As, not the Es.

The NAV

Next find the NAV—that's the *net asset value* per share of the securities held in the fund. If the fund lists a different *offering price* (the price at which it will sell to new investors), that means it assesses a sales charge. Usually, no-load funds will contain the abbreviation NL in that space. *NAV chg, daily chg* or *net chg* tells you how much the fund went up or down in value from the previous day. Some fund listings, including those in the *Wall Street Journal* and *Barron's*, also tell you how many percentage points a fund has risen or fallen since the start of the year, over the past 12 months, and sometimes over the past three and five years.

A quick note on your *real* rate of return

Just because a fund is up, say, 20% so far this year doesn't mean you've made 20% on your investment. You may have bought the fund on a different day than Dec. 31 of last year, or on several different dates. This can change your personal rate of return significantly. (I get more angry letters on this subject than perhaps any other, and, alas, the fund companies are almost invariably right.) Figuring out your personal rate of return, unfortunately, takes more mathematical computations than most people want to undertake. There is hope for change, though. The Securities and Exchange Commission is considering regulations that would require all mutual funds to funds furnish each investor with his or her personal rate of return. Meanwhile, some money-management software such as *Quicken* and *Microsoft Money* will compute your personal rate of return.

Performance ratings

In some newspapers, fund-research firms such as Morningstar and Lipper also provide ratings of how well a fund has done in the past. These are superficial and not worthy of your attention. Similarly, ignore fund advertisements boasting that Morningstar rated a fund "Five Stars." Morningstar maintains that the star system gives you only a few clues about a fund. I agree. To pick funds, you'll want to dig much deeper. For that, you'll want to look in Part Three, particularly Chapter 15, "How to Pick Winning Stock Funds."

12b-1 and other fees

The letter *p* or *b* next to the fund's name usually means it charges a *12b-1 fee*, which funds use to cover marketing and other expenses. No-load funds can't charge a 12b-1 fee of more than 0.25% of assets.

An *r* stands for *redemption charge.* Most no-load funds that levy these charges, designed to discourage short-term trading, impose them only if you sell a fund within say, a year of buying it. Load funds, however, may assess sales charges whenever you redeem shares, even years after investing.

Ex-dividend

An *x* next to a fund stands for *ex-dividend,* meaning only current shareholders will get the next dividend or capital-gains payout, which is imminent. New buyers won't get the dividend.

Key Points

- *Don't let the blizzard of mail that mutual fund companies may send distract you. Some companies will heed requests to reduce mail.*
- *Filling out fund forms is an easy matter if you follow the directions in this chapter.*
- *Buying funds through an online broker can save a lot of time and trouble, but may cost a little money.*

Paying Uncle Sam

Six rules for minimizing your tax bills— and tax headaches

ANY FUND INVESTORS PAY MORE THAN THEIR fair share to Uncle Sam. That's not just my opinion. It's the belief of no less an authority than Fred Goldberg, former head of the Internal Revenue Service (and no relation to yours truly). In this chapter, I'll show you six ways you can minimize the income taxes on profits from your taxable funds. (Funds in tax-deferred accounts require little tax record keeping until you begin withdrawing money, usually between ages 59½ and 70½.) The most important thing is to keep good records—whether on a computer or with pencil and paper. That'll keep you from overpaying your taxes. However, if you're like many people who find keeping detailed records burdensome, I'll also describe some shortcuts. Some of these may cost you a tiny bit in return, but they'll save you time. And, after all, one of the main advantages of mutual funds is that they make your investing life simpler.

Rule 1:
Keep Careful Records

THE BIGGEST MISTAKE MANY FUND INVESTORS MAKE WHEN they pay their income taxes is suffering amnesia about their reinvestment of dividends and capital gains in additional shares of a fund. Let's say you buy 100 shares of the Makemerich stock fund at $10 per share, for a total of $1,000. At the end of the year Makemerich pays you a distribution of $1 per share in long-term capital gains (profits on stocks the fund sold after holding them for more than 12 months) and 50 cents per share in dividends—or a total of $150, which is reinvested in additional shares. The fund company sends you a 1099-DIV form listing those distributions, and you dutifully copy the numbers onto your income-tax return for that year. (Funds that hold bonds and some income-oriented stock funds often pay distributions quarterly or monthly.)

The following year, you sell your shares of the Makemerich fund and replace them with the Pot of Gold fund. The Makemerich fund sends you a final 1099 form—this one listing the total amount you received when you sold the fund. Let's say you sold your shares for $1,500. When you sit down to do your income taxes for that year, you record that you paid $1,000 for your shares of Makemerich and sold them for $1,500. Therefore, you have a capital gain of $500—from which Uncle Sam gets his cut. Not so fast!

When they sell, many investors neglect to add to the cost of their original investment the value of the money they reinvested.

The problem here is that many investors forget about the $150 in capital gains and dividends that they had reinvested in additional shares. *You've already paid taxes on that $150.* Since you reinvested that money in extra shares, you really paid $1,000 *plus* $150, or $1,150, for the shares you sold. Subtracting $1,150 from $1,500, your real capital gain on selling the fund is not $500, but only $350. Many investors hold a fund five, ten or 20 years, reinvesting dividends and capital gains every year. Unfortunately, when they sell their shares, they neglect to add to the cost of their original investment (called the *cost basis* in tax lingo) the value of all the money they reinvested over the years.

On page 113 is a worksheet that shows you how to keep a pencil-and-paper record of all purchases, sales and reinvestments in each mutual fund you own. If you use *Quicken, Microsoft Money* or any Internet record-keeping service, such as Microsoft Money's at www.moneycentral.msn.com, you'll need to enter the same numbers to avoid overpaying taxes.

Record keeping, however, can be a minor nightmare because funds tend to pay these distributions in dribs and drabs. For instance, a fund might pay you:

- **1.4414 shares in dividends** worth $34.91,
- **0.4806 shares in short-term capital gains** (gains on securities held

by a fund for a year or less) worth $11.64 (short-term gains distributed from your fund are treated just like dividends on your tax return and are taxed as ordinary income), and

• **3.6837 shares in long-term capital gains** (gains on securities held more than 12 months) worth $89.22.

Anyone who owns funds can attest that—whether transcribed with pencil and paper or on your computer—it is a tedious job to enter all those numbers. (Most people who use computer software or the Internet find the job less of a hassle.) Also, remember you'll need to track the reinvestment dates to determine your holding periods.

I've labeled this section Rule 1. If you keep good records you'll have no need for the shortcuts described in some of the following sections. You do need to make a choice, however: Either resolve to keep good records, or follow the shortcuts.

Rule 2:
Use the Average-Cost Method

THE IRS ALLOWS YOU TO USE ANY ONE OF THE FOLLOWING three methods for calculating the cost basis of fund shares that you sell.

FIRST-IN, FIRST-OUT

This method assumes that the *first shares* you bought are the first shares you sell. Say you bought your first 100 shares of the Makemerich fund at $10 a share (for a total of $1,000) and then bought 60 more shares at $15 (for a total of $900). If you sold 40 shares at $20 a share (for a total of $800), you would owe taxes on a capital gain of $400—that is, the $800 you sold your 40 shares for minus the $400 you paid for 40 shares (40 of the first 100 that you bought at $10 apiece). Unless you choose otherwise, the IRS assumes you're using the first-in-first-out method.

SPECIFIC IDENTIFICATION

If you keep good records, this is the method to use. You'll delay paying some of your taxes. When you sell, the IRS allows you to designate *which shares* in a fund you are selling. By choosing the highest-cost shares to sell first, you can cut your tax bill for that year. In the example above, this is clearly to your advantage unless you have a loss to absorb. Flexibility is key to specific identification. Instead of selling the first 40 shares you bought at a lower price, you can sell the 40 shares you bought at the higher price—in this instance, 40 of the 60 shares you purchased at $15 per share. Your cost basis on these shares is $15 times 40 shares, or $600. Since you sold your 40 shares for $800, you now have a taxable gain of just $200—half what you'd have using first-in-first-out.

The specific-identification method will add to your paperwork. Each time you sell shares, you have to write a letter to the fund company stating which shares you are selling and asking for a written confirmation. You also must keep track of which shares you sold when for your own records.

For all that paperwork, your savings from using the specific-identification method are likely to be minuscule unless you hold your remaining shares for 15 years or more. Why? Because when you sell your remaining shares in the fund, the tax bite you so artfully dodged will catch up with you—since you've already sold your high-cost shares.

AVERAGE COST

This is far and away the easiest method for most taxpayers to use. You simply average the cost of the shares you bought and use that as your cost basis. You bought 100 shares of Makemerich at $10 per share, and 60 shares at $15. You compute average cost by taking the $1,900 you invested altogether and dividing by the 160 total shares you bought, which gives you an average cost of $11.875 per share. Since you sold 40 shares, you multiply 40 times $11.875 to get your cost basis, which is $475. Subtract that from the $800 you made from selling your 40 shares, and you have a capital gain of $325.

Doesn't sound simple? Well, it's not. But the trick is that many mutual funds—and some online brokerages from which you can buy funds—automatically provide you with average-cost-basis information. All you have to do is copy onto your tax form the information from the statement the fund sends you at the end of each year in which you've sold shares—and, voilà, you've satisfied the IRS. "You might as well use the funds' figures," says Tom Ochsenschlager, a partner with the accounting firm of Grant, Thornton. "You'll usually end up with

Tracking Your Funds

YOU CAN USE the worksheet below to track your mutual funds—that is, unless your fund supplies you with average cost basis and you plan to employ it.

The example filled in below uses the average-cost method, although the worksheet can be used with any of the three IRS-approved methods. Using first-in-first out, the sale would have resulted in a $23.80 gain. Using specific identification, and selling from the lot purchased on 6–15–00, when the price was highest, you'd have a loss of $23.82. (*Note:* The purchase on 12–28–00 was a dividend reinvestment.)

Date	Buy/ sell	Dollar amount	Number of shares	Share price	Share cost basis	Total basis	Total shares owned	Average basis	Dollar gain (or loss)
3–15–00	Buy	$1,000	100	$10.00	$10.00	$1,000	100	$10.00	
6–15–00	Buy	1,000	90.91	11.00	11.00	2,000	190.91	10.48	
12–28–00	Buy	99.76	8.56	11.65	11.65	2,099.76	199.47	10.53	
4–15–00	Sell	500.00	47.62	10.50	10.53	1,598.32	151.85	10.53	–$1.44

the same money, and you'll save a lot of work."

Before you rely on a fund to provide you with average-cost data, make sure your fund does, indeed, provide it. Even better: Pick an online broker from pages 96–98 that supplies year-end, average-cost data on all funds. And, to be safe, keep at least each year-end statement from your funds—just in case something goes wrong. Fund companies usually charge for copies of old records.

Also, keep in mind that the IRS lets you switch between first-in-first-out and specific-identification methods, but once you choose the average-cost method, you're stuck with it until you sell all the shares of that fund.

The average-cost information that many funds give you includes data on reinvested dividends and capital gains. If you could be sure that all the funds you own would provide you with this data, you would be freed of all the record keeping involved in tracking reinvested dividends and capital gains. Alas, many good funds still don't provide this information, and until they do, it's better to be safe than sorry: Keep your own records.

Rule 3:
If You're Going to Sell a Fund, Sell All of It

THE MORE TRANSACTIONS YOU HAVE IN ANY INDIVIDUAL mutual fund account, the more complicated your tax preparation becomes. If a fund company provides you with average-cost tax information, that's no problem. But if it doesn't, you will have to be mighty good with a calculator—or have software to do the job for you. Things get the diciest when you decide to sell off a portion of your holdings in a fund and hold on to the rest. By the time you decide to sell off the third or fourth lot of shares, you may be ready to pull your hair out unless you've kept scrupulous records.

The easiest solution: When you sell shares in a fund, sell all of them. Then you don't have to worry about which accounting method to use. Your cost basis is simply the total amount you invested in the fund. In the example above, you have invested a total of $1,900, which is your cost basis. Instead of selling just 40 shares, sell the entire 160 shares at $20 per share, or $3,200. Your capital gain is $3,200 minus $1,900, or $1,300. Even true math phobics can do that calculation with aplomb. Then, to maintain the proportions in your portfolio, invest your money in a similar fund.

WHY IT PAYS TO HANG ON

Selling all your shares can be tricky, or impossible, if you are invested in a fund that is closed to new investors and you wish to keep your place in the fund. Call the fund and ask whether there's a minimum number of shares you must hold in order to remain an investor. Even if you sell all your shares, some funds will give you several months to buy back in. Of course, the easiest way to reduce your tax record keeping is to avoid selling funds if you can. Don't hold on to a lousy fund, but being a long-term investor makes sense for lots of reasons, including making your taxes simpler. If you want to routinely switch from fund to fund, at least confine those activities to a tax-deferred account such as an IRA.

The tax law provides more incentives for staying put. If you hold fund shares for more than 12 months your maximum tax rate when you sell is 20% (10% if you're in the 15% tax bracket). If you sell a fund after owning it 12 months or less, you'll have to pay taxes on it as ordinary income. Ordinary rates range from 15% to 39.6%.

Rule 4:
Don't Write Checks on Bond Funds

I T'S SO EASY TO SWITCH FROM ONE FUND TO ANOTHER WITH A mouse click or a telephone call, or to withdraw money simply by writing a check on many bond funds, that it's easy to lose sight of the fact that the IRS considers each of those transactions a "taxable event." If you have a bond fund and write a dozen checks on it over a couple of years, your tax records may well become impenetrable, unless you keep careful records.

If you know that you don't keep good records, take the checkbook your fund company sends you when you open a bond fund and tear it into little pieces. Keep a money-market fund at the same fund company and hold on to that checkbook. If you need money, transfer a big, round number, say $10,000, from your bond fund to your money-market fund. Then write checks on that fund. Since money-market funds endeavor to keep a constant price of $1 per shares, and pay only dividend income, you don't need to worry about capital gains or figuring a cost basis on these funds.

Rule 5:
Don't Buy a Fund Just Before It Distributes Gains

FUNDS ARE REQUIRED TO DISTRIBUTE ALMOST ALL OF THEIR capital gains and dividends to shareholders every year. Most stock funds make distributions just once, usually in December. The date the fund declares the dividend is known as its *ex-dividend* date. If you have the misfortune to buy shares just before that date, you probably will immediately get hit with a taxable distribution from the fund.

For this reason, it's best to be wary of investing large amounts in funds late in the year. Call a fund's toll-free number and ask for its ex-dividend date. Then make sure to buy after that date. Some funds are considerate enough to estimate, in advance, how big a distribution they intend to declare on the ex-dividend date. If the distribution is a small one, say 5% or less of the fund's net asset value, you might want to go ahead and buy the fund anyway. But if it's a big one, you're better off delaying your investment.

Late-year distributions can sometimes add insult to injury. Sometimes funds that have had a horrible year will, nevertheless, have large taxable distributions. This is a matter of fund accounting, and there is little that funds—or shareholders—can do to control it. If you do have the misfortune to buy a fund just before it goes ex-dividend, there is some solace. When you eventually sell your shares, your cost basis will be higher than it would otherwise have been, because you bought your shares at the higher price. But you will have lost use of the money you paid in taxes for the time you hold the shares.

For instance, suppose you buy the Makemerich fund at $10 a share just before it declares a $2 distribution. The share price will drop to $8. You'll pay taxes on the $2 distribution the next time you file your income taxes. But when you sell the fund, say a year later, your cost basis on your original shares will be $10 rather than the $8 it would have been had you bought it *after* the ex-dividend date. That will save you money on taxes.

In other words, when you buy a fund before it goes ex-dividend, you pay some of your taxes up front. If you buy after it goes ex-dividend, you don't have to pay those taxes until you sell the fund.

Rule 6:
Dealing With the IRS Is Never Really Simple

OKAY, THIS LAST RULE DOESN'T MAKE THINGS SIMPLER. BUT it's the truth: As you've seen already in this chapter, investing in mutual funds (or anything else, for that matter) requires that you learn some arcane rules (or pay an accountant to do the work for you). Here are some of the less simple things you need to know about funds and taxes:

INHERITED OR GIFT FUNDS

While your cost basis is usually the amount you invested in a fund, that's not the case if you inherit fund shares. In that event, your basis is generally the value of the shares on the date of the death of the person who bequeathed you the shares.

However, if you receive shares as a gift and sell them at a loss, your basis is whichever is *lower*: the value of the shares on the day you were given them, or the price that your benefactor paid for them. In other words, you don't get to deduct any decline in value before you got the gift. If you sell for a profit, your basis is the same as your benefactor's.

MUNICIPAL MISCELLANY

Income from municipal bond funds is exempt from federal tax, but it must be reported on your federal return. Many states and localities make you pay taxes on some or all income from muni funds. Also, a muni fund can realize a capital gain if it sells bonds for a profit. These capital gains are taxable. In addition, to avoid Alternative Minimum Tax complications, try to steer clear of muni funds that hold so-called "private-activity bonds," which might be taxable to you under the Alternative Minimum Tax.

DIVIDENDS, NOT INTEREST

Income from mutual funds, even money-market funds and bond funds, is dividend income, not interest income, as far as the IRS is concerned. This is so even though these funds generally hold debt instruments that pay interest to the funds. Remember this when you're filling out your tax return so you don't enter the information in the wrong place.

A TAX BREAK FOR FOREIGN TAXES

If you own a fund that invests some or all of its money in foreign securities, you can get a tax break for foreign taxes paid by the fund; those taxes should be reported on the 1099-DIV forms your fund mails you. You can take this amount as a deduction if you itemize deductions. Or you can take it as a tax credit, which is usually worth more. Taking it as a credit, however, requires filling out an additional tax form (IRS Form 1116, *Foreign Tax Credit for Individuals*).

SALES CHARGES

Any initial sales charge you pay (called a *front-end load* in fund-speak) is included in your cost basis, because it's part of the cost of your shares. If you invest $1,000 in a fund with a 4.5% front-

Selling Your Losers?

HAD A BAD YEAR in the markets? Uncle Sam wants to help—really. If you own a stock or bond fund that gets pummeled to a level far below what you originally paid for it, consider selling it and buying a similar fund. You can deduct the loss when you file your taxes. (IRS wash-sale rules, however, prevent you from taking a tax loss if you sell a fund at a loss and rebuy the same fund before 31 days have elapsed.) Assuming you buy a similar fund (you replace an aggressive-growth fund with another aggressive-growth fund, for instance), you won't lose an opportunity to make money when the market rebounds.

Selling a losing fund and buying another is most easily done with bond funds because it's usually an easy matter to find another bond fund that's almost identical to your loser. You could sell *Vanguard Long-Term Tax-Exempt,* for instance, buy *Vanguard High-Yield Tax-Exempt,* and have little change in your portfolio. It's trickier with stock funds, though—it's often very difficult to find two that are almost identical because their portfolios are likely to be diverse, even if their goals are similar.

Bear in mind that selling a losing fund and buying a winner will likely yield you only a very small savings because you'll eventually sell the winning fund and owe taxes on its gains. Moreover, selling your losers will complicate your financial record keeping. So use this technique sparingly.

end load, your cost basis is $1,000, even though you will have bought only $955 worth of shares. Brokerage transaction fees are similarly deductible.

FUNDS THAT INVEST IN U.S. GOVERNMENT SECURITIES

If you own a fund that gets all or part of its income from investing in U.S. government securities, you'll have to pay federal tax on the income, but you usually don't have to pay state or local tax on it. However, interest on securities issued by government agencies—such as federally insured mortgage-backed securities and student loans—is not exempt from state taxes. When you receive your Form 1099 from a fund, you'll also receive an accounting of what percentage of income came from government securities of various types.

Key Points

- *Keeping careful records, on a computer or with pencil and paper, is essential to managing the tax aspects of fund investing. Computers are the best method for most people.*
- *If you don't want the aggravation of keeping good records, there are some shortcuts you can employ. They include:*
- *Using the "average cost" method of accounting (with the fund or an online broker doing the record keeping).*
- *Selling all shares of a mutual fund if you sell any.*
- *Even if you use these shortcuts, complying with IRS rules on funds is tedious.*

13 Investment Pitfalls

And how to avoid them

A S YOU CAN SEE FROM THE PRECEDING CHAPTERS, investing wisely isn't that difficult. All you need to do is determine your time horizon and tolerance for losses; decide how much you're going to invest in stocks, bonds and cash; pick solid funds; and invest regularly. Unless you want to learn more of the nitty-gritty about funds, you don't need to read beyond this chapter to create a first-class investment plan.

However, gremlins lurk to throw you off course—largely because, when it comes to investing your money, your emotions tend to come into play as much as your brain. Here are 13 pitfalls that can snare investors—novices and veterans alike—and tips on how to avoid them.

Pitfall 1: Waiting for Stocks to Fall

T HIS TRAP CAN BE ESPECIALLY EASY TO FALL INTO FOR fledgling investors who are afraid to get their feet wet—especially if they have a large sum to invest. At the end of 1994, for instance, the dividend yield on the average stock in Standard & Poor's 500-stock index fell below 3% of the average stock's price. The only other times that had happened were a few months prior to the 1929 crash, just before the onset of the 1973–74 bear market, and a few months preceding the 1987 crash—the worst three markets of the century. It seemed prudent to put off investing until stock prices fell, which would push up yields. When dividend yields are low compared with stocks' prices, it traditionally means companies don't have the confidence to share much of their profits with shareholders. But those who waited for stock prices to fall watched as the S&P 500 soared an annualized 28.5% over the next five years. By late 2000, the dividend yield on the S&P was just 1.1%. The lesson is clear: If you are going to invest, put in a little bit regularly; don't wait for stocks to get cheaper.

Pitfall 2: Timing the Market

WHAT IF YOU KNEW IN ADVANCE WHEN STOCKS WERE GOING to plunge? What if you could step to the sidelines in advance of the bruising bear markets that take the market down by 20% or more? The answer, of course: You could do wonderful things. James Stack, editor of the investment letter *InvesTech*, calculates that an investor who bought the stocks in the Standard and Poor's 500-stock index and held them for the long term would have earned 317% in the ten years that ended in mid 1994. But if that same investor had presciently jumped out of the market on just the ten worst days each year, he or she would have earned 4,576%!

Advocates of market timing counter that the mettle of most buy-and-hold investors hasn't really been tested.

Even after following the market for more than 20 years, I find market timing beguiling. It is nearly as satisfying to sit safely on the sidelines in a money-market fund while stocks plunge as it is to watch your stock funds rise. I experienced it once. I sold all my stocks just days before the 1987 crash. Unfortunately, it took me one and a half years to fully reenter the market because I kept waiting for the market to fall again. As a result, I ended up no better off than if I had patiently stayed in stocks through the crash and the subsequent recovery.

The sad fact is, virtually no one has ever been able to time the stock market well enough and consistently enough to outperform long-term holding. Says John Markese, president of the American Association of Individual Investors: "Good timing can't be beat." The problem is, "It just can't be done."

Advocates of market timing counter that the mettle of most buy-and-hold investors hasn't really been tested by a nasty, drawn-out bear market. The overwhelming majority of assets in stock funds has been poured in since the last bear decline in 1990 and that one lasted only three months, and many investors have never experienced a drop of anywhere near 20% in the S&P. The 37% plunge in Nasdaq in early 2000, timers argue, was likewise too short-lived to wear the bulls out. Market timers doubt that buy-and-holders will hang tough in a protracted down market. Indeed, when stocks fall, mutual fund investors, on the whole, tend to slow their investing. If a market decline extends over a long period, fund buying tends to dry up and investors begin redeeming shares, several studies show. Then, when the market is buoyant again, investors flock back into stocks. It's not just individual investors who fall victim to this buy-high, sell-low malady; professional investors do it, too. Mutual fund managers, as a whole, tend to hold the highest percentage of assets in cash on the eve of bull markets; conversely, they tend to have little cash just before bear markets begin.

The dismal failure of most daytraders provides further evidence of the beauty of a buy-and-hold strategy.

Years ago timers promised that they could outperform the market with lower risk. In recent years they've lowered their claims by promising good returns adjusted for the risks they take. In other words, they say, they'll produce decent returns and keep you safely in cash during bear markets—and make it easier to sleep at night.

But from the highest-paid, most-quoted brokerage strategists on Wall Street to the shoeshine boys, no one really knows what the stock market is going to do today, tomorrow, next month or next year. (Remember that, the next time you hear some strategist telling you which way the market is headed.) The best way to invest for maximum gain is to buy stock funds (or individual stocks) and hold them. The dismal failure of most daytraders provides further evidence of the beauty of a buy-and-hold strategy. Consider the flip side to Stack's perfect market timer: If you missed the ten best days in the market each year during the decade ending in mid 1994, you wouldn't have profited at all. *Not* to be invested in stocks is risky.

In addition to the poor record of market timers, timing presents another problem: It's a lot of work. While good performance is anything but guaranteed, it's a certainty you'll spend hours watching quotes stream across your computer screen. If you're timing in a taxable account, moreover, you condemn yourself to more agony at tax time each year.

Avoiding market timing is easy intellectually, though sometimes terribly difficult emotionally. If you are tempted to try it, remind yourself of the long-term gains of the stock markets and the difficulty of anticipating market turns. And follow this rule: Invest conservatively for the short term and aggressively for the long term, and forget about what the market may or may not do, because you're covered either way.

Pitfall 3: Chasing Performance

PICK UP *KIPLINGER'S PERSONAL FINANCE* MAGAZINE OR ANY other personal-finance publication and you'll see advertisements for funds that have shot the lights out over the past year. These funds aren't spending their money on ads for nothing: They know that great results attract money.

Take Wasatch Mid-Cap. In 1994, it was a sleepy little fund with just over $1 million in assets and fund manager Karey Barker piloted it to an 8% return while the S&P 500 gained just 1%. Then, in 1995, the fund erupted. It rose 59%—beating the S&P by more than 20 percentage points. Money flooded in. By the end of 1995, the fund had $130 million in assets. But just as quickly, Barker's hot hand turned ice cold. Wasatch Mid-Cap earned just 4% in 1996, while the S&P rose 23%. Shareholders jammed the exits, and by the end of the year the fund held only $100 million. Assets have since dwindled to $56 million. The fund, which has changed its name to Wasatch Ultra Growth, has stayed erratic, at best, putting up good numbers in 1998, but providing subpar results in other years.

If you missed the ten best days in the market each year during the decade ending in mid 1994, you wouldn't have profited at all.

What went wrong? Barker hadn't proven in 1995 whether her performance was due to talent or luck. In fact, her fund had badly lagged the indexes in 1993, her first year running the fund. Nor had she shown she could run a $100 million fund—which is much harder than managing $1 million. (For more detail on the difficulties of running bigger funds, see Chapter 16.)

Buying a top-performing fund isn't necessarily a bad idea—just look for one with at least three and preferably five years of good numbers under its belt. (These numbers are available for many funds in Chapter 17 of this book, as well as in personal finance magazines or at www.Kiplinger.com.)

MOMENTUM INVESTING

As with so many investment rules, the rule against chasing performance has a caveat. One style of fund investing, known as momentum investing, buys funds that have chalked up the best performance over relatively short periods. You hold those funds as long as they continue to outperform their peers. When they lag, you switch to other top performers.

If you want to employ momentum investing, do it with only some of your money, because it's a fairly risky strategy. The bulk of your money belongs in good, solid funds that you can hold for years and years. Also, to keep your tax preparation manageable, practice momentum investing only in a tax-deferred retirement account. For best results, subscribe to a good newsletter that exploits momentum investing in a disciplined way; don't simply try to wing it. Perhaps the best of the momentum newsletters is *Equity Fund Outlook* ($125 per year; 800-982-0055; www.efoutlook.com). Edited by Thurman Smith, this newsletter is very technical and can be hard to understand. But its model portfolios are easy to read and follow, and they gained an annualized 22.3% for the eight years through June 30, 2000. Smith recommends top-performing funds in a variety of investment styles to minimize the risk in the overall portfolio.

> **Buying a top performer isn't necessarily a bad idea—just look for at least three and preferably five years of good numbers.**

ADHERE TO YOUR STRATEGY

A variation of chasing performance is hopping from strategy to strategy. Some investors will be fans of buy-and-hold investing only as long as the market is going up. When it starts going down, they decide to become market timers. They might then subscribe to the hottest-performing newsletter of the previous couple of years, only to switch to another newsletter when the first newsletter's performance wanes. Next, they may decide they should hire a broker instead of going it alone. Hopping from one approach to another is a recipe for lousy returns. Pick your investing strategy and stay with it through thick and thin. Why?

Because all too often investors switch approaches at just the wrong time—when their method has been out of favor for a long period and is about to rebound.

Pitfall 4: Putting Too Much Money in One Industry Sector

T HROUGH MOST OF THE 1990S, GARRETT VAN WAGONER WAS near perfect. His Govett Smaller Companies beat every other diversified stock fund in 1993 and 1994 and finished third in 1995. Van Wagoner went into business for himself in 1996, and in the first six months of that year, his flagship fund, Van Wagoner Emerging Growth, climbed 50%. But his hot hand abruptly turned cold and remained so for two years. The fund lost 20% in 1997 and went down another 20% through the third quarter of 1998, before recovering, in the final quarter. Then, Van Wagoner Emerging Growth returned an extraordinary 291.2% in 1999. But when Nasdaq foundered in the spring of 2000, the fund plunged 50.8% before rebounding.Why was this fund acting like a Mexican jumping bean?

Unlike Wasatch's Barker, Van Wagoner was an experienced manager implementing a highly disciplined and well-thought-out strategy. This fund belly flopped for much the same reason as it soared—close to 80% of assets were in technology stocks. The fund doesn't say technology in its name. But careful investors knew this fund bought risky small companies, most of them in the high-tech arena.

There's nothing wrong with taking some of your more aggressive investment money and putting it into a fund like Van Wagoner Emerging Growth, knowing it's chock full of tiny technology stocks. In investing, high risks are often the price you pay to reap high rewards over the long term. But investors make a huge mistake if they concentrate massive portions of their assets in one or two industries. After all, one of the biggest advantages of mutual funds is diversification. When you concentrate your investments in one or two industries, you're defeating that purpose. Putting too much into an industry sector can be a problem whether you invest through a sector fund, or in a diversified fund that is really a "closet" sector fund.

How can you protect yourself? Before you buy a fund, check

out its description in this book or look at another source, such as Morningstar.com or Kiplinger.com. Or visit the fund's Web site or call its 800 number and request either a list of its investments by industry sector or an annual report, which will contain this data.

Pitfall 5: Falling in Love With a Fund (or Failing to Clean Out Your Attic)

DONALD YACKTMAN HAD GREAT YEARS, FIRST AT SELECTED American Shares, and then at Yacktman Fund, which returned 30.4% in 1995, 26% in 1996 and 18.3% in 1997. In fact, Yacktman's returns were so solid, and his investment strategy seemed so coherent that I included his fund in the first edition of this book, which went to press in mid 1998. What a mistake! Yacktman Fund gained 1% in 1998, lost 16.9% in 1999 and was down another 5.2% through July 2000. A fund that was once excellent has been mediocre, at best, for 2½ years. Yet, despite the fund's awful performance, as well as a nasty fight between Yacktman and his board of directors, I had no way (until now) to tell investors who read the first edition of my book to sell. Indeed, much of the reason for the fund's poor performance was that undervalued stocks did poorly for everyone in the last several years. But Yacktman did worse than his value-style peers (see Chapter 14 for more on styles of mutual funds), significantly worse, clinging to huge holdings in falling stocks like Philip Morris. It's time to pull the plug—at least until Yacktman can put up decent numbers again for several years.

Carefully watch a fund that fails to keep up with its peers for a year or two.

A fund that fails to keep up with its peers for a year or two should be watched carefully. If it doesn't turn around fairly quickly, it should be sold—unless you can satisfy yourself that the problems are, indeed, temporary (for more detail on when to sell a fund, see Chapter 16). Of course, if a manager has a long and superior record, such as Yacktman had, or is investing in a part of the market that is out of favor, you'll want to give it the benefit of the doubt. But eventually, you have to bail out. In Yacktman's case, his performance hasn't been just below par for 2½ years, it's been close to horrible. Such dismal performance is often a signal to cash in your chips.

Don't let fear of a taxable capital gain stop you. When you

sell usually makes little difference from a tax standpoint. You'll take a tax hit on a fund with big gains, but whenever you sell, you'll eventually take such a hit.

Too many investors, once they buy a fund (or even inherit it) can never quite bring themselves to sell it. Don't fall into that trap. Look on your mutual funds for what they are— investments, not cherished possessions to be held on to forever. And if their best times have passed, it's time to let them go.

Pitfall 6: Following Your Instincts

L ETTING YOUR EMOTIONS CONTROL YOUR INVESTMENT decisions can lead to trouble. Are you a worrier? If so, you likely scored fairly low on the risk-tolerance test in Chapter 3. But once you've decided what percentage of your money to invest in stock funds, bond funds and money-market funds, don't let the ups and downs of the market spook you into selling or slowing your buying. Don't look at what's happening to the Dow Jones industrial average, the Nasdaq or the S&P 500. Remember that your own carefully constructed portfolio will probably fall a lot less than those averages in a bear market. Moreover, you are probably considerably ahead of where you started when you first got into the market. And, if you keep investing money regularly, you will almost certainly be well ahead by the time you need your money.

Are you a person who gets depressed easily, who thinks the worst is likely to happen to you? Again, your score on the risk-tolerance test probably has you partly invested in bonds for all but the longest-term goals. Remind yourself, whenever you feel like selling, that the market goes up most of the time. Over the long run, the bulls tend to beat the bears. Hang on and hold a steady course.

Are you an optimistic person, who assumes that the best will happen to you? Then, like the DiBenedettos, you'll probably have the bulk of your money in stock funds. Don't get too carried away, though, and be tempted to overload on speculative funds. Don't use borrowed money to invest. Remember to pay off your credit cards and other bills before putting more money into stock funds. And don't keep money in stock funds that you may need to spend within a year or two.

Pitfall 7: Holding On Until You Get Even, and Selling Too Soon

MANY INVESTORS HAVE A TENDENCY TO WANT TO "LOCK IN" their profits. If a fund goes up 20% or 30%, they may decide it's time to bail out. But a rise in a fund's price shouldn't prompt you to sell if the reasons you bought the fund are still in place: The fund has a good manager and a good long-term record, it still fits into your investment program, and your goals haven't changed. You should generally hold on at least until a fund shows signs of weakening—such as a long-term deterioration in performance when compared with similar funds or the departure of a good manager. Many people sell funds too quickly.

Conversely, as I mentioned in Chapter 3, it can be hard to trim losers from your portfolio. If a fund you buy swoons immediately, you may be tempted to hold on at least until you get even. But sometimes that can take years—years in which you could have been profiting in a better fund. The question to ask yourself when deciding whether to sell a fund is: Would I buy this fund today? If you discover the answer is no, you should generally pull the plug.

Pitfall 8: Being Too Plugged In

WHILE YOU NEED TO BE WELL INFORMED, DON'T PUT MUCH stock in day-to-day market moves, much less minute-to-minute market moves displayed on the Internet. It's the news media's job to tell you what's new. If you hang on every word, you can miss the real message—that over the long term the market's direction is always up and stocks will appreciate more than bonds or short-term investments.

Former psychologist turned money manager Paul Andreassen performed an experiment with graduate business students at the Massachusetts Institute of Technology. Half of the business students received frequent news bulletins about stocks, and the others received no information. Those who got no news were more successful stock traders. "People are paralyzed by fear caused by too much information," says Bob Wacker, a financial planner in San Luis Obispo, Cal. "I have clients putting their retirement savings into money-market funds because they get so many conflicting reports."

Here's the remedy: Limit yourself to one or two good sources of current investing information, and don't spend too much time even with them. For instance, CNBC might be a good source of current market movements, but if you watch it all day, you can drive yourself crazy. Likewise for tracking the micro movements of the markets on the Web. Several studies have shown that the more information investors take in, the more frequently they tend to buy and sell stocks and funds. And the more frequently investors trade, the less money they tend to make.

Pitfall 9: Remembering Too Well

W E DEVELOP OUR ATTITUDES ABOUT INVESTING FROM OUR parents, and we rarely examine those attitudes," says Rennie Gabriel, a financial planner in Encino, Cal., and self-described "financial coach." Many of today's investors grew up hearing stories about how the 1929 market crash wiped out a relative. Such family legends can lead people to avoid stocks altogether. "The average American has a Great Depression mentality," adds financial planner Harold Evensky of Coral Gables, Fla. "Ask people what's safe and they'll say Treasury bills, bank certificates of deposit and money-markets." Those types of investments were safe during the Depression, but they're less so today, when the bigger threat is inflation. Don't confuse safety with an investment that doesn't change much in value. When investing for the long term, the ups and downs of the stock market generally work to your advantage.

I have a good friend who keeps all of her money in real estate, even though she hates renting out the properties she has purchased. When I asked her why she invests in real estate, she explains how well her grandfather did in real estate. Such family stories are often handed down from parents to children, and they dictate how people determine whether an investment is a good one, or whether it is one to be avoided.

Instead of relying on what you heard around the dinner table decades ago, look at what has really worked over the long run. There's nothing wrong with investing in real estate, by the way: It's just a lot of work.

Pitfall 10: Seeking Perfection

W ITH THOUSANDS OF INVESTMENTS TO CHOOSE FROM, YOU can search forever for a flawless fund. Call off the hunt. "Every investor has to be prepared to lose money," says Maury Elvekrog, a former psychologist who's now an investment adviser in Detroit. "If you're not, you're not doing much of a job of investing." Don't expect to own *the* top-performing fund. Be satisfied with a solid portfolio of funds—some of which will lag the market averages at any given time.

One sure-fire way to raise your investment comfort level— and increase your odds of success, to boot—is to have a friend or relative with whom you talk at least occasionally about your investments. Warren Buffett, probably the most successful investor of our time, never makes a move in the market without talking to his alter ego, Charlie Munger, vice-chairman of his firm. Talking over ideas with someone else can prevent you from acting impulsively and help you make sound decisions. Many people hire a financial advisor solely for the handholding he or she can provide. Barton Biggs, a global investment strategist at Morgan Stanley, once observed: "It may seem corny, but when the market or a stock goes against you, it always seems to help to have someone else to complain to and commiserate with."

Internet message boards provide advice and consolation for many investors. Just be careful that you don't get talked out of your buy-and-hold strategy by fellow posters. And try to pay attention only to posters who impress you over several months as knowledgeable and conservative investors. Most message boards are dominated by rapid-fire traders, as well as people with a financial interest in pushing particular stocks.

Pitfall 11: Owning Bear-Market and All-Market Funds

C RABBE HUSON SPECIAL EQUITY MADE HUGE GAINS IN THE early 1990s. It beat the S&P 500 by 25.8 percentage points in 1992, 24.5 percentage points in 1993, and 10.4 percentage points in 1994. Like a lot of people, manager James Crabbe got nervous toward the end of 1995. He decided to wager that some of the high-flying technology stocks would fall on their keisters. Investors bet that a stock will go down by a complicated process known as "short selling." A short seller borrows shares of stock from one investor and then sells it to a second investor, hoping he or she can buy it back later at a lower price. Crabbe put a large proportion of his fund's assets in these short sales—which turned out to be a disaster, as the stocks continued to climb higher. Crabbe Huson Special Equity proceeded to trail the S&P by 26.7 percentage points in 1995, 17 percentage points in 1996, 22.1 percentage points in 1997, 71.4% percentage points in 1998 (the fund lost a staggering 42.9% that year) and 12.9 percentage points in 1999.

Since the stock market has a long-term upward bias, betting that it will go down—or even that certain stocks will go down—is like casino gambling: The odds are not on your side, because stocks go up more than down. A number of funds (such as Rydex Ursa and Prudent Bear) put all or part of their money into investments that will profit only if stocks decline. Or they may put their assets into gold, which, although it's supposed to do well during times of inflation and global uncertainty, hasn't delivered on that promise in many years. Gold did poorly even during the Persian Gulf War. Ignore these funds. You can tell if a fund is a bear-market fund by calling the toll-free number and asking what percentage of the fund is in gold stocks and what percentage is in short sales or in index *puts*—bets that a market average will decline. Anything over 10% of assets in these usually indicates a bearish fund. They offer the *illusion* of insurance against market declines—although many of them, surprisingly, have failed to do well even in market plunges—and retard your overall returns. The Crabbe Huson fund, incidentally, was taken over by Liberty in late 1998, and the fund has stopped selling stocks short.

Although gold is supposed to do well during inflationary and uncertain times, it hasn't delivered on that promise in many years.

If you want to purchase some protection against inflation by investing in a natural resources' fund, T. Rowe Price New Era is probably the best of the lot. It also invests in other stocks that its manager thinks will benefit from inflation, giving it much-needed diversification. But keep this mutual fund to a small percentage of your portfolio, or, better still, don't buy this type of stock fund at all.

Pitfall 12: Owning Too Many Funds (or, How Many Are Enough?)

M ONEY MANAGER ROGER GIBSON LIKES TO COMPARE unskilled fund investing to a ramble on the beach picking up shells: "That's a pretty one; I'll pick that one up. And that's a pretty one, too." Trouble is, if you buy too many funds, your portfolio can become so unwieldy that you may find it difficult to tell how you've really deployed your money. Your holdings in stocks, bonds and cash can be out of kilter without your even knowing it. And you're unlikely to do as well as the market averages when you own dozens of funds.

How many funds are enough to reduce risk without sacrificing performance? There's no magic number. Most financial planners and money managers believe a portfolio should contain at least three but probably no more than a dozen funds, and money managers who invest in funds generally recommend a number in the middle of that range. Or as Tim Medley, a financial planner and asset manager in Jackson, Miss., puts it: "The ideal number is somewhere between a basketball squad and a baseball team." The portfolios in this book are generally in Medley's ballpark. For beginning investors, even fewer funds may suffice. Investors with large portfolios, on the other hand, might want to own more funds.

If you suspect that you own too many funds, go back over them one by one and try to recall why you bought each one. Are those reasons still valid? Would you buy the fund today? If not, the fund is a candidate for selling. Do you own two funds that seek largely the same objective and go about it in largely the same manner? Sell one of them.

Funds should make life simpler. Don't buy so many that you defeat that purpose.

Pitfall 13: Not Investing Enough in Stock Funds

O NE OF THE BIGGEST MISTAKES MADE BY MANY INVESTORS with long-term goals is putting too little into stock funds. The stock market may be too high, or too low, or too frightening to invest more of your money. But remember, over the long haul, the biggest enemy you face is not the loss of money in stocks, but the slow whittling away of your purchasing power through inflation. Stock funds can afford you long-term protection against that unhappy outcome.

Every year or so, check your funds. Ask yourself: Do you have enough in stock funds? If you're not sure, take the risk-tolerance test on pages 30–31 and look at the "How Much to Invest in Stocks" tables on page 32. Of course, this advice applies mainly to long-term investing. When investing for short- and intermediate-term goals, you'll want to trim your stock exposure gradually as you get closer to your deadline.

Key Points

- *Don't try to time the market.*
- *Don't chase short-term, top-performing funds.*
- *Don't invest too much in one industry sector.*
- *Don't fall in love with a fund.*
- *Don't let your emotions get in the way of sound decisions.*
- *Do invest enough in stock funds.*

Want Someone to Do It for You?

How to find a good planner or broker, or to get help from a mutual fund company

 HILE I WAS WRITING THIS BOOK, I SPOKE OFTEN with Nancy and Paul DiBenedetto to see whether they—as busy, intelligent people with virtually no knowledge of mutual funds—could easily understand the points I was making. For the most part, they did quite well. But one topic—the different types of funds—totally bewildered them. "I am definitely confused," Paul said after I attempted to explain them. "I am so confused I want to just take my money and hire someone, and pray I don't lose my shirt. This is just too mind-boggling." Fortunately, the more Nancy and Paul learned, the more their fears subsided. They had simply hit a temporary roadblock. You may hit a roadblock or two yourself and decide, for at least a moment, that you don't want to go it alone.

It's the raison d'être of this book that almost anyone can do his or her own investing. This book gives you all the tools you need to accomplish that task. And take my word for it: Investing on your own should consume little, if any, more time than you would spend finding and working with a broker or financial planner. Plus, investing on your own guarantees you will save a ton of money in commissions and fees. (Not only that, you'll be in control, and you won't have to take a close-your-eyes-and-hope-for-the-best attitude.)

However, lots of people who invest in mutual funds don't

do all the work themselves—determine their goals; figure their time horizon; estimate their tolerance for risk; decide how much to invest in stock funds, bond funds and money market funds; and select their mutual funds. For a variety of reasons, you may decide you want to hire a professional to handle your money. You may decide you'll never get started unless you hire someone to help you. You may feel you'll make mistakes if you invest on your own. You may think you'll panic and sell when the market falls. Whatever your reason, this chapter will help you find a good professional.

Still, I'd suggest you continue to learn about investing. After a year or two of working with a broker or financial planner, you'll likely feel more confident about handling things on your own. So, whatever you do, hold on to this book. Even if you decide to let someone else make your decisions for you now, you may well change your mind.

A HYBRID STRATEGY

What if you feel nervous about investing on your own but aren't sure you want to turn your affairs over to a financial planner, either? Here's an excellent way to become more confident about investing and keep your costs down, as well: Pay an hourly fee to meet two or three times, for an hour or two each time, with a planner—and implement his or her recommendations on your own. Expect to pay about $100 to $150 per hour. Tell the planner up front that you want temporary help. Many will be glad to oblige you.

If you proceed this way, make sure you have all your financial files organized before you go visit the planner, and, once the clock starts, spend all your time discussing your financial affairs. Don't get distracted by other topics. Don't get talked into turning all your affairs over to the planner, which is much more lucrative for the planner.

In a year or two—or sooner if you feel adrift—visit again for an update. "Renting a planner" is a good course of action if you feel you need a little advice or handholding before putting an investment plan into action, or if you don't have a lot of money to invest. Many planners don't want long-term relationships with you unless you have $100,000 or more to invest. Many advisers and virtually all brokers welcome clients with significantly less.

Finding the Right Adviser

O NCE YOU HAVE DECIDED THAT YOU NEED HELP, THERE ARE hundreds of thousands of people—bankers, insurance agents, stockbrokers, financial planners, mutual fund representatives and money managers—who would love to handle your investments for a fee. It sometimes seems as if everyone is hanging out a shingle these days, on the Internet and elsewhere, and offering to help you invest in mutual funds.

Unfortunately, it doesn't take any training whatsoever to call yourself an investment adviser or financial planner. Those who manage more than $25 million of clients' money—or work for a firm that does—must register with the federal Securities and Exchange Commission (SEC). That involves filling out a voluminous (and revealing) form called an ADV (short for "adviser") that includes information about an adviser's education, compensation and investment strategy. All the SEC requires is full disclosure. So if a financial adviser is a convicted felon, that's fine—as long as the ADV notes it. If he or she picks mutual funds by using a Ouija board, that's okay, too, if it's disclosed on the ADV.

Rent a planner if you need advice or handholding before putting an investment plan into action, or if you don't have a lot of money to invest.

Advisers or planners managing less than $25 million need not register with the SEC. Instead, state regulations cover them. To locate the state agency that can give you information about a financial adviser or planner, call the North American Securities Administrators Association at 202-737-0900 or visit its Web site at www.nasaa.org.

PLANNER, ADVISER OR BROKER?

While planners, investment advisers and brokers all offer financial expertise, most brokers still make their money by getting you to buy or sell stocks, bonds or mutual funds. Many planners and advisers make their money the same way.

But a growing number of "fee-only" planners and advisers will give you advice for an hourly fee or manage your portfolio for an annual fee of 0.5% to 3% of the assets you place under their management. The advantage of a fee-only planner is that he or she is "on the same side of the table" as you are. In other words, the bigger your portfolio grows, the more money the planner makes. Some planners call themselves "fee-based," which means they derive some of their compensation from fees but the rest from commissions.

One of the most encouraging developments in the brokerage industry is that a growing number of full-service brokerage firms are also beginning to offer fee-only services to customers who request them. Merrill Lynch offers a notable plan that assesses you a fee of 1% or less of your assets under management annually and doesn't charge you any commissions. You can be charged extra if you buy mutual funds—even for those that are otherwise sold without sales charges—because they have underlying expenses, which you must pay regardless of how you buy them. If you go with a broker like Merrill Lynch (Prudential and PaineWebber offer similar similar programs), make sure that you enroll in a fee-only plan—except for those investments that you already own and plan to hang onto for a good long time. In your fee-only plan, you might want to rely on your broker's expertise and purchase individual stocks—because you'll save money compared with investing in mutual funds.

Full-service brokerage firms are only too aware that they have a poor image with many members of the post–World War II generation. Online brokers, commission-free mutual funds and fee-only planners have lured away many potential customers. Fee-only brokerage plans are designed to win over these people. But most brokers and commission-based planners and advisers can make money simply by persuading you to buy or sell. They generally get a commission on everything you trade—whether it's stocks, bonds or mutual funds. Commission-based planners and advisers, like most stockbrokers, typically make their money from mutual fund companies, which pay them around 5% of the amount you invest in a fund.

Because stockbrokers are less popular than they used to be, many have taken to calling themselves by all manner of other titles: financial consultant, financial planner, account executive, vice-president—anything, it seems, but stockbroker. Since fee-only planners and advisers are growing in popularity, many brokers are migrating into that business. At the same time, as I noted above, some brokerages are changing the way they charge to fee-only, at least for some clients. All these developments make it harder to ascertain much difference between a generic planner, adviser or broker. More than ever, the key is how good the individual professional is—not what his or her title may be.

Fee-only planners, fee-only advisers and fee-only brokers make their money by charging you an annual percentage of the assets they manage. But planners typically offer more than investment advisers, and some charge little or nothing extra for the additional services. (Beware: Other planners charge quite a bit more for such services.) Planners should look at your entire financial situation—estate planning, insurance, the value of your home and other assets, taxes, and so on. In most instances, this may make them a better choice, particularly for beginners, than investment advisers who may offer additional services, but who focus on money management. Investment advisers, on the other hand, argue that they are better at investing simply because it's their primary endeavor. Some brokers are beginning to offer the same extra services that financial planners do, for free or little extra.

WHERE TO LOOK

Try any of these leads:

Family and friends

The best way to find a good broker, planner or adviser is to talk with your friends and relatives about who helps them manage their money. If a friend has someone he likes a lot, try to find out if your friend's ideas about investing are similar to yours. Is your friend a fund investor? Does he buy and hold funds for long periods—as opposed to trading frequently, which is usually a money-losing strategy? Also, ask other questions: Does the broker or planner return his calls promptly? Does the adviser seem to understand your friend's investment needs and temperament?

Accountant or lawyer

Lacking a friend who is happy with a broker, adviser or planner, your next step may be to turn to your accountant or lawyer for a recommendation. Be aware that a lawyer or accountant may regularly send clients to the same investment professional, who in turn may send clients to the lawyer or accountant.

Referral services

Still running into a brick wall? *Kiplinger's Stocks 2000*, an annual publication, awarded its top rankings of brokerage firms to A.G. Edwards, Salomon Smith Barney and Edward D. Jones in that order. For planners, the best strategy may be to contact professional associations that will provide you with lists of credentialed financial planners in your area:

The Financial Planning Association (3801 E. Florida Ave., Suite 708, Denver, CO 80210; 800-282-7526; www.fpanet.org)

The American Institute of Certified Public Accountants (Harborside Financial Center, 201 Plaza 3, Jersey City, NJ 07311; 888-777-7077; www.aicpa.org)

The National Association of Personal Financial Advisors (fee-only planners; 355 W. Dundee Road, Suite 200, Buffalo Grove, IL 60089; 888-333-6659; www.napfa.org)

The trouble with these referral services is that they don't give you any idea which planners are good and which are mediocre. But membership in the National Association of Personal Financial Advisors is particularly meaningful because a screening committee takes a close look at prospective members. It requires them to have clean disciplinary records and to produce a financial plan that passes muster with the organization's membership committee.

A rating service

You can also locate a financial planner through Dalbar Inc. This Boston-based research firm rates financial planners (as well as other money managers) on performance, trustworthiness, and the quality and scope of services provided. It rates only planners with clean regulatory records and at least 50 clients. The information is available at by calling 800-296-7056. Or visit www.therightadvisor.com, where you will be asked questions and matched with local planners and advisers from Dalbar's database, who may suit you individual needs.

Although Dalbar provides the service free to consumers, planners pay Dalbar to rate them. "People are reluctant to check references, and to the degree that the ratings provide that, they offer some potential information," says Barbara Roper, director of investor protection for the Consumer Federation of America. "But any time we have people buying ratings, it raises questions." Well-respected planners with booming businesses are unlikely to be willing to pay for inclusion on Dalbar's list.

Charles Schwab

Broker Charles Schwab will help you find a planner or invest-ment adviser in your area if you call 888-774-3756 or visit www.schwab.com. Schwab makes no effort to ensure that the planners it refers you to have had good past performance. It does insist that they have at least five years of experience man-aging money and at least $25 million under management. As with Dalbar, managers pay Schwab for referrals.

A FIRST INTERVIEW

If you use Schwab, Dalbar or one of the associations above to find a financial planner or investment adviser, or if you decide to pick a broker, make sure to interview at least three. The first interview should be free. Try to get a feel for whether his or her personal-ity and approach to investing matches yours. If you're not com-fortable when you talk, you're not going to be comfortable with his or her investment recommendations. Below are some things to ask about at a first meeting. You may not find some of these questions easy to ask, but ask them even if it makes you a little uncomfortable. The relationship you have with a financial pro-fessional is one of the most important (and expensive) you'll have. Don't be embarrassed to politely decline the person's ser-vices if he or she won't answer these straightforward questions or won't provide you with information. Even if he or she acts oth-erwise, a financial professional expects these questions and requests. To put it bluntly, don't allow yourself to be taken.

His or her educational background

While education is no guarantee of competence, a certified finan-cial planner (CFP) designation shows the planner had a willing-ness to get an education, as opposed to simply hanging out a shingle. Other credentials that reflect training are the chartered financial consultant (ChFC), which is the insurance-industry equivalent of a CFP, and the personal financial specialist (PFS) designation awarded to certified public accountants. Many bro-kers also have these designations.

A résumé

You're mostly looking for evidence that this person isn't just getting his or her feet wet. While an ex–real estate agent may become a top-flight financial planner or broker, let him or her make the rookie mistakes with other people's money. Look for someone who's been in financial planning for at least five years.

An investment strategy

Look for evidence that a planner's or broker's main concern isn't "beating the market," but rather learning your goals and assembling a good, long-term portfolio for you. Get nervous if he or she spends time bragging about clients' investment returns. Run if he or she promises to outperform the market. Steer clear of planners, advisers or brokers who try to "time the market" by guessing when to sell stocks or bonds. Likewise, it's time to end the interview if he or she talks of frequent moves among funds. Good financial professionals almost always hold funds for years, not months.

A sample investment plan

It should show evidence of a well-thought-out, long-term approach to investing. A planner will almost certainly want to do such a plan for you if you retain him or her. Some planners charge extra—sometimes quite a bit extra—for this initial plan. Many brokers also offer such plans. Usually, they are less comprehensive, but they are typically free or much less expensive than what you'll get from a planner.

Amount of interaction

Ask how often your broker, planner or adviser will be in contact with you, and what sort of ongoing monitoring of your portfolio he or she will do. He or she should send you at least quarterly reports showing how your portfolio is doing, and should be available to discuss your portfolio whenever you feel it's necessary.

A Form ADV

Ask to see a planner's or adviser's ADV form, if he or she has one (refer back to the discussion on page 137 for more on this). If a planner or adviser or the firm he or she works for manages less than $25 million and, therefore, is not registered with the SEC, he or she must have a similar form filed with the state. He or she must give you Part II of the ADV or its state equivalent, but not

Part I, which records any disciplinary actions. If the planner or adviser doesn't voluntarily give you Part I, it's time to look elsewhere. (Both parts of the ADV are also available from the SEC for 24 cents-a-page plus tax and postage if you submit a written request. You can send a letter to the Securities and Exchange Commission, 450 Fifth Street, N.W., Room 1300, Washington, DC 20549; fax it to the SEC at 202-628-9001; or email a request to: publicinfo@sec.gov.)

References
A broker, planner or adviser should give you several references to satisfied clients. Naturally, he or she won't refer you to someone who has had a bad experience. But when you call references, ask detailed questions about the kind of assistance they have received. By probing a bit, you may learn useful information. For instance, ask whether they feel the planner has put them into good mutual funds or merely adequate ones. Also ask if they've been able to get through to the planner easily to discuss their investments or changes in their financial situations. Ask whether the planner seems on top of their financial situation and keeps in touch on a regular basis.

Bonding
Before you sign on the dotted line, make sure a planner or adviser is bonded, meaning you're insured if he or she walks off with your money. That protects you if you give the planner or adviser direct access to your money. In rare instances, crooked planners and advisers have vanished with their clients' money. (You're safer if an online brokerage, like Charles Schwab, holds your money. The planner or adviser has access to the money to make trades, but can't withdraw money without your knowledge and approval.)

Compensation
Be sure you understand precisely how you will pay the planner or adviser. Will you pay only a percentage of assets (fee-only), commissions, or some combination of the two? You can sometimes bargain for lower fees. *Don't hire anyone who will charge you more than 1% annually.* One advantage of fee-only planners and advisers is that you can tell what your costs will be in advance.

With a commission-only planner or fee-based planner, you'll pay part of your money in sales charges on investments your planner gets you into and out of. Most of these fees are invisible to you, so you may not really know how much you are paying.

Many fee-only financial planners and advisers have Charles Schwab, TD Waterhouse or another brokerage do the book-keeping on all their accounts because it saves them time and money. You'll usually get monthly statements from the brokerage firm. Be aware that the funds the planner buys for you at a brokerage have expenses of their own, so whatever the planner charges you amounts to an extra layer of expenses. You'll occasionally have to pay small trading fees to the broker, as well.

CHECKING ON A BROKER

Look for many of the same qualities in a broker that you would in a financial planner or adviser. The National Association of Securities Dealers Regulation, the brokerage industry's self-regulatory organization, is the main source of information on a broker's history. By calling the NASDR, at 800-289-9999, or visiting its Web site at www.nasdr.com, you can find out about:

• **customer complaints** against a broker,

• **whether he or she has been the target of any disciplinary actions** by the NASDR or other agencies, and

• **whether he or she has lost arbitration claims** (almost all broker-ages require you to settle disputes by arbitration rather than by going to court).

State securities agencies maintain similar information. If you can't readily find the right agency, visit the North American Securities Administrators Association's Web site at www.nasaa.org, or call the organization at 202-737-0900 and ask for your state's telephone number.

Avoid the house brands

Once you settle on a broker, you should generally stay away from the firm's "house-brand" funds. Funds managed and distributed by the brokerage firm usually have the firm's name in them. Thus, there's Merrill Lynch Capital and Salomon Smith Barney Aggressive Growth. Broker-run funds have tended to be poor performers. Moreover, a broker may be more objective in sizing up funds sold by outside firms. Some of the best fund families among broker-sold funds, include the American funds (managed by Capital Research & Management), Franklin Templeton funds and Putnam funds.

Alphabet Soup

N OT TOO MANY YEARS AGO, WHEN A BROKER OR PLANNER sold you a mutual fund, it came in only one variety: Class A shares. These shares had huge sales charges, typically 8.5%. As investors began to understand how hefty those commissions were, many stopped buying the funds. The financial-services industry reacted in two ways: It lowered its commissions to a more reasonable 5% or so, and it introduced a jumble of fee structures so bewildering it's a wonder any broker or planner—much less an investor—can keep up with them. They include:

Class A shares, which usually assess their entire sales charge when you first invest.

Class B shares, which have no initial sales charge but nick you for as much as one percentage point more than no-load funds in annual expenses. If you sell Class B shares before, say, five years are up, you pay a redemption fee, too.

Class C shares, which have no initial sales charges, leading some dishonest brokers to say they have no sales charges. Actually, C shares typically charge the same high annual expenses as B shares. Moreover, those expenses on C shares often continue for as long as you own the fund, while the annual fees on B shares often reduce to the level of the A shares after five or six years.

Confused? You don't have to be a skeptic to think that the fund industry came up with this alphabet soup precisely for the purpose of confounding investors. My advice:

If you're buying a fund for a long period—say, five years or more—go ahead and pay the front-end sales charge for the Class A shares. You'll likely end up better off, and you won't have to learn the fine points of differentiating among share classes.

Better yet, if you stick with a fee-only planner or adviser, you will invest entirely in funds that levy no sales charges. That will make life simpler, though not necessarily cheaper, because the planner will generally charge you up to 1% of assets under management annually.

Help From the Funds

AS FUND COMPANIES SEEK TO EXPAND THEIR MARKETS, MORE are going into the advice business. Sometimes, fund-company advice is as expensive as what you'd pay a planner or broker. Other times, it's free. In all cases, you need to be a little wary, because fund companies usually recommend only their own funds. (Fidelity, T. Rowe Price and Vanguard also offer excellent educational materials on investing—however, you'll find most of what they offer covered in this book. Good fund newsletters also can help; see pages 194–197 of Chapter 15 for some suggestions, as well as some Web sites devoted to mutual funds.)

Here's a thumbnail sketch of some of the services offered by fund companies. They change constantly, so check for details.

DREYFUS (800-782-6620)

Dreyfus will give you access via a toll-free number to a financial planner, who will help you determine how much you need to save for various goals and provide you ongoing advice on fund selection, and financial planning issues including insurance, tax questions and estate planning. While many Dreyfus stock funds have been poor performers, clients of this noteworthy program, called the Lion Account, have access to more than 800 no-transaction-fee funds out of more than 8,000 mutual funds from today's top mutual fund companies. Best of all, the program is free.

FIDELITY (800-544-3455)

For investors with a minimum of $200,000, Fidelity offers its Portfolio Advisory Services, which will allocate your money among Fidelity and other funds and move it to different funds as market conditions and your personal situation warrant. But Fidelity charges up to 1% annually for this service on top of its ordinary annual fund expenses and provides little financial planning.

STEIN ROE (800-322-8222)

The Stein Roe Counselor plan will provide fund-selection advice—for nothing—to anyone who fills out a questionnaire. If you decide to open an account with at least $50,000, the firm will monitor your account and periodically recommend changes in your funds. It's your decision whether to implement the suggested changes. Some Stein Roe funds have been good performers, but the company lacks a full menu of consistent top performers.

USAA (800-382-8722)

Unlike other phone representatives (the people who answer the toll-free numbers when you call a mutual fund), USAA's trained representatives give clients advice. They work in clusters of seven to ten, and each group's supervisor has at least five years' experience in the investment business and usually holds a financial-planning designation, such as CFP. A state-of-the-art computer system enables phone reps to call up information from previous times you've contacted USAA. While USAA has only a few stand-out funds, its funds tend to be steady performers, and they charge among the lowest fees in the industry. If you want someone you can call for free advice periodically, USAA is a fine place to go, particularly if you're a beginning investor without a lot of money to invest.

Vanguard (800-635-1511)

The mutual fund company with among the lowest expenses, Vanguard charges $500 for an investment plan that includes guidance on how much you should invest and which funds to invest in (or $500 for a retirement-savings plan or an estate-planning plan) or, if you have more than $500,000 in assets, 0.65% of assets annually (with a minimum fee of $3,250) for continuing investment advice. (For slightly higher fees, Vanguard will include advice on non-Vanguard funds, too.) Vanguard has great bond and index funds, as well as some good actively managed stock funds. So long as you don't mind doing business solely on the phone and through the mail, Vanguard's 0.65% service offers comprehensive financial planning at about half the price you'd pay elsewhere.

Key Points

- *It takes no training to become a registered investment adviser.*
- *Friends are your best source of information on good brokers, financial planners and investment advisers.*
- *Be prepared to spend time interviewing brokers and financial planners, and to ask them blunt questions.*
- *Make sure to check disciplinary records.*
- *Load funds come in a bewildering assortment.*
- *Fund companies can help.*

PART THREE

How to Pick Good Stock Funds

This section provides the nuts and bolts of how to pick funds yourself. The first chapter takes a look at how stocks and other investments have performed over the long haul—something surprisingly few investors know. It's certain to make you feel more comfortable about investing in stock funds. The other chapters in Part Three explain how to select and monitor good stock and bond funds, and how to assemble them into solid fund portfolios.

A Look at the Long Term

How stocks, bonds and cash have performed and what to expect from them in the future

T HIS CHAPTER IS ONE OF THE MOST IMPORTANT IN the book. While I touched on how investors can expect stocks, bonds and cash to perform over the long term and short term in Chapter 2, this chapter, in a few pages, gives you a comprehensive picture of returns of different investments over time so that you can make intelligent decisions about how to deploy your money. After you've finished, you'll have all the data you need about why it makes so much sense to invest as much of your long-term money in the stock market as your gut will allow. Once you've completed this chapter, you may even want to retake the risk test on pages 30–31. The additional knowledge may have increased your tolerance for the market's ups and downs.

Because of this chapter's significance, I've placed it at the beginning of the part of the book that is aimed at investors who want to delve more deeply into the whys and hows of mutual funds. Aside from a couple of cameo appearances, incidentally, the DiBenedettos have decided to bow out of these later chapters. "We've gotten all we want for now," says Nancy. I'll catch up with them in the Afterword, on page 249.

The Short and Long of Stocks

STOCKS CAN BE TREACHEROUS TO OWN OVER SHORT PERIODS. IN October 1987, the Dow Jones industrial average plummeted 23% in a *single day*—an even worse drop than the "Black Tuesday" 1929 stock market crash that ushered in the Great Depression. But imagine if you had been "unlucky" enough to buy stocks on August 25, 1987, just before the three-month, 33.5% decline in the market began. You would have been back to even within 21 months, and by August 22, 1997, you would have more than tripled your original investment. That's not bad, to say the least, for a ten-year span.

No one can foretell the future, but the past is clear: Despite crashes and protracted down markets—through wars, depressions, inflation and all manner of political and economic crises—since 1926 stocks in large companies have returned an annualized 11.3%, as measured by Standard & Poor's 500-stock index. By contrast, five-year government bonds have returned an annualized 5.2% since 1926, and cash has returned only 3.8%. By cash, I mean 90-day Treasury bills, which return roughly the same as money-market funds, ultra-short-term bond funds and bank certificates of deposit.

ACCOUNTING FOR INFLATION

Over those years, inflation has risen at an annualized 3.1%. Inflation, which measures how much more expensive things get every year (remember nickel Cokes and $3,000 new cars?), is the enemy of investors. In *Through the Looking Glass*, the Red Queen informs a distraught Alice that she has to run as fast as she can just to stay in the same place. Similarly, inflation gives you a benchmark for how fast your investments need to grow just to keep you from losing ground in terms of spending power. The *annualized returns* (see the box on the opposite page) *after inflation* since 1926 have been 8.2% for stocks, 2.1% for bonds and 0.7% for cash. Once you factor in taxes, you can actually fall behind each year by investing in "low-risk" cash.

Strikingly, over holding periods as short as five years, stocks have been far better at outpacing inflation than either bonds or cash. Since 1926, stocks have failed to beat inflation in only 20% of all five-year periods, while bonds have fallen behind inflation in 30% of those periods, and Treasury bills have failed to best inflation 37% of the time. So, even over five-year-periods, stocks are more predictable inflation fighters than either bonds or cash.

(Note: To make the data more reliable, I've used "rolling" five-year periods. The first period started in 1926 and ended in 1930. The next started in 1927 and ended in 1931, and so on. I've done the same thing throughout this chapter. After all, just because you're investing for ten years doesn't mean you're necessarily starting at the beginning of a decade.)

RISK AND REWARD OVER TIME

Over long periods, stocks have been, without question, the best investment. During rolling five-year periods, stocks have lost money only 10% of the time, and have lost more than an annualized 10% only 3% of the time—or in only two of the five-year periods since 1926 (both of those were during the Great Depression). So why not invest every dollar you can in stocks, no matter what your goal? Because over short time periods, bonds are more reliable and cash is the most predictable of all. In investing, as with most other endeavors, the amount you stand to gain is roughly commensurate with the amount of risk, or volatility, you accept—at least over the short term.

WHAT THE TABLES SHOW

The "Performance Snapshots" table on page 155 shows the best,

What Does "Annualized" Mean?

FROM HERE ON, I use the word *annualized* when discussing returns on investments. It means the same thing as "compound annual," a term sometimes used in other publications. Both terms describe how much an investment earns *per year.* For instance, if a stock doubles in five years, its annualized return is 14.9%.

But annualized returns are not quite the same as average annual returns, which you should steer clear of. Here's an example that demonstrates why: You buy a fund at $10 per share. The price rises 100%, to $20 per share, the first year you own it. The second year, it drops in price by 50%, to $10 a share. Your *annualized* return is 0%. But your *average annual* return (100% + −50% = 50%) divided by two equals 25%. Bottom line: You can't spend average annual return.

worst and annualized performance of stocks, bonds and cash over periods of one, five, ten and 20 years. It also shows the percentage of time that stocks have failed to outperform bonds and cash. Here's what those results mean for you:

Investing for one-year periods

Over one-year periods, cash is clearly the most prudent option. Stocks have plunged as much as 43.3% in one year, while five-year government bonds have never lost more than 5.1%, and the worst performance for cash has been a minuscule loss of 0.02%. That's why when you're investing for a period of a year or two, as the DiBenedettos are for their new house, your money belongs in money-market funds, bank savings accounts, certificates of deposit, or short-term bond funds. While stocks, on average, do better than bonds or cash, stocks have lost money in nearly one out of every three years.

Investing for five years or more

Over five years, however, stocks have never lost more than an annualized 12.5%, and five-year government bonds have never lost money. With a five-year time horizon, it makes sense to divide your money among stocks, bonds and cash. If stocks go up, you'll get the benefit of being in the stock market, but if they go down, you'll have the bonds and cash to cushion your losses. Over five-year periods, stocks have outperformed bonds and cash 79% of the time.

Investing for ten years or more

Over periods of ten years or longer, stocks look the best. Since 1926, stocks have outperformed both five-year government bonds and cash in 85% of the ten-year periods; the have outperformed bonds in 98% and cash in all of the 20-year periods. Their worst ten-year return was an annualized loss of 0.9% (from 1929 to 1938). That's why investors with more than ten years before they need their money will want to put the bulk of it into stocks.

Average returns

The tables also show the average of the annualized returns over each time period. That's a mouthful, and forgive me for using it,

Performance Snapshots: Stocks Versus Bonds Versus Cash, 1926–1999

ONE YEAR	BEST ONE-YEAR RETURN	WORST ONE-YEAR RETURN	PERCENTAGE OF TIME INVESTMENT LOST MONEY	PERCENTAGE OF TIME INVESTMENT BEATEN BY STOCKS	90% OF RETURNS BETTER THAN	
Stocks	54.0%	−43.3%	27.0%	—	−10.8%	
Bonds	29.1	−5.1	10.8	66.2%	−0.4	
Cash	14.7	−0.02	1.4	64.9	0.2	

FIVE YEARS	BEST ANNUALIZED FIVE-YEAR RETURN	WORST ANNUALIZED FIVE-YEAR RETURN	PERCENTAGE OF TIME INVESTMENT LOST MONEY	PERCENTAGE OF TIME INVESTMENT BEATEN BY STOCKS	AVERAGE OF ANNUALIZED RETURNS	90% OF ANNUALIZED RETURNS BETTER THAN
Stocks	28.6%	−12.5%	10.0%	—	11.0%	−0.2%
Bonds	17.0	1.0	0	78.6%	5.3	1.56
Cash	11.1	0.01	0	81.4	3.8	0.2

TEN YEARS	BEST ANNUALIZED RETURN	WORST ANNUALIZED RETURN	PERCENTAGE OF TIME INVESTMENT LOST MONEY	PERCENTAGE OF TIME INVESTMENT BEATEN BY STOCKS	AVERAGE OF ANNUALIZED RETURNS	90% OF ANNUALIZED RETURNS BETTER THAN
Stocks	20.1%	−0.9%	4.4%	—	11.1%	3.3%
Bonds	13.1	1.3	0	84.6%	5.3	1.6
Cash	9.2	0.2	0	84.6	3.8	0.2

20 YEARS	BEST ANNUALIZED RETURN	WORST ANNUALIZED RETURN	PERCENTAGE OF TIME INVESTMENT LOST MONEY	PERCENTAGE OF TIME INVESTMENT BEATEN BY STOCKS	AVERAGE OF ANNUALIZED RETURNS	90% OF ANNUALIZED RETURNS BETTER THAN
Stocks	17.9%	3.1%	0%	—	11.2%	6.8%
Bonds	9.9	1.6	0	98.2%	5.0	2.1
Cash	7.7	0.4	0	100	3.9	0.6

SOURCES: T. ROWE PRICE ASSOCIATES, IBBOTSON ASSOCIATES

but let me explain. Let's look at the five-year periods. Fund company T. Rowe Price took the annualized returns for each rolling five-year period from 1926 through 1999. It then *averaged* the returns for those periods over the long term to compute the answers you see in the tables. While the process is a bit complicated, the results are not. For instance, if you invested in stocks, the average of the annualized five-year returns was 11%. So, if you held stocks five years, on average, you would have earned

11% per year. By comparison, in bonds, the average of the annualized five-year returns was only 5.3%.

A measure of your risk

Finally, the tables present a useful look at risk. The last column shows the *worst return* you could expect in each investment type 90% of the time. In other words, it presents your near-worst-case scenario. Another way of looking at the last column: *90% of the time you would have done better than the percentage return it lists.* Since most people are willing to take a risk when the odds are stacked 90% in their favor, this is a meaningful number.

Don't Bet Against History

OF COURSE, THERE'S ALWAYS THE CHANCE THAT THE NEXT ten or 20 years will not be like the last 70 years. The past, after all, is not always prologue. But a longer time period should inspire even greater confidence that the past 70 years were not a historical fluke. Jeremy Siegel, a finance professor at the University of Pennsylvania's Wharton School, examined the returns of stocks, bonds and cash since 1802—the earliest date for which he could find meaningful data. (Some academics, to be fair, assert that there is *no* reliable data going back that far.) Remarkably, he found that stocks have returned an annualized 6.8% after inflation since 1802—*just a bit less* than what they

---

Combining Stocks, Bonds and Cash

THIS TABLE LOOKS at how you would have done with various mixtures of stocks and bonds in your investment portfolio in the 73 years between 1926 and 1999.

	ANNUALIZED RETURN	WORST ANNUAL LOSS	NUMBER OF YEARS WITH A LOSS
80% stocks, 20% bonds	10.5%	−34.9%	19
60% stocks, 40% bonds	9.5	−26.6	17
40% stocks, 40% bonds, 20% cash	7.9	−17.7	14

Source: The Vanguard Group

The Calming Effect of Time

THIS BAR GRAPH ILLUSTRATES how little risk there is in stocks over long time periods. It uses the same numbers—the best and worst annualized returns for stocks, bonds and cash in each of four periods—as the "Performance Snapshots" table on page 155. Over one-year periods, stocks are unpredictable, but over 20-year periods they are actually more predictable, as well as more profitable than competing investments. (*Note:* Some values are so small that, given the scale of the graph, they appear as zero.)

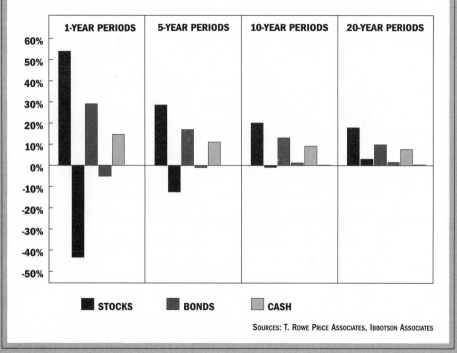

SOURCES: T. ROWE PRICE ASSOCIATES, IBBOTSON ASSOCIATES

have returned since 1926. Before inflation, stocks have returned an annualized 8.1% since 1802.

In addition to examining returns for U.S. stocks, Siegel looked at stock-market returns since 1802 in Great Britain and since 1926 in Germany. Those markets produced approximately the same results as the U.S. stock market despite nearly being destroyed in World War II. In the U.S., there has been no 30-year period since 1802 in which stocks failed to outperform bonds and cash. In his book, *Stocks for the Long Run,* Siegel found that U.S. bonds historically have returned an annualized 4.7%

before inflation since 1802—a little less than they have since 1926. Cash has returned an annualized 4.3% since 1802. Inflation, meanwhile, has taken a toll of 1.3% annually.

It's possible that history won't repeat itself—that stocks will lose money over the next 20 years, or fail to outperform other investments. But the odds are overwhelmingly against such an occurrence. As Sir John Templeton, the legendary investor who pioneered overseas mutual fund investing for Americans, said, "The four most dangerous words in investing are, 'This time is different.'" In this context, it means simply: Never bet against stocks over the long run.

How Bad Can It Get?

WHILE STOCKS OFFER THE BEST ROUTE TO LONG-TERM investment success, don't delude yourself about how bumpy the road to wealth can be. Understanding how the stock market behaves will make it easier to stay invested, however. "If people are emotionally prepared for a bear market, they are more apt to stay the course, which is what they should be doing when the tough days come," says John Bogle, chairman of the Vanguard funds.

Imagine for a moment that in August 1929 you decided it was the perfect time to put all your money into stocks. The market fell a staggering 86.2% between then and June 1932, when it hit bottom. Just to break even, an investor who bought at the peak in 1929 would have had to wait until July 1944, about a month after the Allied landing in Normandy on D-Day.

Unfortunately, there's been a more recent bear market in stocks (a bear market is a decline in the S&P 500 of 20% or more) that cruelly depressed prices. Starting in early 1973, the stock market lost 48% over two years. An investor who got in at the top wouldn't have broken even until late 1976, and, if you factor in inflation, not until October 1983.

The average bear market since 1926 has meant a drop in value for Standard & Poor's 500-stock index of 35.3%, and it has taken people who invested at the top two years and five months to break even. On average, there is one such bear market about every five or six years. Investors can also expect the stock market to decline by 10% or more twice in every three years. Most of these declines do not become bear markets but, in retrospect, represent buying opportunities.

Some of the best advice on preparing for bear markets came from a stockbroker who later became a minister. He jokingly equated them with the Second Coming of Christ. He quoted from the book of Mark: "Watch therefore, for you know neither the day nor the hour."

The clear lesson of stock-market history is that stocks are the place to be for the long haul. Moreover, the market has a lot more safeguards in place than it did in 1929. The volatility of the U.S. stock market in 1929 is arguably more akin to what exists in today's emerging stock markets, such as Argentina, Thailand and Russia. Nor is there any sign at this writing that circumstances like those of 1973–74—which included high inflation, recession, an oil embargo and the resignation of a president—are on the horizon.

Key Points

- *Stocks can be volatile and dangerous to own over short periods.*
- *Over longer periods, stocks offer the best returns.*
- *Studies going back to 1802 in the U.S. and Great Britain and to 1926 in Germany support the idea that stocks return about an annualized 7% after inflation.*

Starting the Search for the Right Funds

There are funds for every purpose, though their names may not tell you so

F SCOTT FITZGERALD ONCE SAID THAT A TEST OF A first-rate intelligence is the ability to keep two contradictory ideas in your head at the same time and still be able to function. While you don't have to be a genius to invest well in mutual funds, it will help to keep these two somewhat contradictory rules in mind:

● **Learn the precise name** of every mutual fund you are considering.
● **You can't count on funds' names** to tell you much about how they invest.

Rule one comes into play partly because fund companies— which have created more than 13,000 mutual funds—sometimes get carried away and create funds that aren't much different from other funds. For example, Dreyfus has a fund called *Dreyfus Muni Bond*. The name is simple and straightforward—this fund invests in tax-exempt municipal bonds, which we'll discuss in Chapter 18. But how does this fund differ from *Dreyfus General Muni Bond*? Not by a lot. Then there's *Dreyfus Basic Muni Bond*. And *Dreyfus Premier Muni Bond*, which is sold by brokers and comes in A, B and C share classes. Think that should about cover it? Guess again. Dreyfus also sells a line of *intermediate muni bond* funds in all these same flavors (muni, general, basic and premier), as well as a similar number of *limited-term muni bond* and *insured muni bond* funds. In all, Dreyfus has more than 75 municipal bond funds—all of which have pretty similar names, but some of which do different things.

I read the last few paragraphs to the DiBenedettos after work one day, and the number of choices appalled them. Paul said that, lacking any further guidance, he would probably have chosen the Dreyfus Basic fund. "Since I'm a novice investor, I guess the basic one would be the one I would want to buy. Basic means simple, doesn't it?" Paul has a wry sense of humor; he wasn't serious. And Dreyfus's Basic line of funds isn't for beginners. "All these different names are confusing," added Nancy. "How can anyone keep them straight? The fund companies are in business to make money, so they keep coming out with new things. If you figure out how funds work, you might get ahead for a while. But it seems like you're taking one step forward and two steps backwards."

Nancy's comments are worth remembering. Mutual fund companies are not in business just to make money for you; they are in business to make money. Unfortunately, coming out with a seemingly endless procession of new funds is one of the best ways many fund companies have hit on to drum up more business. They're frequently variations on the same theme, but occasionally fund companies come up with bizarre funds. One short-lived fund, Pauze Tombstone, focused on companies in what its sponsor termed the "death-care" industry, running funeral homes, making caskets and providing grave markers. OpenFund (www.metamarkets.com) not only lets investors see the trades its managers make almost as they make them, but it allows you to see constantly updated photographs of the managers at work.

Just as in buying a car or a refrigerator, it takes work to sort through the thousands of funds—and plethora of names—to find the ones that are the best values for you. Before you invest, you'd better know exactly which fund you're buying—its precise name and what it does. Otherwise, you might end up owning one you didn't want or a type of fund that doesn't lend the proper balance to your investment plan.

This chapter will help by describing the different types of funds. I've also provided some guidance on which of them belong in long- and short-term portfolios. Even if you don't remember all the types of funds enumerated in this chapter, you can always turn back to it for reference.

Remember that Part Two gave you portfolios of specific funds that match your goals. As a check of any portfolio you assemble yourself, you may want to turn back to Part Two and see what percentage of each fund type I've included in portfolios for different goals.

Once you assemble a good portfolio, fund investing is pretty low-maintenance. Despite Nancy DiBenedetto's fears, you won't have to keep up with every new mutual fund that comes to market; you'll find that most are retreads of similar funds and you can ignore them.

How Fund Followers Type the Funds

Y OU'D THINK THAT A NAME WOULD AT LEAST REALLY TELL YOU what a fund does. Unfortunately, that's not always so. Consider Fidelity Utilities. In 2000, it held a mere 15% of assets in gas and electric utilities, the traditional fare of utility funds. Its largest holdings included such stocks as Voicestream Wireless, Spring PCS and Nextel. Or consider T. Rowe Price Capital Appreciation, a fine fund, which typically has only about half its assets in stocks, although capital-appreciation funds are considered the highest-octane of all stock funds. There are many other examples of misnamed funds—stock funds that own few stocks, and supposedly well-diversified funds that have most of their money stuffed into one or two sectors. The bottom line: When it comes to mutual funds, you can't judge a book by its cover.

Before you buy a fund, you need to examine its semiannual report to determine what it actually does. Or consult resources such as *Morningstar* (www.morningstar.com), which gives detailed descriptions of most funds.

To help you see through the fog of misnamed funds, most sources of fund information—including *Morningstar* and *Kiplinger's Personal Finance* magazine (or Kiplinger.com)—go beyond names when they classify funds into different groups. They scrutinize the holdings of each fund to see what it actually does, and take a careful look at how volatile each fund is relative to its peers. Then they divide funds into broad categories, also called investment objectives. Unfortunately, every fund-rating service classifies funds in slightly different ways. Be aware of this when you are consulting more than one source on funds.

I'll describe the way *Kiplinger's* classifies funds. Don't feel as though you have to memorize these categories and what they

Keep Your Eye on Total Return

THE NUMBER TO FOCUS on when evaluating funds is *total return*. Most funds pay dividends and capital gains to their shareholders at least once a year. Payment of those distributions shrinks the per-share price (or net asset value per share) of the fund, but doesn't change your stake in the fund—so long as you reinvest the distributions in additional shares.

Suppose the XYZ fund has a net asset value of $10 per share on January 1, and you buy 100 shares with a total value of $1,000. Over the course of a year, the share price rises to $11, and in late December, the fund pays out dividends of $1 per share and capital gains of $1 per share. Because of the $2-per-share distribution, the net asset value of the fund is now only $9. But you haven't lost money because you have your $2 per share in distributions. If you reinvest those distributions, you now own 122.2 shares at $9 per share, worth $1,100. That's a $100 increase in value from the beginning of the year, and $100 divided by $1,000 gives you a *total return* for the year of 10%.

Total return also takes into account how much a fund charges you in expenses. In short, a fund's bottom line is its total return. As shorthand, I sometimes use the word "return" to refer to total return. Total return figures in newspapers and magazines typically don't reflect sales charges, but those in prospectuses do.

Even if you are living in retirement and require income from your funds, don't pay too much attention to a fund's yield—that is, how much monthly or quarterly income it pays you. The problem with investing for yield is that you can end up with funds that don't grow enough to keep you ahead of inflation. Instead, you should buy funds likely to produce good total returns. Then spend some of the yearly distributions rather than reinvesting them—or even sell some shares of your funds to meet your needs.

mean. Each time I discuss a fund in detail, I'll explain again what it does and where it fits into the scheme of things. Moreover, you'll likely do just fine without ever investing in most of the fund types listed.

Stock Funds

KIPLINGER'S BREAKS DOWN STOCK FUNDS INTO EIGHT investment categories, or objectives. Here are descriptions of each:

AGGRESSIVE-GROWTH FUNDS

Aggressive-growth funds seek maximum gains. Often they invest in risky stocks of small companies, and usually they pay no attention to dividend income. These funds tend to outperform the market in rising (or "bull") markets but to fall sharply in declining (or "bear") markets. They are best suited for investors with ten years or so before they'll need their money. As you get closer to your goal, you'll want to scale back on these funds.

LONG-TERM-GROWTH FUNDS

Long-term-growth funds also aim for big gains. But they tend to invest in stocks of larger, more stable companies. These funds typically mirror the market—rising about as much as Standard & Poor's 500-stock index when the stock market is on a roll. When the market falls, they also tend to fall just about the same amount. They should typically make up the biggest part of long-term portfolios.

BALANCED FUNDS

Balanced funds generally have 30% or more of their assets in bonds, no matter what the market looks like. They tend to underperform the stock market when it's rising, but will usually hold up better than all-stock funds when the market turns down. Most investors are better off creating their own "balanced" funds, by buying both pure stock funds and pure bond funds. That way *you* decide how much to invest in stocks and bonds, rather than a fund manager who doesn't know your individual situation.

GROWTH-AND-INCOME FUNDS

Growth-and-income funds tend to be conservative. They typically don't concentrate on trying to earn stupendous gains. These funds usually invest in large companies and, in addition to stocks, often own bonds and other income-producing securities. They generally produce lower returns than aggressive-growth and long-term-growth funds in good times (though they outpaced their more aggressive brethren, on average, over the 15 years through July 31, 2000), but should decline less than those two categories of funds in a bear market. Growth-and-income funds are often the ballast of long-term portfolios. In shorter-term portfolios, though, they may be your largest stock-fund holding.

You can subdivide the growth-and-income category into additional types:

Plain growth-and-income funds (sometimes called equity-income) usually own few or no bonds.

Total-return funds use a variety of strategies but typically vary their percentage of bonds depending on the manager's prognosis for the markets.

Asset-allocation funds usually have a flexible division of assets in stocks and bonds. Some asset-allocation funds invest 100% in stocks in good times and nothing in stocks in bad times. Others vary their percentage of stocks only slightly.

I mention these subcategories because you may see a fund referred to in these ways. But for the most part, the growth-and-income moniker tells you what you need to know.

INTERNATIONAL FUNDS

International funds generally have all, or almost all, of their assets invested in foreign companies. These funds allow U.S. investors to take advantage of growth opportunities in other parts of the world. But they are usually riskier than domestic funds because foreign political upheaval, looser regulatory environments and changes in the value of the dollar against foreign currencies can affect them. The chief advantage of owning international funds is that foreign markets often do not move in tandem with the U.S. market, so they reduce the volatility of your overall portfolio. They usually invest some money in risky emerging markets. Most long-term investors will profit by placing 20% to 25% of their money in these funds. A subcategory of international funds is:

International-specialized funds, which invest either in developing nations, mostly in Asia and Latin America, or in a single country or a single region of the world. These funds tend to be extremely volatile but sometimes produce big gains. Most investors will do well to use these specialized funds sparingly, if at all.

GLOBAL FUNDS

Global funds invest most of their assets overseas, but they also invest in the U. S. These funds often vary in the percentage of assets that they invest in the U.S., depending on where managers perceive the most value. Most investors will do better with pure international funds because you can more reliably and easily track how much of your money is invested abroad. Global funds are sometimes called *worldwide* funds.

SECTOR FUNDS

Sector funds invest in a single industry, such as automobiles or software, or in a broader economic sector, such as transportation, technology or the Internet. These funds tend to be extremely volatile, and you can often find some of them atop the market leaders' lists for the preceding 12 months. Alas, you can usually find some sector funds on the laggards' list for the same 12 months. Predicting which sectors will do well is nearly impossible, so take these funds in small doses or abstain from them altogether.

There are exceptions, though. If your funds don't own enough technology stocks (the S&P 500 is about one-third tech stocks), you might want to put 5% or so of your stock money into a tech fund. Biotechnology offers immense promise, but, at this writing, few diversified funds have more than a tiny percentage of their assets in biotech stocks. Up to 5% of your most speculative money could go into this sector (see pages 227–229 for more on tech and biotech funds). Real estate funds, which provide a high-level of dividend income and tend to be much less risky than other kinds of sector funds. You'll see them in some of the lowest-risk portfolios in Part One.

UTILITY FUNDS

Utility funds are really a subset of sector funds. *Kiplinger's* groups utility funds separately because there are a lot of them and they've traditionally been more conservative than other sector funds. But the utility industry has become much more competitive in recent years, and it's likely to become even more cutthroat in the future. That has reduced the dividend yields of these funds and made them somewhat more volatile. A utility fund, however, is still likely to be safer than most other sector funds.

PRECIOUS-METALS FUNDS

Precious-metals funds invest in stocks of gold-mining companies. Some also own stock in silver-mining companies, as well as in gold and silver themselves. Many financial planners in the 1980s considered these so-called "hard assets" to be ideal hedges against inflation. Planners often recommended that investors hold 5% or so of their stock money in these funds, to cushion against declining markets. But since the mid 1980s these funds haven't acted well as an inflation hedge. They've even done badly in times of global political upheaval, such as the 1990 Gulf War.

Bond Funds

A S A GROUP, BOND FUNDS ARE LESS RISKY, AND LESS REWARDING, than stocks. Think about it. If you had bought shares in Microsoft years ago, your money could have grown a hundredfold or more. On the other hand, if you had had the misfortune to own shares of one of the many Microsoft wannabes, you may have made little or no money—or even lost it all. But if you had bought bonds from any company, regardless of how rosy its future, the best you could have hoped for is the return of your money with interest. Unless the company went bankrupt, you'd be repaid—but your potential for gain would have been limited. During periods of rising inflation and interest rates, such as the 1970s, bonds actually paid you back less *after inflation* than you had invested in the first place. Since the early 1980s, however, long-term bonds have been unusually profitable—as interest rates have dropped, thus driving up bonds' prices.

You can ordinarily count on bond funds to reduce risk in your portfolio and provide steady income. They are an essential part of shorter-term portfolios and portfolios for people living in retirement. Most investors will do well to put most of their bond money into high-grade bond funds and a smaller amount into high-yield bond funds (see below), because owning the two types tends to minimize your portfolio's overall volatility. Even with a fairly short time period until you'll need your money, you'll want to own different types of bond funds. It's only when you're within two or three years of your goal that you'll want to stick largely to short-term bonds.

Kiplinger's divides the bond universe into the following investment objectives:

HIGH-GRADE CORPORATE FUNDS

High-grade corporate funds emphasize safety by owning mostly bonds that bond-rating agencies have rated as "investment grade." (That means Standard & Poor's ratings of BBB–, A, AA or AAA, or Moody's Investors Service ratings of Baa, A, Aa or Aaa.) There's little likelihood that the issuers of these bonds will default (fail to make payments on time), so investors will want to put most of their bond money into high-grade bonds—either corporates or municipals depending on their tax brackets. The risk in high-grade bonds comes from rising interest rates. All bonds lose value when rates rise (see page 22 in Chapter 2 for an explanation of why), but lower-quality bonds rise and fall more with the fortunes of the issuing company, so rising rates tend to affect them less.

HIGH-YIELD CORPORATE FUNDS

High-yield corporate funds are also called "junk" bond funds because they invest in lower-quality bonds. These bonds tend to pay high rates of interest because they are low-rated or unrated and are issued by corporations that have a real risk of defaulting or going bankrupt. When the economy is growing, the companies that issue junk bonds tend to prosper and junk-bond funds likewise do well. But when the economy falls into recession, some junk-bond issuers default, and junk-bond funds do badly. These funds are almost as risky as stock funds. At the same time, in small to midsize helpings they can increase the yield in a portfolio without raising your overall risk, because junk bonds often rise and fall in value at different times than high-quality bonds.

HIGH-GRADE MUNICIPAL FUNDS

High-grade municipal funds own mostly tax-free bonds classified as investment-grade. States, municipalities and other tax-exempt agencies issue tax-free bonds. Like their taxable cousins, muni funds tend to be sensitive to interest-rate swings. They are usually a better bet than taxable bond funds for investors in the 28% federal tax bracket or higher who are investing in an account that's subject to income taxes. While municipal bond funds are free from federal taxes, they are usually not exempt from state and local income taxes.

HIGH-YIELD MUNICIPAL FUNDS

High-yield municipals invest in lower-quality muni bonds. They offer higher yields but also carry more risk than high-grade munis. While defaults have been rare in recent years, these funds yield only a bit more than safer funds.

SINGLE-STATE MUNICIPAL FUNDS

Single-state municipals invest in the municipal bonds of a single U.S. state or territory. Their advantage to investors is that they are free not only from federal income taxes but also from the state (and often local) taxes of the state in which they are issued. Single-state munis often make sense for high-income investors who live in states with an income-tax rate of 6% or more. But tread carefully here; not all states treat income from their own state bonds in such a favorable way. A few states allow you to deduct the dividends from national municipal bond funds; others don't allow you to deduct dividends even from single-state funds. Moreover, single-state muni funds generally charge higher expenses and are less diversified than other muni funds. People in low-tax or no-tax states, such as Florida and Texas, should avoid them.

GOVERNMENT FUNDS

Government bond funds are the safest in terms of credit quality, because they invest mostly in securities issued by the U.S. Treasury or other government-related agencies. These bonds are not without risk, however. Their prices will fluctuate with changes in interest rates. Investors will often do better with high-quality corporate bonds than with government bonds.

MORTGAGE FUNDS

Mortgage bond funds own mortgage-backed securities, most of which are issued or insured by the government or government-related entities such as Ginnie Mae (the Government National Mortgage Association), Fannie Mae (the Federal National Mortgage Association), and Freddie Mac (the Federal Home Loan Mortgage Association). While Ginnie Mae only insures mortgages, Fannie and Freddie Mac bundle hundreds of mortgages together and sell them to dealers who, in turn, sell them to mutual funds and other large investors.

Mortgage bonds do best in times of relatively stable interest rates. When rates rise, their prices decline just as do the prices of most other bonds. When rates drop a lot, however, homeowners refinance their mortgages at the lower rates, so the yields from these funds falls. Despite their disadvantages, mortgage-security funds make a great addition to your portfolio if you are seeking high income. Moreover, they tend to zig when other funds are zagging, smoothing your portfolio's volatility.

Mortgage securities can be relatively straightforward, or among the most complicated investments available. Investments in complex mortgage-backed bonds triggered several bond fund disasters during the 1990s. It's best to keep it simple here: Rather than trying to get a bit of extra yield, stick with funds that invest in government-guaranteed Ginnie Maes. We'll get into more detail on specific funds in Chapter 18.

GLOBAL BOND FUNDS

Global bond funds invest all or most of their assets in bonds of foreign countries. These bond funds are quite volatile, because changes in currency valuations influence them as much as interest rates.

Key Points
- *Learn a fund's precise name before investing.*
- *Fund names are sometimes misleading.*
- *Funds are divided into numerous categories and subcategories.*

Investing With Style

Make sure part of your portfolio is always "in"

HEN YOU THINK OF STYLE, DO YOU THINK OF designer dresses or spiked hair? Do you think of people who have a certain panache, who light up a room when they enter it? Well, it might surprise you to learn that mutual funds have style, too. "You've got to be kidding," says Paul DiBenedetto. "Well, you've got my attention now." Just as with fashion, funds' styles of investing are quite distinct. Understanding how they vary is important, and while the concepts in this chapter are the most difficult in the book, once you grasp them you'll be a much better investor.

As important as it is to know a fund's objective, which we discussed in the last chapter, that tells you only what the fund aims to accomplish. It doesn't tell you *how* the fund attempts to achieve its goal. A fund's style describes the method by which a fund seeks to meet its objective. Let's pursue our fashion analogy just a little further. Say two young women go to a party hoping to meet attractive young men. Their objective is the same. But one may wear a Versace gown and diamonds, while the other sports a miniskirt and nose ring. Their styles are quite different.

Determining a stock fund's style depends on the answers to two questions:

• **Is it a fund that invests in stocks of large companies** or stocks of small companies?

• **Is it a growth-style fund** (looking for fast-growing companies) or a value-style fund (seeking bargain stocks)?

Investors who don't understand style often end up buying a portfolio of currently top-performing funds without realizing that all of them use the same investment approach. Then, when that style goes out of favor, the funds lose their sparkle, and the investor ends up replacing them with new funds—all of which again follow a common style. By contrast, when you understand fund styles, you can build portfolios of funds with different styles that work in harmony. When one style goes out of favor and another one comes in, your overall portfolio may barely miss a beat; in other words, your portfolio's volatility will be much lower. Just as important, you'll be able to compare funds with their real peers—other funds with the same objectives and styles—so that you don't end up buying an average or below-par fund simply because its investment style is currently working.

If you're a beginner without a lot of money to invest, you probably won't want to go to all the work of tearing apart each top-performing fund's innards to determine whether it's a large-company fund or a small-company fund, a growth-style fund or a value-style fund. You'll find you can do okay by selecting for your portfolio:

• **one aggressive-growth fund,** which is likely to contain smallish, growth-style stocks;

• **one long-term-growth fund,** which is likely to contain medium-size or large stocks;

What's a Stock's Market Value?

A STOCK'S MARKET value is the value that shareholders collectively place on a company's stock. It's computed by multiplying the stock's share price by the total number of shares the company has issued. For instance, in mid 2000 General Electric traded at about $52 a share, and there were roughly 10 million shares of GE outstanding. Multiply those two numbers and you get GE's market value, which is about $520 billion. (General Electric just happens to have the highest market value of any U.S. stock.)

A stock's market value is use-ful for mutual fund investors chiefly because it gives you an idea of whether a fund is investing in small, medium or large stocks. A stock's market value doesn't necessarily tell you anything about the company's earnings or sales, or the value of its physical plant and other assets. In other words, market value is not necessarily what the company would be worth if it were sold. In 2000, for instance, many stocks of Internet companies, such as Yahoo and Amazon.com have had huge market values, but scant earnings or assets.

- **one growth-and-income fund,** which will probably contain large, value-oriented stocks; and
- **one international fund.**

Then, as you become more proficient in sorting out funds, you'll want to refine your methods. For the purposes of this book, I've tried to make things easy. Chapter 17, "Twenty Great Stock Funds," tells you the investment style of each fund, allowing you to easily pick top funds from each category.

If you do well enough on your basic investments, you may want to use some of your earnings to spice up your wardrobe. Then you can truly say that you are in style.

Is the Fund Large-Company or Small-Company?

L ET'S START LEARNING FUND INVESTMENT STYLES BY LOOKING at just two funds. *Skyline Special Equities* and *Janus Mercury* are both considered aggressive-growth funds because they seek to increase your capital without regard to dividend income. But the two funds employ very different investing styles:

The average stock that Skyline Special Equities buys has a market value (see the box on the preceding page) of just over $812 million. Some of its largest holdings recently were BancWest, IDEX, Heller Financial and Arthur J. Gallagher. Haven't heard of any of them? Stocks with market values of less than $1 billion represent smaller companies, many of which are obscure.

Now let's look at Janus Mercury. Its average stock has a market value of $48 billion—or about 66 times the value of the Skyline fund's average stock. The fund's top holdings at this writing included such household names as Cisco Systems, Nokia and Time Warner.

To put it simply, Skyline Special Equities invests mostly in stocks of small companies, while Janus Mercury prospects among big companies.

WHAT'S IN AND WHAT'S OUT?

That wouldn't be especially noteworthy to investors except that the stock market goes through fads that are just as extreme (and sometimes as nonsensical) as those in the world of fashion. It's not unusual for small stocks to be hot for two or three years, as they were in the late 1970s and early 1990s, while big stocks are as out-of-favor as polyester leisure suits. Then things change. In 1997, 1998 and 1999, for instance, investors couldn't get enough of large stocks, especially technology stocks. Behemoths like Cisco, Microsoft and Intel, with growing global franchises, were the darlings of investors and money managers, while smaller stocks were wallflowers. Investing in large stocks almost guaranteed that a fund manager would do well in those three years, while even the most talented managers of funds specializing in small companies fell behind.

COMPARING APPLES WITH APPLES

Why does this matter? For two reasons:

You need to make a valid comparison

First, if you compared Janus Mercury's performance with Skyline Special Equities' for the three years ending in mid 2000, knowing only their objective (aggressive-growth), you'd decide that Janus Mercury was a far better fund than Skyline Special Equities. Janus Mercury rose an annualized 41.6% over the three years, while Skyline Special Equities actually lost an annualized 1.47% in the same period. But Standard & Poor's 500-stock index, the benchmark large-company stock average against which to judge Janus Mercury's performance, rose an annualized 16% during the three-year period, while the Russell 2000, a small-company-stock average against which to judge Skyline Special Equities' performance, rose only 7.73% during the same period.

Definitions of precisely what constitutes a small, medium or large stock often differ—confusing even the most conscientious investors.

What you can conclude is that, by comparison with their benchmarks, Janus Mercury still outshone Skyline Special Equities during those three years, but not by quite as much as it seems at first blush.

Only by comparing a stock fund against a suitable index or against stock funds employing similar styles can you come to an intelligent conclusion about how well the fund has performed. Just as you wouldn't learn anything about the abilities of two football players by comparing a lineman's total touchdowns against those of a quarterback, you can't learn much about a fund's performance unless you compare it with its peers.

You can reduce your portfolio's volatility

There's another reason it's important to know what size stocks a fund invests in. That's because the goal of a good portfolio is to attain maximum returns with minimum fluctuations in the value of your holdings. Now, remember how small stocks stalled in the mid 1990s. If you had held a portfolio that consisted only of funds investing in small stocks, the value of your holdings wouldn't have grown nearly as much as that of the overall stock market. You would have done better by owning some large stocks as well.

Over the long haul, however, small stocks are almost certain to catch up with large stocks. As I noted earlier Chapter 4, since 1926 small stocks have outperformed large stocks by roughly one percentage point per year. But to minimize your portfolio's volatility—which is especially important if your time horizon isn't very long—you'll do best owning some funds that invest in small stocks and others that invest in large stocks.

DIFFERENCES IN COMPARING FUNDS

Definitions of precisely what constitutes a small, medium or large stock often vary—and that can be a bit confusing to even the most conscientious investors. Standard and Poor's Micropal, which supplies fund data to Kiplinger's (which can be viewed at www.kiplinger.com), describes small stocks as those with a market value of less than $1 billion. Micropal defines large stocks as those with market values of more than $10 billion, and those with values in between as medium-size.

But another popular information source, Morningstar (at www.morningstar.com), uses somewhat different definitions. It first ranks the largest 5,000 U.S. stocks by market value. It calls the top 5% large, the next 15% medium-size, and the remaining 80% small. At this writing, Morningstar defined large stocks as those with market values of more than $10.5 billion, small stocks as those with market values under $1.7 billion, and medium-size as those with values in between.

Micropal and Morningstar both use data from the funds to classify them as small, medium-size or large. Funds must release a list of their holdings only every six months, and these listings are often out of date the day they are released. That can make it difficult to get current information on precisely what a fund is up to. Most funds, however, are fairly consistent in what kinds of stocks they own, so this usually isn't a major problem.

Growth Versus Value

UNDERSTANDING WHETHER A FUND INVESTS IN LARGE-company stocks or small-company stocks is half the battle in determining its investment style. The second half of the struggle is concluding whether the fund invests in growth stocks or value stocks. Janus Mercury and Skyline Special Equities differ in this regard just as they differ in the size of the stocks they buy.

Janus Mercury hunts for companies with growing earnings. (A company's earnings are its profits after taxes and other expenses have been deducted. The relevant number for investors is earnings per share—that is, earnings divided by the number of outstanding shares of common stock.) As a result, Janus Mercury's investment *style* is labeled "growth." What's confusing here is that the fund's objective is aggressive-growth, and growth in that context has an entirely different meaning. If you remember from the previous chapter, a fund with an objective of aggressive growth seeks capital gains rather than dividends, and often invests in stocks of small companies. I say often because the fund research services also classify Janus Mercury, which buys stocks of large companies, as having aggressive-growth as its objective. *Be careful to differentiate between a fund with "growth" as an objective and a "growth-style" fund—which is one that specializes in stocks with growing earnings. The two terms mean different things.*

Analyzing funds' styles: There is no perfect way to capture what a fund does statistically and place it into a neat little box.

Some growth-style funds hunt for stocks with steadily rising earnings; others, like Janus Mercury, look for companies with rapidly growing or accelerating earnings. These companies usually are Wall Street's glamour stocks, stocks that investors are willing to pay high prices for (expressed as a multiple of their earnings). Janus Mercury's average stock traded at 51 times the previous 12 months' earnings in mid 2000. (During the same period, the average S&P-500 stock traded at 36 times earnings.)

Skyline Special Equities buys a totally different type of stock than Janus Mercury does. It looks for so-called "value" stocks—

stocks that Wall Street has so pummeled or ignored that they sell at bargain prices relative to their earnings, sales or assets—that is, relative to what an informed buyer might be willing to pay for the whole company. These stocks typically reach their depressed prices because earnings have been disappointing, investors have no faith in the company's management, or some other perceived failing. So Skyline Special Equities is a "value-style" fund. Value stocks tend to be less volatile than growth stocks because their share prices already reflect much of the bad news; they usually don't have as far to fall as growth stocks. Skyline Special Equities' average stock sold at 15 times earnings in late 2000 (about one third what Janus Mercury's average stock sold for).

So what is an investor to do? One good solution is to stick to a single data source, especially when you are first analyzing funds.

One example of a growth stock is software giant Cisco, which increased 13-fold in price from 1996 through mid 2000. The stock was on fire because investors believed Cisco would continue to see fast-growing earnings as it increased its dominance over other networking suppliers amid the mushrooming growth of the Internet. But Cisco was not cheap by mid 2000. Its share price of $65 amounted to more than 175 times what the company had earned per share in the preceding 12 months (meaning the stock traded at a price-earnings ratio of more than 175), while the S&P 500 traded at 36 times earnings (or had a P/E ratio of 36). Stocks trading at high P/E ratios are vulnerable to even the smallest whiff of bad news. One disappointing quarterly earnings report, and Wall Street takes the stock out and shoots it. Declines of 15% and 20% in a single hour are not uncommon for high-flying growth stocks. For instance, Qualcomm, a telecommunications firm, experienced such a plunge in early 2000. Many growth stocks, however, offer the promise of increasing earnings without too much regard to the ebbs and flows of the economy.

Fortunately, there is more agreement among the experts over what a value stock is and what a growth stock is than over the size of stocks. Morningstar looks at the price-earnings ratios and the price-to-book ratios of all the stocks in a fund (see the box below for definitions of these terms). Micropal analyzes only price-to-book ratios. Morningstar and Micropal then compare a fund's weighted price-to-book ratio (and, in the case of

Morningstar, a fund's weighted price-earnings ratio) and those of an index, such as the S&P 500 (weighting accounts for the proportion of each stock in a fund's portfolio). Those funds owning stocks with low price-to-book ratios (and in Morningstar's case, low price-earnings ratios) are considered value funds, while those with high ratios are considered growth funds. Funds somewhere in the middle are considered to "blend" growth and value styles.

The Four Food Groups of Funds

SKYLINE SPECIAL EQUITIES HUNTS FOR SMALL UNDERVALUED stocks. Other funds specialize in small growth stocks. Janus Mercury buys large growth stocks, while other funds invest

Two Ways to Value Stocks

PRICE-EARNINGS RATIOS and price-to-book-value ratios are the two most common measures used to ascertain the value of a stock. While the terms will surely sound confusing to new investors, they are simple to understand if you take a minute to learn them.

A PRICE-EARNINGS RATIO is determined by dividing a stock's earnings per share into its share price. So, if a company earned $2 per share over the previous 12 months and it now sells for $40 a share, the stock has a P/E ratio of $40 divided by $2, or 20. All other things being equal, the higher a stock's price-earnings ratio, the more expensive it is and the faster investors anticipate its earnings will grow in the future. Essentially, a price-earnings ratio represents the number of dollars investors are willing to pay for each dollar of a company's profits.

BOOK VALUE is how much is left after all assets and liabilities of a company are

taken into account. Say a stock has total assets (things such as the value of its buildings, products in its inventory, its cash on hand, and what customers owe) of $100 million, and total liabilities (things such as bills due to suppliers and loans it must repay) of $80 million. Book value is $100 million minus $80 million, or $20 million. If the company has a million shares outstanding, each share has a book value of $20 ($20 million divided by one million shares). And if the stock sells at $40 a share, that's two times its book value. As with price-earnings ratios, the higher a stock's price-to-book ratio, the more expensive it is and the faster investors expect its earnings will increase. It can also mean, however, that a company doesn't have much physical plant.

P/E ratios of stocks are listed daily in newspaper stock tables, and price-to-book ratios are available in most other stock- and fund-information sources.

in large value stocks. These four variations are the main styles of investing. Although it takes work to determine which funds are truly peers, the result is well worth the effort. Comparing the funds in each of these four groups against their peers is the best way to identify outstanding funds. Academic studies show that by comparing funds that are similar you have a better chance of predicting which funds will outperform others in the future.

Furthermore, to have a truly diversified portfolio, it's best to have some representation from each of these four styles, as well as an international fund. Then, if one or two of these styles are out of favor, your whole portfolio won't fall apart on you. Diversifying is the only way you can maximize your potential return while minimizing your portfolio's volatility—the amount it bounces around from month to month.

You can also think of these fund styles as personality types. **Small-company growth funds** tend to be tightly wound, high-energy creatures, soaring in good times and crashing to Earth in bad times.

Large-company growth funds are still mighty peppy.

Small-company value funds are typically more sedate.

Large-company value funds are the most somnolent of all stock funds—moving slowly compared with the market when stock averages are careening to new highs or plunging sharply.

Like Fund, Like Manager, Like Investor?

IT'S STRETCHING THE TRUTH TO SAY THAT MOST FUND managers reflect their fund's investment styles. But there are enough examples of managers who match the personalities of their funds to make it seem more than mere coincidence. The prototypical growth fund manager is impatient, and keeps his eyes glued to a computer screen and his ears attached to several telephones. Foster Friess, manager of Brandywine, a growth-style fund, has only one chair in his office—so he holds all meetings with everyone else standing up. That tends to keep meetings short. Friess doesn't even like his employees talking to one another—on the phone or in person. He says e-mail and faxes are far more efficient for quickly exchanging information, even for, say, inviting a colleague to lunch.

Meanwhile, value managers, though they may put in as

many hours studying stocks as their growth counterparts, tend to trade less frequently. They can be slower-moving, thriftier types. The late Max Heine, founder of the Mutual Series funds (now part of the Franklin fund group) and a multimillionaire, was known for taking the subway to work, wearing the same suit every day and, once he got older, always insisting on senior-citizen discounts.

Investors may find themselves drawn to one style or another. Technology-laden, small-company growth funds may attract those who crave excitement. Conservative investors, on the other hand, are often more at ease with large-company value funds. To a certain extent, it's fine to overweight your portfolio with funds you feel comfortable with. But you'll profit more as an investor if you also fight your instincts to a degree—and, say, buy some shares in a volatile growth fund even if its thrills and spills unnerve you at times.

Fund Mini Styles

TO MORE ACCURATELY compare funds, some analysts go beyond the four styles explained in detail in this chapter. Most of these subcategories lie on the cusp of two of the broader styles. Commonly used mini styles include:

• *blend,* a cross between growth and value

• *growth at a reasonable price,* growth funds that also consider value criteria

• *relative value,* which buy stocks that are cheap relative to other stocks in the same industry sector, even if they aren't cheap in comparison to the whole market.

• *earnings momentum,* a substratum of growth funds, which specialize in stocks with accelerating earnings and rising share prices. Some analysts also identify:

• *medium-size company funds,* which fall between small-company and large-company funds, and

• *micro-cap,* which invest in companies that have smaller market values than those in small-company funds.

You usually don't need to use these fine points to effectively evaluate funds, because the narrower style slices don't generally behave all that much differently from the broader ones. But you should be aware of them for the rare times that mini styles do diverge significantly. For instance, small-company momentum-style funds were in a terrible slump from mid 1996 through early 1998, while most other small-company growth-style funds didn't suffer as much.

SHIFTING STYLES

It's wise to own funds that represent all four styles of investing. But some investors—and many pension-fund managers—take that maxim so seriously that they won't consider buying a fund that strays even slightly from its investment style. That can be a mistake. Some fund managers shift styles as they perceive changes in the market. Switching from a growth style to a value style can be a tricky business, however, and many more managers fail at it than succeed. Also, the rise in their funds' assets forces most successful fund managers to shift style from smaller to larger companies. Some execute that transition flawlessly, while others fall flat on their faces.

It's best to be a little skeptical of those funds that aren't consistent. Morningstar shows a fund's style, as well as the style it has followed in previous years, so you can tell whether the fund has been consistent.

Key Points
• *A fund's style tells you what kinds of stocks it specializes in.*
• *Telling small-company funds from large-company funds is difficult, partly because the experts disagree on their definitions.*
• *Growth funds buy stocks with growing earnings.*
• *Value funds buy cheap, undervalued stocks.*
• *A portfolio with funds that use different styles will be less volatile than a portfolio that owns stocks of only one style.*

How to Pick Winning Stock Funds

Performance, risks, management, method and costs

P ICK UP MOST FINANCIAL PUBLICATIONS AND YOU'LL
see a list of the top-performing stock funds for the
past 12 months. If only you could figure out, in
advance, which funds would fill those pages 12 months from
now! You may receive junk e-mail promising you sure-fire methods for picking those funds. Fact is, picking next year's top funds
is as hard as hitting the trifecta at the race track.

But that's no reason to despair. You *can* identify funds with
good odds of beating their peers. By comparing funds that are
similar in both their investment objective and their style, you can
identify which ones have a good chance to be top performers. I
emphasize a *good chance* here, because picking funds is three
parts number crunching and one part instinct.

Focus on the Long Term

T HIS CHAPTER SPOTLIGHTS THE SIGNPOSTS OF EXCELLENCE TO
look for when sizing up funds. While past performance is
no guarantee of future success, it's the best indicator we
have. Just make sure to compare funds against their peers. As
you've learned already, comparing a large-company growth fund
against a small-company value fund is pointless. As noted in the
previous chapter, academic studies have found that stock funds
that have done well in past years *against their peers* tend to continue to outperform.

When evaluating past performance, statisticians tell us, the longer period you can consider, the better. Performance of a fund over three months means virtually nothing. *American Heritage*, among the worst-performing funds around, put up terrific numbers in the first quarter of 2000. In fact, American Heritage was the number-one aggressive-growth fund in 1997. But even one-year performance has little long-term predictive value. *(Note:* Momentum investing relies on past fund performance over short periods to predict future *short-term* performance; I discuss it in Chapter 10, "13 Investment Pitfalls and How to Avoid Them.")* Performance over three years has more meaning, and performance over five years is, perhaps, the best single number to employ.

From a purely statistical standpoint, it would be better to consider ten or 20 years. But very few funds have been run by the same managers for that long, and, even if they have, often the

Keeping Up With the Indexes

TO TELL HOW a fund is doing compared with the indexes, you may want to go beyond looking at the S&P 500 large-company index and the Russell 2000 small-company index. Several companies, most notably BARRA, Russell and Wilshire, maintain value and growth indexes, as well as large-company and small-company indexes. You can find information on performance of those indexes in most of the fund sources mentioned in the this chapter, as well as on page 212 and on numerous Web sites. You can also find BARRA indexes on the Internet at www.barra.com, Russell at www.russell.com, and Wilshire at www.wilshire.com

Many newspapers publish averages of various composites of stock funds: small-company value, large-company growth, and so on. If your newspaper doesn't contain composites, use the Vanguard index funds as benchmarks.

Vanguard Small Cap Index (NAESX) mirrors the Russell 2000 index,

Vanguard Value Index (VIVAX) tracks the S&P BARRA Value, which tracks value stocks of all sizes.

Vanguard Growth Index (VIGRX) reflects the S&P BARRA Growth, which tracks growth stocks of all sizes.

Vanguard 500 Index (VFINX) fund is also a good source of total-return data of the S&P 500 (unlike many data sources, which neglect dividends when reporting the S&P 500's performance).

Vanguard Total International Stock Index (VGTSX) tracks the Morgan Stanley Capital International's combined Europe, Australasia, Far East (EAFE) and Emerging Markets Index. It's a good proxy for international funds.

Vanguard Extended Market Index (VEXMX) tracks the Wilshire 4500 Index, which represents all stocks except those in the S&P 500.

nature of the fund has changed radically during that period. By all means, though, examine ten- and 20-year performance, if a fund has had the same manager that long, as well as five- and three-year performance. Some long-term top performers, such as *Acorn* (begun in 1970) and *Davis New York Venture* (started in 1969) are still great funds. The more useable data you have, the more likely a fund's top-notch performance wasn't a fluke.

But don't stop with long-term total returns. Consistency is also important. Examine how a fund has done *each year* of the period you're looking at relative to its peers or against an appropriate benchmark (such as Standard & Poor's 500-stock index for large-company funds or the Russell 2000 for small-company mutual funds).

Performance isn't everything. How risky is a fund relative to its peers or an appropriate stock-market average?

If a fund's performance is consistently above average, it is likely be a winning fund. For instance, Selected American Shares has finished in the top half of growth-and-income funds every year since Christopher Davis became a co-manager in 1995. Conversely, if a fund beat the pants off its competitors for a year or two, only to slump badly in other years, you'll want to steer clear of it. For instance, CornerCap Small Cap Value finished in the top 20% against its aggressive-growth peers in 1996 and 1997, but it the fund finished in the bottom 20% in 1998, 1999 and the first half of 2000. This is probably a fund to avoid unless you can satisfactorily account for the substandard years and gain a measure of faith in its long-term potential.

Look at Risk

PERFORMANCE ISN'T EVERYTHING IN PICKING A FUND. YOU'LL want to determine how risky a fund is relative to its peers or an appropriate stock-market average. Think of risk as the chance that you won't achieve as high a return as you expect or that you'll lose money. For instance, large-company stocks have returned an average of more than 10% annually, but that doesn't mean you can expect to earn 10%-plus in large-company stocks next year. The stock market is volatile over the short term, rising 30% one year, then falling 20% the next. It's only over periods of ten and 20 years that returns smooth out and stocks become (or, at least, have been in the past) fairly predictable investments.

Similarly, when you are evaluating funds, you want to know how much they tend to fall when the overall market tumbles. The simplest way to estimate this is to compare a fund's performance during the last two market downturns with that of its peers or with an appropriate benchmark. In 1998, Standard & Poor's 500-stock index lost 19.1% from July 17 through August 31. But if you were unlucky enough to have invested in *Frontier Equity*, your fund would have plunged 38.7% during that six-week span. By contrast, *Merger* fund lost just 5.6% in that period.

A Measure of the Future

An even better way to determine how a fund will do during a downturn is to look at its *standard deviation*. Standard deviation measures a fund's volatility—how much it tends to bounce around from month to month. By knowing a fund's standard deviation compared with that of its peers or a market average, you can estimate how it will fare relative to a benchmark when the market plunges. Merger fund, for example, has a three-year monthly standard deviation (standard deviations can be measured over different periods) of 1.39, which is less than one-third of the 5.03 three-year-monthly standard deviation of Standard & Poor's 500-stock index. In the 1998 sell-off, Merger fund lost less than a third of what the S&P did.

Risk Measures

STANDARD DEVIATION is a rather weighty-sounding mathematical term. Trust me, you really don't need to know how it is computed. Just remember that it measures to what degree returns of a fund vary during some period of time. That may be month to month or year by year, depending on how the number is expressed; it doesn't matter much what time period you use, so long as you are consistent. While many data sources provide standard deviation, if you stick to one data source, you'll be sure of getting consistent information. The higher a fund's standard deviation, the more the fund's net asset value is likely to plunge during a down market. Other measures of risk that you may have heard of, such as beta, measure a fund's volatility compared with a stock index. They're not nearly as useful as standard deviation.

Frontier Equity has a standard deviation of 16.5, three times that of the S&P 500. Frontier Equity actually did a little better than its standard deviation predicted, losing about twice what the S&P did. But it may not be so lucky next time. Because of its low standard deviation, odds are that in the next bear market the Merger fund will lose less than a third of what the S&P does, while Frontier Equity will likely lose about three times as much as the S&P. When stock prices have been rising virtually unchecked, it's particularly important to monitor a fund's volatility. That will give you a better feel for how the fund will likely do in more normal times, when bear markets more frequently follow bull markets.

Is It Still the Same Fund?

L ONG-TERM PERFORMANCE AND RISK ARE THE MOST IMPORTANT numbers you need to know about a fund compared with its peers. But don't stop there. There are several other items you need to consider before settling on a fund. Skip one and you may find you've bought a lemon. Following are things to keep your eyes peeled for.

A CHANGE OF MANAGER

Fund companies spend millions of dollars every year on advertisements aimed at persuading consumers that they offer the best funds. But only a small percentage of those advertisements ever name the fund company's managers. Fund managers earn fat salaries, and other companies constantly court the good ones. No fund company wants to tout its manager in advertisements only to have him or her leave for another firm.

A lot of things go into the success—or failure—of a mutual fund. The culture of a fund company matters a lot. The quality of its research analysts, the working conditions, how well managers work with one another and with research analysts are all important. But at the end of the day, when you invest your money in a fund, you're hiring a manager. When Troy Aikman leaves the Dallas Cowboys, the next player to quarterback the team isn't likely to be as good at throwing footballs. By the same token, if Aikman were traded to another team, he would take his skills with him.

So when a manager leaves a fund, think of the fund as a new, untested creature. Most of its past record will be of little value in judging how it will do going forward. In evaluating a fund's performance, you'll usually want to look at only its record under the current manager or managers. If a manager hasn't been at a fund for at least five years, call the new fund family to ask for the manager's pedigree—which fund he or she ran previously and the results he or she produced. For the greatest likelihood of success, you'll want a manager whose previous fund used a similar investing style and contained as much money as the new one. As I've noted, running bigger funds undoes some managers. Be a little skeptical of a record chalked up as a manager of private money. These numbers are not as reliable as mutual fund performance records.

When a manager leaves a fund, think of the fund as a new creature. Most of its past record will be of little value in judging the future.

Some funds are "team managed," making it more difficult to tell which manager is really calling the shots. In that case, you should be less willing to invest in a fund. But some firms, such as the American funds, managed by Capital Research & Management, as well as Dodge and Cox funds, have chalked up superb long-term records with team-managed funds. Similarly, some firms, especially Fidelity, have a habit of rotating managers about as often as the Yankees change managers. Fidelity and T. Rowe Price generally hire good people to run their funds, so the new manager's previous record (or lack of one) may be of less importance at these firms.

What should you look for in a fund manager?

Start by looking for experience. Some new managers are great, but let other investors test these newcomers. Until a manager has at least three years, and preferably five years, under his or her belt, be skeptical.

You also want a manager who has a disciplined approach to investing. Managers who can clearly articulate their approach to picking and selling stocks, and who have demonstrated an ability to stick with that method through thick and thin, tend to have the best long-term records.

Finally, just as in other endeavors, the best managers tend to love their work. You're not looking for a workaholic here, but you want someone with a passion for investing.

Unfortunately, most of these personal qualities are not on view to individual investors. As a journalist, I spend a good deal of time talking with managers, trying to determine which ones have the right stuff. I've attempted to put that knowledge to use in selecting the funds in Part Four. However, by reading interviews with managers on the Web, in newspapers, and in *Kiplinger's* and other personal-finance and business magazines, you can gain insight into a manager's approach. And some managers, particularly at smaller funds, are willing to take calls from prospective investors who want to quiz them on their approach.

A CHANGE IN INVESTMENT METHOD

A change in managers isn't the only way a fund can be fundamentally altered. Sometimes managers change their investment methods, so the fund that you're considering buying isn't using the same approach as it did when it chalked up a good record.

Managers most frequently run off the rails by losing faith in their own methods. This typically happens during a long period when the stock market is not favoring their investment style. Rather than stick to it, trusting that eventually their style will come back into vogue, they lose their nerve and begin following whatever style seems to be working right then. This kind of capitulation, alas, often happens just as the market is finally making its long-awaited turn to the management style the manager had practiced in the first place. Growth's domination over value in the past several years has led many value managers to buy stocks that they ordinarily wouldn't. Many managers of value-oriented funds bought technology stocks. Nicholas Fund, for instance, a long-successful fund that was always wary of stocks selling at pricey valuations, bought a fistful of technology stocks. Alas, it bought many of the stocks just before the roof caved in on technology stocks in the spring of 2000.

> **Managers most frequently run off the rails by losing faith in their own methods, typically when their investment style is out of the market's favor.**

Inexperience may also cause a manager to change methods. Veteran managers often relate stories of their own early mistakes in this regard. And poorly run fund companies put pressure on managers to boost short-term performance, sometimes to the point of firing them if results don't improve, even if their investing style is currently out of vogue.

Too Much of a Good Thing

Perhaps the most common way once-successful funds fail is that they become victims of their own success. They put up such good numbers that more and more money flows in. Pretty soon they can't buy the same stocks they used to—particularly if they built their record by specializing in fast-growing, small-company stocks. Funds that invest in such stocks tend to trade frequently, and it's a lot easier for a small fund than a big fund to buy or sell a stock without disturbing its price. I'll get into more detail about fund size, and how it can hinder performance, in the next chapter.

In general, however, be wary of small-company growth funds that have more than, say, $2 billion in assets. Don't count just the assets in the fund you are studying, but all the money run by that manager—whether in other funds or in private accounts. A call to the fund's toll-free number should quickly tell you how much money a manager has under his or her purview.

Add Up the Costs

While predicting future performance of a fund is no sure thing, you can be pretty certain of one thing: how much a fund will charge you in expenses every year. The higher a fund's expense ratio, the less is left for you. All things being equal, the more expensive a fund, the less likely it is to perform well. That's because it has to work that much harder to overcome its expense ratio and still produce a good return. Moreover, a fund that charges a high expense ratio demonstrates its lack of respect for you as an investor. You want your fund's manager and research analysts to earn a good living, but you don't want the company to fleece you.

The average stock fund annually charges about 1.26%—or about one-quarter of your long-term, after-inflation, after-tax gain.

In a bull market, when stocks are soaring, it's easy to overlook the importance of expenses. Don't make that mistake. The average stock fund charges expenses of 1.26% annually, excluding most of one type of fee, known as a 12-b1 fee, which is used to compensate brokers and pay other marketing expenses, not to run the fund. (When they are over 0.25%, I have excluded these fees from the average, because they are charged only by load funds.) Assume that stocks will continue to return an average of 11.3% a year—as they have since 1926. Inflation has averaged 3.1% annually, and federal and state income taxes take about another 3% annually in a taxable account. That leaves you with only 5.2% after inflation and taxes. So the expense ratio of the typical fund is equal to almost one-quarter of your long-term, after-inflation, after-tax gain.

Excessive trading also drives up your costs. The fund's expense ratio doesn't reflect these trading costs, although funds must disclose in their annual reports to shareholders how much, on average, they have paid per share in brokerage commissions. The more a fund trades, the more it pays in commissions. In addition to brokerage commissions, trading adds further costs, because the firms your fund trades with mark up the prices of the stocks they sell so that they can earn profits.

The average stock fund has a turnover ratio of 110%, which means that every stock in the fund, on average, gets traded a little more than once per year. It doesn't necessarily mean all of the stocks in the portfolio change. For example, it's possible that half of the assets could turn over twice during a year. In general, be wary of fund turnovers that creep much over 100%—although there are exceptions here; some gifted managers trade more rapidly and still come out ahead of their peers.

Don't be penny-wise and pound-foolish, however. Good funds often require lots of resources to be run well; some really good funds charge a little more than might appear reasonable at first blush, particularly if they are funds without much money invested in them. Such funds have fewer shareholders to split their costs.

How high an expense ratio is too high? The average varies by category. The following averages exclude most 12-b1 fees:

STOCK FUNDS	EXPENSE RATIO
Growth-and-income	0.99%
Long-term-growth	1.13
Aggressive-growth	1.36
Sector	1.39
International	1.53
Global	1.51

Where to Look It Up

Wᴵᴛʜ ᴛʜᴇ ʙᴏᴏᴍɪɴɢ ʙᴜʟʟ ᴍᴀʀᴋᴇᴛ ɪɴ ʀᴇᴄᴇɴᴛ ʏᴇᴀʀꜱ ᴀɴᴅ Americans' growing love affair with mutual funds, new sources of information on personal finance are springing up everywhere from bookstores to magazine racks to newspapers to the Internet. Moreover, publications that previously didn't cover personal finance are hiring writers to do so. The hard job is to separate the wheat from the chaff. Following are some suggested sources of information.

Tʜᴇ Iɴᴛᴇʀɴᴇᴛ

These are just a few of the best sites:

www.fundalarm.com keeps you up-to-date on funds you might consider selling. It's written from a refreshingly skeptical viewpoint.

www.fundspot.com gives you a directory of mutual funds' Web sites, as well as a compilation of good articles on fund investing from all over the Web.

www.kiplinger.com provides articles from *Kiplinger's Personal Finance* magazine, articles on funds written for the Web site (including my own weekly column), and several databases.

www.moneycentral.com, a feature of Microsoft's MSN, is perhaps the most comprehensive financial Web site on the Internet. It gives a variety of ways to search for funds that meet your criteria. Check out the "Research Wizard" feature.

www.morningstar.com contains lots of helpful articles and data about fund investing, as well as message boards (see the discussion of Morningstar on the following page).

www.Quicken.com offers much of the same information as MSN's Money Central. If you're accustomed to using Quicken, you'll likely find it superior.

www.sageonline.com offers sensible advice on funds and news, and some of the most active fund message boards.

www.sec.gov contains Securities and Exchange Commission filings by all funds, including annual and semiannual reports and prospectuses.

www.smartmoney.com and www.money.com offer current articles and data on funds and other investments.

www.thestreet.com offers good coverage of fund news, as well as stock news.

www.vanguard.com, www.fidelity.com, www.estrong.com and **www .troweprice.com** are probably the best sites, run by mutual fund advisers, for obtaining educational materials.

MAGAZINES

Kiplinger's Personal Finance, Business Week, Forbes and *Money* magazines all publish annual mutual fund issues, mostly in late summer, that provide data on thousands of funds. *Kiplinger's* also publishes an annual mutual fund guide (available on newsstands in February) that provides key fund data and advice.

MORNINGSTAR MUTUAL FUNDS

Morningstar Mutual Funds, both the software version (Principia Pro Plus, $595 annually; 800-735-0700) and the paper version ($495 annually; 800-735-0700), offer a wealth of material, although the most up-to-date information can be found in the premium version of Morningstar.com ($99 annually). Although its offerings are expensive, Morningstar often runs introductory specials. A single copy or short-term subscription may be all that you need, since most of the information doesn't become outdated quickly. The software and paper versions are also available at many public libraries. A Morningstar page will give you almost all the information you need to size up a fund. Trouble is, many beginners find these pages about as comprehensible as quantum physics. If you stick with it awhile, you'll find the information begins to make sense.

New sources of information on personal finance are springing up everywhere.

MUTUAL FUND NEWSLETTERS

Most mutual fund newsletters are mediocre at best, but a handful provide solid advice, including funds to consider and portfolios of funds for conservative, moderate and aggressive investors. Before you subscribe, request a sample issue. Is this a newsletter you feel comfortable with and will use? If you can't read, understand and agree with the logic of its investment strategy, the newsletter is not for you.

Also consider cost. If a newsletter costs $200 and you're investing just $20,000, the newsletter costs you 1% annually. But if you're investing $200,000, the cost is a negligible 0.1% annually.

Once you pick a newsletter, stick with it for at least several years; even the best newsletters have periods when their recommended portfolios underperform the market averages.

Following are a few top newsletters that novices should find easy to understand. (All are independent of the mutual fund companies they report on.)

Fidelity Insight and FundsNet Insight ($177; 800-444-6342). Editor Eric Kobren offers one newsletter aimed at Fidelity mutual fund investors, and another aimed at investors who buy funds through Charles Schwab, Fidelity's brokerage or other online brokers. Both letters are easy to understand and have solid performance records.

Fidelity Monitor ($116 per year; 800-397-3094). Editor Jack Bowers follows only Fidelity mutual funds. Its performance has been better than that of *Fidelity Insight,* and his advice is sensible.

Independent Adviser for Vanguard Investors ($99.95 per year; 800-777-5005). Former journalist Daniel Wiener's newsletter offers common-sense advice in an easy-to-read format, on allocating money among Vanguard mutual funds.

No-Load Fund Investor ($129 per year; 800-252-2042). Sheldon Jacobs has written about mutual funds since the early 1970s. His newsletter offers portfolios for investors at different stages of life. The newsletter also offers portfolios for investors who invest only in mutual funds offered by Vanguard, T. Rowe Price or Fidelity.

THE MUTUAL FUND'S PROSPECTUS AND REPORTS

Before investing, you'll want to take a look at a fund's prospectus. These used to be impenetrable documents written by lawyers, but the Securities and Exchange Commission has ordered them to be written in "plain English." Read the section on the fund's investment objectives and policies, which tells you what types of securities it may invest in. Also make sure to read the sections that describe the fund's risks and expenses.

A fund's annual and semiannual reports are even more valuable. Here you will get a snapshot of the fund's holdings. Scan them to get a sense of what securities the fund invests in. Also look at which industry sectors a stock fund is emphasizing. If the prospectus says a fund invests in blue-chip stocks and you don't recognize any of the names of the stocks in the annual report, that should set off an alarm. Call the fund to find out what's going on—before you invest. Prospectuses and semiannual and annual reports are available online at fund Web sites and at the SEC's Web site.

SOFTWARE

Several computer programs, besides Morningstar's Principia, supply data useful for analyzing funds. One to consider: **Alexander Steele's Mutual Fund Expert** ($29.95; 800-379-0679) offers the most speed and variety in screening funds.

Key Points

- *Compare stock funds against their peers.*
- *Long-term returns are the most important numbers to examine.*
- *Short-term performance means little; consistent long-term performance means a lot.*
- *Look carefully at funds' volatility.*
- *Look at the managers' past records.*
- *Low costs are important.*
- *Many good sources of fund data are available on the Internet.*

When to Sell a Fund

How to tell when it's time to cut bait

B Y MUTUAL FUND STANDARDS, MICHAEL FASCIANO'S Fasciano fund was a midget, ending 1994 with a mere $18 million in assets—not much more than he had when he started the fund in 1987. But then Fasciano, whose prior results had been middling, put together three fine years, returning 31%, 27% and 22% respectively in 1995, 1996 and 1997. All of a sudden, the money poured in. The fund ended 1997 with just $59 million, but assets topped $233 million the following year. But a funny thing happened to Fasciano's returns: They plunged. The fund returned just 7% in 1998 and 6% in 1999, and it was flat through July of 2000.

Fasciano suffered from an all-too-common phenomenon in mutual fundom: It turned red-hot for a few years, money flooded in the door, and performance chilled. So far, the fund hasn't recovered. Despite your best efforts, count on making a few mistakes in your fund picks. One of the most common: buying a top performer like Fasciano just before it nose-dives. The important thing is to recognize your mistakes and sell them before they become disasters.

Once you've assembled your portfolio, you should review it at least annually. If things go wrong at a fund, you'll want to know why before you consider replacing it. Don't be too hasty about selling funds, though. More investors make the mistake of selling funds whose styles are temporarily out of favor (see Chapters 14 and 15) than of holding on to losers too long.

Why Investors Sell Too Soon

FIGURING WHETHER TO KEEP A FUND IS LIKE SELECTING A NEW fund: it's most important to keep your eye on the fund's performance relative to its peers. Value-style investing had been out of favor for years when this book went to press. Technology stocks seemed the only key to stock-market success, and the performance of most value funds was mediocre, at best. But these funds were still worth holding—unless they lagged against other value funds. If a fund's total return compared to that of similar funds deteriorates over two or three months, don't even give it a second thought. The best funds can have terrible three-month periods. If performance lags for a year, it's time to begin watching more closely, but not to sell. Few funds are able to avoid an occasional bad year. Usually you should sell only if a fund underperforms over an extended period—say, two or three years.

USING THE WRONG YARDSTICK

A common mistake investors make is to compare a fund against the wrong index or the wrong group of funds. *Janus* fund, among the most successful long-term growth funds of the past 20 years, had poor returns relative to the market for four straight years, from 1994 through 1997. It lagged Standard and Poor's 500-stock index by more than 22 percentage points over that stretch. But investors who sold missed out on the fund's resurgence in the subsequent years. From 1998 through 1999, the fund gained in excess of 36 percentage points *more* than the S&P 500.

How could you have known that this fund was worth holding on to? You couldn't have, without knowing more about then fund manager James Craig and his investment style. (Craig relinquished the manager's job at the end of 1999 and resigned from Janus in September, 2000.) If you hadn't known that Craig was a growth-at-a-reasonable-price investor (see "Fund Mini Styles" on page 182), who looked for large, growing companies selling at reasonable prices, you might have sold his fund without knowing that there was nothing wrong with him—it was just that his style of investing lay becalmed for four miserable years.

Other managers who invested the way Craig did—such as Bert Mullins, manager of Dreyfus Disciplined Stock, and Beth Terrana, former manager of Fidelity fund—also had wretched slumps then. So by comparison with its peers in the market,

Janus wasn't doing badly. In fact, Craig, a crafty manager, altered his style in 1998, becoming a pure growth manager—which led to his comeback.

THE MANAGER'S LONG-TERM RECORD

The other reason to hang on to Janus through its long drought was Craig's long and successful record. He had been with the fund since 1986. If a relatively new manager stumbles for two or three years—or occasionally even one year—you may want to pull the plug. On the other hand, if you have a manager with a proven long-term record, give him or her longer to pull out of a slump.

Warning Signs to Heed

USUALLY, IF A FUND'S PERFORMANCE IS COLLAPSING, A BIT OF detective work will tell you why. Often it turns out to be one of the following reasons, which can be signals that it's time to consider ditching a fund, even if performance has not yet begun to slump:

A CHANGE IN MANAGERS

When a manager changes, you may own what amounts to an untried fund, and you should question whether it remains worthy of your money. Sometimes you can assuage your doubts.
- **Did the new manager run another fund previously?**
- **If so, what was its record relative to its peers?**
- **Did the new manager assist the departing manager?**
- **If so, for how long and in what capacity?**

Such was the case when Shelby Davis left Selected American shares at the start of 1997. His son, Christopher Davis, who took over as manager, had been co-manager since 1994 and had been steeped in his father's style of stockpicking since he was a boy. He had mastered Shelby's methods well—as the fund's subsequent returns have demonstrated.

TOO MANY ASSETS: WHEN IT'S A PROBLEM, WHEN IT'S NOT

In the case of Fasciano, the warning sign that the fund was facing trouble was a rapidly growing asset base. It's one thing to manage a couple of million dollars in a fund. It's quite another

How Assets Weigh Down a Fund

THIS GRAPH graph shows how a popular fund, Kaufmann, stumbled under the weight of burgeoning assets. In the graph, the benchmark Wilshire 4500 index (see page 212) is shown as a flat line to better illustrate the fund's performance relative to the index, which tracks stocks of small- and medium-size companies. Piloted by Hans Utsch and Lawrence Auriana since its inception in 1986, Kaufmann had $1.6 billion in assets in 1994 and proceeded to post three benchmark-beating years. But as assets topped $6 billion in 1997, performance stumbled, and remained lackluster even as half the assets disappeared from the fund by the end of 1999. In the first seven months of 2000, the fund was up 11%, but it was doubtful that Kaufmann would ever regain the glory of its first decade, when it regularly creamed its peers.

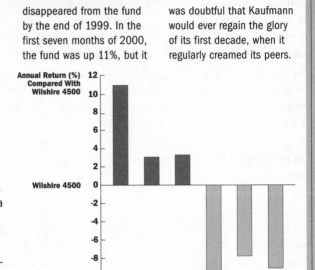

to manage hundreds of millions or billions of dollars. Small fund companies that lack the infrastructure to handle huge growth are especially vulnerable to catastrophe when assets balloon. A bigger company that can throw more seasoned analysts in to help a fast-growing fund and allow the manager to devote full-time efforts to picking stocks is much more likely to handle growth effectively. Don't be too quick to pull the trigger on a fund that's grown, though. It's usually best to watch for a year or two to see if the fund can continue to do well against its peers.

Small-company growth versus value funds

Sometimes a fund can thrive even as assets mushroom. But that's uncommon in a fund that buys small-company growth stocks. Cast a wary eye at such a fund whose assets are much over $2 billion.

Value funds—which usually trade less frequently than

growth funds, and typically sell stocks that many investors want to buy and buy stocks that many investors want to sell—can usually handle much more in assets. A small-company value fund should be able to handle $3 billion in assets—and sometimes more. *Acorn* fund, a small-company value fund, is still doing well despite assets of almost $4 billion. (One reason: Manager Ralph Wanger was prescient enough to close Acorn to new investors for several years while he trained additional analysts and adjusted to his fund's newfound popularity.)

Too many stocks to handle
Time after time, funds start off with hot performance, only to cool as they gain in popularity. To cope with exploding size, fund managers typically start buying stocks of bigger, more well-established companies because big funds can't easily profit from investing in small companies (to learn why, see the box on page 204). A manager who specialized in small stocks might start buying medium-size stocks, for example. Such was the case with Fasciano. The problem is two-fold: the manager might not be as talented at picking bigger stocks and the nature of the fund changes.

Another way managers deal with swelling assets is to own more stocks. Instead of owning, say, his or her 40 or 50 favorite stocks, a manager may buy 200 or 300 stocks. This can also hurt performance, because a manager's favorite stocks typically do better than those in which he or she lacks the same level of con-

New Funds With Proven Managers

OCCASIONALLY, THE MANAGER of a fund that has outgrown its ability to turn in top numbers will open a new fund to invest in the smaller stocks that helped the old fund make its name in the first place. When that happens, investors can often do very well. Such was the case when William Miller, who piloted Legg Mason Value to great returns, launched Legg Mason Opportunity. The new fund invests in smaller stocks and is more nimble than his old one, which he still manages, too. An opportunity to invest with a manager like Miller at the helm of a smaller fund doesn't come along too often, but it's worth grabbing when you spot it.

Trading a Stock Without Getting Killed

UNLIKE AN INDIVIDUAL investor who buys, say, 100 shares of a stock, fund managers often buy hundreds of thousands of shares of a stock. That's tricky to pull off, and it's why fund companies employ traders, whom they pay handsome salaries to trade stocks without roiling the markets.

The problem is that when a manager wants to buy a large quantity of a stock, its price will tend to go higher—because too few investors want to sell at the lower price. The manager creates extra demand, which drives the price up. If a fund specializes in small-company stocks, which

tend not to trade in great volumes, buying even a couple of thousand shares will send the price higher *before* the manager has finished buying.

Traders at small-company funds, or at funds that have huge amounts of money invested in them, will try to buy stock slowly, sometimes over months, to avoid disturbing the price. Then, when the fund manager wants to sell, the same agonizing process is repeated in reverse. That's why smaller funds have an edge. They can be more nimble, buying and selling smaller quantities of stock more quickly to execute the ideas of their manager.

viction. "Why would I want to buy my 81st–most attractive stock?" wonders L. Roy Papp, who limits the Papp funds to 30 or fewer stocks each. It's also tough for a manager to really keep up with 100 or 200 companies—unless he or she has a lot of help.

Difficulties finding small, proven funds
Good funds that have grown too big are a huge problem in fund investing. "Let there be no doubt that I could manage $100 million better than $50 billion," Fidelity Magellan fund manager Jeffrey Vinik said before leaving the fund in 1996 to manage a smaller, private investment fund available only to wealthy investors. But there's often a Catch-22 at work when you're hunting for small, proven funds. In general, you want to avoid unseasoned funds. But by the time a fund has a good five-year record, it's often bigger than you'd like—or it's closed to any new investors.

What large-company funds can do
In contrast to small-company funds, large-company growth

funds seem to be able to keep up with their peers as assets grow to about $10 billion, and sometimes more—so long as the fund company is willing to hire enough analysts to research stocks. *TCW Galileo Select Equity* beat most of its competitors even as manager Glen Bickerstaff's total assets under management, including private accounts as well as the fund, soared past $10 billion. Large-company stocks are much easier to buy and sell without disturbing the stock's price. And large-company value funds can sometimes outperform their rivals even after assets reach $25 billion or more.

An opportunity in soon-to-close funds

The best-run funds will close their doors to new investors before size becomes a problem. For that reason, it sometimes pays to buy a small stake in a promising small-company fund if you think it might close soon, even if you aren't totally convinced that the fund will be a great one. These funds will often stumble a bit immediately after they close, as they digest their surfeit in assets. But, over the long term, most of them will prosper. Putting a little seed money in such a fund to preserve your right to buy more shares later can turn out to be a great long-term investment.

Other Times to Sell

NOT ALL THE REASONS TO SELL A FUND HAVE TO DO WITH A fund's failings. Here are three other equally important reasons to consider:

A BETTER FUND

There's no more appropriate time to sell a fund than when you identify a superior one. If you match the two funds up carefully and the advantages are clearly with the new fund, it's probably time to trade.

A BAD FIT

Sometimes you buy a fund only to realize later that it's not what you needed. Say you own *AIM Aggressive Growth*, *PBHG Growth*, and American Century *Vista*. All invest in stocks whose earnings (and share prices) are accelerating. You'd do better selling one or two of these funds and putting the proceeds into a fund that can better balance out your portfolio. At other times, you'll find you simply made a mistake in buying a fund. Go ahead and sell it.

YOUR SITUATION CHANGES

Go-go growth funds are perfect for a big chunk of your money when you're in your twenties, thirties, forties and early 50s, and can occupy a small portion of your portfolio in later years. In general, though, the closer you get to needing your money, the more conservative you need to be with the funds you own. Don't hang on to a high-octane growth fund simply because it's done well for you in the past.

Key Points

- *Be careful about selling a fund too quickly. Generally, look for poor performance over two or three years before selling.*
- *A change in managers may be a signal to sell.*
- *Funds that grow too big often stumble.*
- *Sell if your situation changes or if you made a mistake buying the fund in the first place.*

Winning Mutual Funds

T his section describes some of what I think are the best stock funds among the thousands on the market. These funds aren't, by any means, a recommended "buy" list. Using what you've learned in Part Three, you're well equipped to pick good funds on your own. But the funds described in Part Four give you a starting point—and they can be a finishing place, too, if you want to build or augment your portfolio from among them. In addition, Part Four explains how to pick bond funds and money-market funds, and describes some top funds in those categories.

Great Stock Funds

Profiles of 20 funds with helpful data

C GARY PILGRIM AND RON BARON BOTH MANAGE top-performing funds that invest in rapidly growing small companies. But while Baron spends two out of every three weeks on the road visiting companies, Pilgrim does most of his work from behind a computer terminal in suburban Philadelphia. The lesson here is that there is no one right way to run a mutual fund. There are good managers like Pilgrim, who use a largely numbers-driven approach to pick stocks, and there are good managers like Baron, who wouldn't dream of buying a stock without talking to the company's management, as well as its competitors, suppliers and anyone else he can think of.

The point here is that even if the numbers and categories indicate that two funds are twins, the odds are that they are very different beneath the surface. In the end, each fund is defined by the distinct investment methods of the person or people who run it. That's why this chapter does more than simply offer the names and statistics of top-flight funds. It also provides descriptions of how each fund works toward its goal.

That makes these fund profiles useful even if you decide to pick other funds, because they offer you signposts of quality to look for in evaluating any fund. By the same token, if you assemble your portfolio from among the funds described in this chapter, you'll have a better idea, from reading the profiles, of why you selected each fund. That knowledge will help you determine when to stick with a fund and when to sell it. The more you understand about why you bought specific funds, the more stalwart an investor you will be. That's important because, at times, your commitment to investing will be tested by adversity.

What This Chapter Will Tell You

IN THIS CHAPTER, I PROFILE 20 GREAT STOCK FUNDS. I'VE INCLUDed a diversified group of funds, so that you'll have no trouble putting together a balanced portfolio from them, if you choose. It's important to remember, too, that even the best funds, over the long haul, are usually only a little better than the average fund with the same investment objective and style. In general, a fund's performance is determined primarily by the waters in which it fishes. That's why it's so important to put together a diversified portfolio of funds representing different objectives and styles of mutual fund investing (see Chapters 13 and 14 for more on this). And because performance is difficult to forecast, it's essential to examine expense ratios and risk—which are more predictable than total return.

THE FUND'S OBJECTIVE

I've divided the funds into general categories by objective (aggressive-growth, long-term-growth, growth-and-income, sector and international) and defined each objective at the beginning of the appropriate section of funds.

THE FUND'S STYLE

I've also indicated the investment style of each domestic, non-sector fund. This tells whether a fund specializes in stocks of small, medium or large companies, and whether it specializes in growth stocks, undervalued stocks or a blend of the two styles. I've used Standard and Poor's Micropal definitions of what constitutes growth and value stocks, as well as small, medium and large stocks.

AND MORE

For each fund, I also give:

Annualized returns: They cover the three, five and ten years ending July 31, 2000 (if the fund has been in existence that long). These numbers show how the fund has held up over long time periods.

Annual expense ratio: The percentage of your investment that the fund company charges each year to run the fund. That number doesn't include any sales fees that you might pay for a fund. Only one fund in this chapter, Fidelity Select Biotechnology, charges a sales fee.

Annual portfolio turnover: How often the fund manager trades stocks. A portfolio turnover of 50% means the manager trades half the assets in the fund annually. Low-turnover funds are sometimes superior, because they incur fewer brokerage commissions and other costs of trading stocks. Though not reflected in fund expense ratios, such costs are passed along to investors in the form of lower total returns.

Best benchmark: See the accompanying box for more on this.

Volatility: How much a fund's return varies from month to month compared with all other stock funds. Volatility is a superb predictor of how funds will hold up in market declines. A score of 1 means that the fund is less volatile than 90% of all stock funds. A score of 10 means a fund is in the top 10% for volatility among all stock funds. These rankings are derived from funds' standard deviations (see page 188).

Same manager since...: How long at least one of the managers has been at the helm. If a fund has more than one manager and one started after the other, that information is included in parentheses.

Total assets: How much money is invested in the fund. Funds whose assets mushroom sometimes lose their touch, particularly if they specialize in small stocks.

Median stock-market value: Market value of the median stock in the fund. (The median stock is the stock halfway between the largest and the smallest in value, after adjusting for each stock's weighting in the fund.) A stock's market value is computed by multiplying the share price times the number of shares outstanding. The median market value indicates whether a fund buys small, medium-size or large stocks. While experts may quibble, for this chapter I've used Micropal's definitions of small stocks as those with a market value of less than $1 billion, medium-size— $1 billion to $10 billion, and large—more than $10 billion. As assets of some small-company funds have increased, their median market values have grown a bit beyond these parameters. Nevertheless, I am still classifying them as small-company funds.

Minimum initial investment: The minimum purchase the fund requires to open an account. The second number is for IRAs.

Phone number: The toll-free number to call for a prospectus, semi-annual report and fund application—and to ask questions. Make sure to ask whether any of the key numbers reported in this chapter have changed since publication.

Best Benchmarks

A BENCHMARK IS the index that can be best used to measure how well a fund is doing. This table allows you to compare funds in this chapter with their appropriate benchmark to see how they have performed. You'll generally do fine comparing large-company stock funds with the S&P 500, medium-size-company funds with the S&P Midcap 400, small-company funds with the Russell 2000, and international and emerging-market funds with the

Morgan Stanley indexes. If you want to delve deeper, I've also provided, whenever possible throughout this chapter, the more specific Wilshire indexes for each fund.

In each case, the table provides the index name, its description and annualized returns for the past one, three, five and ten years through July 31, 2000. You can use the Web sites to look up current returns for the indexes (for more on index funds, see Chapter 4).

INDEX	DESCRIPTION	ANNUALIZED RETURNS		
		3-YEAR	5-YEAR	10-YEAR
S&P 500 (www.standardandpoors.com)	an index of stocks of mostly large U.S. companies	16.04%	22.60%	17.64%
S&P Midcap 400	an index of stocks of medium-size U.S. companies	17.22	20.33	18.47
Wilshire 4500 (www.wilshire.com)	an index of all U.S. companies except for those 500 included in the S&P 500	15.13	17.94	16.35
Russell 2000 (www.russell.com)	an index of stocks of small U.S. companies	7.73	12.26	13.71
Wilshire Large Company Growth	an index of large U.S. companies with growing earnings	23.35	28.63	20.85
Wilshire Large Company Value	an index of undervalued large U.S. companies	2.27	12.65	12.72
Wilshire Mid-Cap Company Growth	an index of medium-size U.S. companies with growing earnings	6.88	11.85	15.21
Wilshire Mid-Cap Company Value	an index of medium-size undervalued U.S. companies	0.28	9.29	13.63
Wilshire Small Company Growth	an index of small U.S. companies with growing earnings	4.20	9.39	13.56
Wilshire Small Company Value	an index of small undervalued U.S. companies	−4.30	6.11	12.05
Morgan Stanley Capital International Emerging Markets Index (www.mscidata.com)	an index of small, highly volatile developing markets around the world	15.82	16.43	9.73
Morgan Stanley Capital International Europe Australasia and Far East Index (www.mscidata.com)	a broad index of foreign stocks in developed markets	6.55	7.47	5.66

Web site: The fund's online address if it exists. Web sites contain a variety of information about funds. Most of them also allow you to print out a fund application.

Ticker symbol: An easier way to buy, sell and track funds on the Internet, as more people buy funds through online brokers (see Chapter 8).

Aggressive-Growth Funds

MOST OF THESE FUNDS SWING FOR THE FENCES WITH FAST-growing companies or small companies. They outperform in bull markets and get clobbered in bear markets. Use them sparingly unless you have fortitude and a long time horizon. However, some small-company value funds, such as Skyline Special Equities, that are classified as aggressive-growth funds aren't all that volatile.

BARON SMALL CAP

What makes Baron Small Cap so appealing is that it has delivered glitzy returns without overdosing on technology stocks. The fund gained 71% in 1999, 50 percentage points more than the Russell 2000 index, a widely followed measure of small-stock performance. This comes on the heels of a 2.2% return in 1998, which may not seem impressive but was still ahead of the Russell small-stock indexes. Cliff Greenberg, with more than 15 years of investment experience, buys only stocks he thinks will double over the following 18 to 24 months. He looks for "good, growing businesses that are down in the dumps" for one reason or another. The company may be an obscure one that few people have heard of or one with a complex story that few have bothered to examine. Or it may be a classic "baby thrown out with the bathwater" story: the poor performance of a few companies causes the stocks of good companies in the same industry to suffer, too. Greenberg wants his companies' earnings to grow at least 20% annually. And he won't buy anything with a stock-market value greater than $1 billion at the time of purchase.

INVESTMENT STYLE: small-company growth
THREE-YEAR RETURN: NA
FIVE-YEAR RETURN: NA

TEN-YEAR RETURN:	NA
ANNUAL EXPENSE RATIO:	1.34%
ANNUAL PORTFOLIO TURNOVER:	43%
BEST BENCHMARK:	Russell 2000, Wilshire Small-Company Growth
VOLATILITY:	9
SAME MANAGER SINCE:	1997
TOTAL ASSETS:	$1.1 billion
MEDIAN MARKET VALUE:	$1.4 billion
MINIMUM INITIAL INVESTMENT:	$2,000, $2,000 for IRAs
PHONE NUMBER:	800-992-2766
WEB SITE:	www.baronfunds.com
TICKER SYMBOL:	bscfx

SPECIAL RISKS. Two big question marks are whether Greenberg can continue to put up good numbers as assets swell and whether he'll close the fund before it gets too big. Another question: Assuming technology stocks continue to beat the market, can Greenberg keep up? He concedes that he can't tell "one guy's computer chips from the next guy's." He has managed to do well in spite of avoiding tech—no mean feat, especially in 1999. Through July 31, 2000, he is down 2.7%.

JANUS MERCURY

The Janus style of investing has been among the most successful in the mutual-fund world over the past several years. The style involves buying stocks of fast-growing companies, most of them large companies and many of them technology companies. While this style will inevitably fall out of favor, it will also surely bounce back again. It makes sense to own at least one fund that buys these kinds of stocks. Mercury is one of the best funds in the Janus stable. Warren Lammert has run this fund since 1993, making him a veteran among new-economy fund managers. He formerly paid more attention to value, but now follows the Janus mantra of seeking out mostly big companies with rapidly growing earnings. Lammert had rough sledding in 1997 because he didn't own the right blue-chip stocks. But he compiled a great record in 1998 and 1999. His fund was down 5.2% through July of 2000.

INVESTMENT STYLE:	large-company growth
THREE-YEAR RETURN:	41.6%

FIVE-YEAR RETURN:	32.3%
TEN-YEAR RETURN:	NA
ANNUAL EXPENSE RATIO:	0.91%
ANNUAL PORTFOLIO TURNOVER:	89%
BEST BENCHMARK:	S&P 500
VOLATILITY:	9
SAME MANAGER SINCE:	inception in 1993
TOTAL ASSETS:	$17 billion
MEDIAN MARKET VALUE:	$49 billion
MINIMUM INITIAL INVESTMENT:	$2,500, $500 for IRAs
PHONE NUMBER:	800-525-8983
WEB SITE:	www.janus.com
TICKER SYMBOL:	jamrx

SPECIAL RISKS: This is an aggressive fund, and when large technology stocks fall, so will this fund. Given its huge size, Lammert can't buy the smaller stocks that powered this fund in its first years.

RS DIVERSIFIED GROWTH A

Unlike many other red-hot funds that focus on small, rapidly growing companies, RS Diversified is still small. Assets recently totaled just $708 million. This is important because a small fund can buy and sell small-company stocks nimbly without moving their prices too dramatically. Co-manager John Wallace, 45, brings a long and distinguished record to the fund. In its first three full-calendar years, Diversified outran the Russell 2000 Growth index by 16, 15 and 107 percentage points, respectively. It trailed the index by 2.7% through July of 2000. Wallace and co-manager John Seabern try to identify a catalyst that could cause a stock to soar. It might be new management, a new product or any number of other factors, says Wallace. More than 40% of assets are in technology issues, and about one-quarter of those are in Internet-related stocks. Wallace is aghast at some of the price-earnings ratios (P/Es) of Internet stocks but says, "This is the most exciting event of our investing lifetimes, and for me to ignore it would be anathema."

INVESTMENT STYLE:	small-company growth
THREE-YEAR RETURN:	42.4%
FIVE-YEAR RETURN:	NA

TEN-YEAR RETURN:	NA
ANNUAL EXPENSE RATIO:	1.89%
ANNUAL PORTFOLIO TURNOVER:	403%
BEST BENCHMARK:	Russell 2000
VOLATILITY:	10
SAME MANAGER SINCE:	inception 1996
TOTAL ASSETS:	$708 million
MEDIAN MARKET VALUE:	$726 million
MINIMUM INITIAL INVESTMENT:	$5,000, $1,000
PHONE NUMBER:	800-766-3863
WEB SITE:	www.rsim.com
TICKER SYMBOL:	rsdgx

SPECIAL RISKS: Make no mistake. This fund is aggressive; on average, its portfolio turned over more than four times in 1999. Its managers sell when they hit their price targets or when the reasons for owning them fail to materialize. They quickly cut losers. Says Wallace: "The worst thing I can do for shareholders is rationalize a mistake." The expense ratio is also high. Be careful if assets climb over $2 billion.

RAINIER SMALL/MID CAP EQUITY

This fund offers a tamer ride than the preceding funds. While its managers like companies with growing earnings, they also keep a sharp eye on valuations. The average stock in this fund sells at less than 28 times last year's earnings. Such relatively mild fare means the fund will rarely give you indigestion. In 1999, when the fund rose just 17.7%, lagging most of the stock indexes. But the fund has also managed to avoid stalling in market sell-offs. Through July of 2000, it was up 6.3%. Like RS Diversified Growth, this fund is small. Assets total $449 million. The managers mix racy stocks like LSI Logic with lower-risks companies, such as energy firm Amerada Hess. In sum, this is a good, middle-of-the-road choice for investing in stocks of small- and medium-size companies.

INVESTMENT STYLE:	medium-size blend
THREE-YEAR RETURN:	11.7%
FIVE-YEAR RETURN:	18.8%
TEN-YEAR RETURN:	NA
ANNUAL EXPENSE RATIO:	1.25%

ANNUAL PORTFOLIO TURNOVER: 199%
BEST BENCHMARK: S&P Midcap 400
VOLATILITY: 7
SAME MANAGER SINCE: inception 1994
TOTAL ASSETS: $449 million
MEDIAN MARKET VALUE: $3.5 billion
MINIMUM INITIAL INVESTMENT: $25,000, $25,000
PHONE NUMBER: 800-248-6314
WEB SITE: www.rainierfunds.com
TICKER SYMBOL: rimsx

SPECIAL RISKS: To keep up with the soaring dot-coms in 1999, this fund put a small percentage of assets into tech stocks without earnings. Tech makes up 31% of its assets. The high initial minimum may keep some investors away, but you can buy it for less through online brokers.

SKYLINE SPECIAL EQUITIES

This fund is a perfect example of the importance of comparing funds with their peers. A small-company value manager, William Dutton lost 7% for shareholders in 1998 and 13% the following year. This abysmal performance led a lot of shareholders to bail out. But in 2000, as many more aggressive funds stumbled, Skyline rose 11%% through July. When its style is in favor, this fund can shine. For the ten-year period ending in 1998, Skyline returned an annualized 19%, making it Morningstar's top-ranked small-company value fund for that period. Dutton, 47, looks for cheap stocks that can deliver 10% to 15% earnings growth over the next 12 months. "Over time, the market's earnings grow at 7% to 8%, so 10% to 15% is better than average, and if we can buy them at prices cheaper than average, that's a good mix," says Dutton. Skyline has another plus: Its size—under $200 million in assets—is ideal for a small-company fund. And Dutton has closed the fund in the past when hot money started pouring in.

INVESTMENT STYLE: small-company value
THREE-YEAR RETURN: −1.47%
FIVE-YEAR RETURN: 9.87%
TEN-YEAR RETURN: 14.60%
ANNUAL EXPENSE RATIO: 1.47%

ANNUAL PORTFOLIO TURNOVER:	68%
BEST BENCHMARK:	Russell 2000
VOLATILITY:	6
SAME MANAGER SINCE:	inception in 1987
TOTAL ASSETS:	$181 million
MEDIAN MARKET VALUE:	$812 million
MINIMUM INITIAL INVESTMENT:	$1,000, $1,000
PHONE NUMBER:	800-458-5222
WEB SITE:	NA
TICKER SYMBOL:	sksex

SPECIAL RISKS: When small-company value is out of favor, don't expect this fund to do much. It can be difficult to hold onto to a fund when it's doing badly.

Long-Term-Growth Funds

STOCKS OF LARGE AND MIDSIZE COMPANIES DOMINATE THESE funds. They tend to be about as volatile as Standard & Poor's 500-stock index. They are the bread and butter of most portfolios.

DELPHI VALUE

Scott Black, manager of the new Delphi Value fund, is a bargain hunter. Digging among undervalued, profitable companies, veteran money manager Black rejects most stocks selling for more than 12 times the next 12 months' "conservatively estimated" earnings. In some industries, such as cable TV and energy, he invests in companies selling at big discounts to the value of their assets. Black also wants companies that can deliver at least 9% earnings and revenue growth over the next three to five years. All of his picks have stock-market values of less than $2 billion. Delphi is Black's first fund available to individual investors. His fund returned 6.6% in the past year.

INVESTMENT STYLE:	medium-size company value
THREE-YEAR RETURN:	NA
FIVE-YEAR RETURN:	NA
TEN-YEAR RETURN:	NA
ANNUAL EXPENSE RATIO:	1.75%

ANNUAL PORTFOLIO TURNOVER:	17%
BEST BENCHMARK:	Wilshire Mid-Cap Company Value
VOLATILITY:	3
SAME MANAGER SINCE:	inception in 1998
TOTAL ASSETS:	$36 million
MEDIAN MARKET VALUE:	$3.1 billion
MINIMUM INITIAL INVESTMENT:	$2,500, $2,000
PHONE NUMBER:	800-895-9936
WEB SITE:	www.kobren.com
TICKER SYMBOL:	kdvrx

SPECIAL RISKS: Like Skyline Special Equities, this is not an all-weather fund. When value investing is out of favor, don't look for great things from Scott Black.

EXCELSIOR VALUE AND RESTRUCTURING

This fund delivered an incredible 42% in 1999, which was a terrible year for value funds. David Williams achieved a good part of that return from a handful of meteoric technology stocks—semiconductor-maker Texas Instruments and wireless-equipment manufacturers Nokia and Qualcomm. Williams bought these stocks years ago when they were bargains and held onto some shares as they skyrocketed. Says Williams, 57: "These companies don't belong in a strict value portfolio. But their fundamentals have been great, and I'm trying to make money for my shareholders." For most of his stocks, Williams looks for cheap companies undergoing some sort of change. "I like good companies that are undermanaged, and then management sees the light," he says. He also likes to see some growth "because a company that doesn't grow is in deep trouble." He buys companies of just about any size.

INVESTMENT STYLE:	large-company value
THREE-YEAR RETURN:	16.98%
FIVE-YEAR RETURN:	22.91%
TEN-YEAR RETURN:	NA
ANNUAL EXPENSE RATIO:	0.93%
ANNUAL PORTFOLIO TURNOVER:	43%
BEST BENCHMARK:	S&P 500
VOLATILITY:	7
SAME MANAGER SINCE:	inception in 1992

TOTAL ASSETS:	$1.3 billion
MEDIAN MARKET VALUE:	$19 billion
MINIMUM INITIAL INVESTMENT:	$500, $250
PHONE NUMBER:	800-446-1012
WEB SITE:	www.excelsiorfunds.com
TICKER SYMBOL:	umbix

SPECIAL RISKS: This fund has outdistanced other value funds by bending its value criteria a bit. When large-company value comes back into season, the fund could fall behind its peers.

HARBOR CAPITAL APPRECIATION

Spiros Segalas has built an enviable record at this fund by buying fast-growing, large-company stocks, many of them technology issues. "We emphasize earnings," Segalas says. For him, that means buying companies with annual 15%-plus earnings growth. It also means being unafraid to buy richly priced stocks, because such fast-growers don't come cheap. In 2000, his average holding sold at 48 times the previous 12 months' earnings. But Segalas, with more than 30 years' experience as a money manager, doesn't overload on technology stocks and stays away from high-risk dot-com stocks. This is a perfect choice for investors who want a growth fund with a high-tech flavor, but don't want the spice of a fund like Janus Mercury (see page 214). It also boasts a low 0.68% expense ratio.

INVESTMENT STYLE:	large-company growth
THREE-YEAR RETURN:	26.52%
FIVE-YEAR RETURN:	26.89%
TEN-YEAR RETURN:	23.44%
ANNUAL EXPENSE RATIO:	0.68%
ANNUAL PORTFOLIO TURNOVER:	70%
BEST BENCHMARK:	S&P 500
VOLATILITY:	8
SAME MANAGER SINCE:	1990
TOTAL ASSETS:	$9 billion
MEDIAN MARKET VALUE:	$101 billion
MINIMUM INITIAL INVESTMENT:	$2,000, $500
PHONE NUMBER:	800-422-1050
WEB SITE:	www.harborfunds.com
TICKER SYMBOL:	hacax

SPECIAL RISKS. You can expect this volatile fund to significantly trail the averages in bear markets.

LEGG MASON OPPORTUNITY

This fund gives investors the rare opportunity to hitch a ride with one of the nation's most consistently successful managers in a relatively new fund (see box on page 203 in Chapter 16). At this writing, William Miller's eclectic style had sparked elder sibling Legg Mason Value Primary to an unmatched nine consecutive years of besting the S&P 500. That's a stock-market feat worthy of Miller's fellow Baltimorean Cal Ripken's consecutive-game record. Newcomer Legg Mason Opportunity invests in smaller companies than Value Primary. Miller looks at the same things that most other value investors do—price to earnings, price to book value, and the like. But some very unvalue-like stocks find its way into his fund because Miller thinks they will prosper in the future. America Online and Dell computer are two of the most noteworthy. They have sky-high price-earnings ratios and price-to-book ratios. Most value investors wouldn't touch them with a ten-foot pole. Yet Miller's unorthodox style of value investing is precisely what has led to his success.

INVESTMENT STYLE:	medium-size blend
THREE-YEAR RETURN:	NA
FIVE-YEAR RETURN:	NA
TEN-YEAR RETURN:	NA
ANNUAL EXPENSE RATIO:	NA
ANNUAL PORTFOLIO TURNOVER:	NA
BEST BENCHMARK:	S&P 500
VOLATILITY:	NA
SAME MANAGER SINCE:	2000
TOTAL ASSETS:	$574 million
MEDIAN MARKET VALUE:	$3.6 billion
MINIMUM INITIAL INVESTMENT:	$1,000, $1,000
PHONE NUMBER:	800-577-8589
WEB SITE:	www.leggmason.com
TICKER SYMBOL:	lmopx

SPECIAL RISKS: Just because Miller has done so well with Legg Mason Value is no guarantee he'll be as successful with this new fund. It's possible, for instance, that he's lost his touch with stocks of small- and medium-size companies.

MASTER'S SELECT EQUITY

Take the seven best stock pickers you can find. Give each of them a portion of your money to invest in his or her favorite eight to 15 stocks. In essence, that's the game plan behind Masters' Select Equity fund. So far, it has succeeded. The brainchild of Ken Gregory, publisher of *No-Load Fund Analyst* newsletter, the fund has top-flight managers representing a variety of styles and approaches. They include value mavens O. Mason Hawkins of Longleaf Partners and William Miller of Legg Mason Opportunity, and growth investors Foster Friess of Brandywine fund and Spiros Segalas of Harbor Capital Appreciation. Occupying the middle ground are Christopher Davis of Selected American Shares and Richard Weiss of Strong Opportunity—growth investors who like out-of-favor companies. Together, their picks for Select Equity have beaten the returns of their own funds by an average of almost five percentage points annualized. "That's huge," says Gregory. Gregory's theory is that managers' favorite stocks tend to do better than their other picks.

INVESTMENT STYLE:	large-company blend
THREE-YEAR RETURN:	15.4%
FIVE-YEAR RETURN:	NA
TEN-YEAR RETURN:	NA
ANNUAL EXPENSE RATIO:	1.38%
ANNUAL PORTFOLIO TURNOVER:	135%
BEST BENCHMARK:	S&P 500
VOLATILITY:	6
SAME MANAGER SINCE:	2000
TOTAL ASSETS:	$478.6 million
MEDIAN MARKET VALUE:	$13 billion
MINIMUM INITIAL INVESTMENT:	$5,000, $1,000
PHONE NUMBER:	800-960-0188
WEB SITE:	www.mastersfunds.com
TICKER SYMBOL:	msefx

SPECIAL RISKS: Some fund experts believe the notion that managers do best when forced to pick their favorite stocks is a bunch of hooey. Also, this fund's success is based on Gregory's ability to continually pick good managers to run it.

OAKMARK SELECT

William Nygren crunches numbers until they beg for mercy. Nygren went from head of research for Harris, the Oakmark funds' parent company, to pilot of Oakmark Select fund. In 1997, its first full year, Select returned 55%, and Nygren hasn't looked back. As its name implies, the fund invests in no more than 20 stocks, and Nygren tries to keep at least half the assets in just five stocks. That strategy takes a feature common to the Oakmark family—portfolios that tend to be concentrated—a bit further. "Diversification is a wonderful tool to help ensure that your results are similar to the broad market results," he says with some disdain. "Playing to win is a lot different from playing not to lose."

INVESTMENT STYLE:	medium-size company value
THREE-YEAR RETURN:	18.01%
FIVE-YEAR RETURN:	NA
TEN-YEAR RETURN:	NA
ANNUAL EXPENSE RATIO:	1.16%
ANNUAL PORTFOLIO TURNOVER:	67%
BEST BENCHMARK:	S&P 500
VOLATILITY:	8
SAME MANAGER SINCE:	1996
TOTAL ASSETS:	$1.6 billion
MEDIAN MARKET VALUE:	$3.4 billion
MINIMUM INITIAL INVESTMENT:	$1,000, $1,000
PHONE NUMBER:	800-625-6275
WEB SITE:	www.oakmark.com
TICKER SYMBOL:	oaklx

SPECIAL RISKS. Being concentrated makes a fund less likely to perform the way the market averages do. Growing assets could hurt Nygren's performance. Besides Oakmark Select, he also manages Oakmark fund.

TCW GALILEO SELECT EQUITY N

Glen Bickerstaff has one of the best and most consistent long-term records of any investment manager. He has beaten the S&P 500 ten years in a row. His streak began with an institutional fund he ran for Transamerica and continued at Transamerica Premier Equity fund. And he's still at it at TCW Galileo Select Equity. Over the ten years through 1999, he returned an annualized 30.8%. Bickerstaff hunts for stocks of large, growing companies that have built-in advantages over their competitors. He seeks companies with valuable patents, or firms that can produce goods for less than others or that can get products to consumers more efficiently. "Those kinds of advantages tend to be intractable," he says. "Over time, the advantages widen, and the companies grow faster." Select Equity owns only about 30 stocks, and they are clustered largely in three sectors: technology, health and finance.

INVESTMENT STYLE:	large-company growth
THREE-YEAR RETURN:	NA
FIVE-YEAR RETURN:	NA
TEN-YEAR RETURN:	NA
ANNUAL EXPENSE RATIO:	1.46%
ANNUAL PORTFOLIO TURNOVER:	48%
BEST BENCHMARK:	S&P 500
VOLATILITY:	7
SAME MANAGER SINCE:	1999
TOTAL ASSETS:	$70 million
MEDIAN MARKET VALUE:	$44 billion
MINIMUM INITIAL INVESTMENT:	$2,000, $500
PHONE NUMBER:	800-386-3829
WEB SITE:	www.tcwgroup.com
TICKER SYMBOL:	tgcnx

SPECIAL RISKS: If the handful of companies or the three sectors Bickerstaff has preferred go out of favor, he could find himself facing a headwind.

Growth-and-Income Funds

THESE LOWER-RISK FUNDS USUALLY INVEST IN LARGE COM-panies and often produce some income, too. They anchor many portfolios. You'll want to increase your holdings in growth-and-income funds and scale back your holdings in aggressive-growth, international and long-term growth funds as you get nearer to needing your money. We've featured only one such fund because of its consistent superiority.

SELECTED AMERICAN SHARES

In 1997, Shelby Davis turned this top-performing fund over to his co-manager and son, Christopher Davis. But Chris, who as lead manager has taken on Kenneth Charles Feinberg as co-manager, has hewed to the same strategy and has enjoyed the same success as his father. Shelby Davis, who also managed broker-sold New York Venture from 1969 until 1997 with consistently superior results, says he "looks for growth at a reasonable price." Chris Davis follows the same path. He dislikes buying stocks whose price-earnings ratios are higher than their expected rates of profit growth. For example, he wouldn't ordinarily buy a stock expected to grow at 15% a year that was selling at 17 times earnings. About half the fund is in financial stocks. Chris Davis thinks that Americans, concerned about retirement, will save more, boosting the fortunes of companies that provide financial services. Yet he has also managed to invest 31% of the fund in tech stocks, mostly by buying stocks such as Hewlett Packard when they were beaten down in price.

INVESTMENT STYLE:	large-company blend
THREE-YEAR RETURN:	15.30%
FIVE-YEAR RETURN:	23.85%
TEN-YEAR RETURN:	18.54%
ANNUAL EXPENSE RATIO:	0.93%
ANNUAL PORTFOLIO TURNOVER:	21%
BEST BENCHMARK:	S&P 500
VOLATILITY:	6
SAME MANAGER SINCE:	1997
TOTAL ASSETS:	$4.7 billion
MEDIAN MARKET VALUE:	$74 billion
MINIMUM INITIAL INVESTMENT:	$1,000, $250
PHONE NUMBER:	800-243-1575
WEB SITE:	www.selectedfunds.com
TICKER SYMBOL:	slasx

SPECIAL RISKS. While Chris Davis seems as savvy as his father, a few more years of running this fund successfully would give us even more confidence. As is always true in funds concentrated in an industry sector, the fund's big stake in financial stocks poses potential risks.

Sector Funds

T HESE FUNDS ARE MOSTLY HIGH RISK. THEY INVEST IN A single industry. Many invest in technology stocks or health care stocks and tend to be very volatile. After all, the manager lacks the freedom to switch to another sector—no matter what happens. That's why you should use these funds sparingly—generally for not more than 5% of your stock holdings. Real estate funds are a special case. They produce high yields and tend to be less volatile, making them suitable for retirees.

COLUMBIA REAL ESTATE EQUITY

David Jellison, manager of Columbia Real Estate Equity, says real estate investment trusts (REITs) offer the best way to buy real estate without midnight calls from tenants with leaky toilets. REITs are high-yielding animals, which generally pay out almost all their annual income to their investors. No REIT fund manager has a better or more consistent record than Jellison. His fund has finished among the top 30% of real estate funds in each of the six years since it started. Such consistency is hard to beat. Yet this fund is also one of the least volatile real estate funds. Jellison's first step in investing is to forecast the outlook for the commercial real estate market as a whole, as well as for different types of REITs. He considers valuations, potential for growth, and whether supply or demand for property is growing faster. Only then does he pick stocks. He sticks with mostly blue-chip REITs with seasoned management and geographic diversity.

INVESTMENT STYLE:	real estate
THREE-YEAR RETURN:	5.09%
FIVE-YEAR RETURN:	15.19%
TEN-YEAR RETURN:	NA
ANNUAL EXPENSE RATIO:	1.01%
ANNUAL PORTFOLIO TURNOVER:	6%
BEST BENCHMARK:	Wilshire REIT index
VOLATILITY:	6
SAME MANAGER SINCE:	1994
TOTAL ASSETS:	$339 million

MEDIAN MARKET VALUE:	$2.8 billion
MINIMUM INITIAL INVESTMENT:	$1,000, $1,000
PHONE NUMBER:	800-547-1707
WEB SITE:	www.columbiafunds.com
TICKER SYMBOL:	creex

SPECIAL RISKS: When REITs are out of favor, even the most adroit management won't help. While Jellison has been successful, most consistently top-performing fund managers pick companies one at a time rather than first forecasting what the economy or an industry will do.

FIDELITY SELECT BIOTECHNOLOGY

Biotechnology, despite its long-term promise, is a volatile sector. Stocks skyrocket and plunge on rumors and sentiment. What's attractive about this fund is that it sticks mainly to blue-chip biotechnology firms, such as Amgen, Immunex and MedImmune. Its top-ten holdings, all similarly well-known names, make up more than half of the fund's assets. Manager Yolanda McGettigan is bullish on biotech. "Over the next five years, the biotech industry is going to evolve like it has never evolved before," she says. Still, she plays the field cautiously. "If you have a company with one drug in early clinical trials, you take a huge risk," she explains. "But if you have an Amgen with five or six drugs on the market and five or six more in trials, if one fails, the stock is not going to zero." McGettigan is new on the job, but Fidelity's biotech research analysts are first-rate. Because it is practically the only biotech fund that emphasizes larger companies, and because it has been the top-performing biotech fund over the past three, five and ten years (despite numerous changes of manager), we've broken our rule here and are suggesting it, even though it has a 3% sales charge.

INVESTMENT STYLE:	biotechnology
THREE-YEAR RETURN:	47.06%
FIVE-YEAR RETURN:	33.58%
TEN-YEAR RETURN:	23.92%
ANNUAL EXPENSE RATIO:	1.3%
ANNUAL PORTFOLIO TURNOVER:	86%
BEST BENCHMARK:	Wilshire 4500
VOLATILITY:	9

SAME MANAGER SINCE:	2000
TOTAL ASSETS:	$4.1 billion
MEDIAN MARKET VALUE:	$6.1 billion
MINIMUM INITIAL INVESTMENT:	$2,500, $500
PHONE NUMBER:	800-544-8888
WEB SITE:	www.fidelity.com
TICKER SYMBOL:	fbiox

SPECIAL RISKS: While hopes are high for biotech, a plethora of blockbuster drugs could take years longer than most experts think before making it to market.

FIRSTHAND TECHNOLOGY VALUE

Kevin Landis, who runs Firsthand Technology Value, was playing volleyball in 1995 with some friends who told him about PMC Sierra and its new communications chips. This was Silicon Valley's "old geek network" in action, and Landis quickly sensed the importance of PMC's breakthrough. He bought the stock, and it rose 70-fold. His fund was the top performer among *all* mutual funds for the five years ending July 31, 2000. An electrical engineer, Landis started Firsthand Technology Value after working in the semiconductor business. The fund is more than two-and-a-half times as volatile as the S&P. Declares Landis: "If there's a dumb way to invest, it's to not go with the Internet." Yet Landis is picky about what technology subsectors he'll invest in. He has never bought stock in a personal-computer company or an Internet retailer. "We need to focus, and we are not retailing analysts," he explains.

INVESTMENT STYLE:	technology
THREE-YEAR RETURN:	48.95%
FIVE-YEAR RETURN:	51.78%
TEN-YEAR RETURN:	NA
ANNUAL EXPENSE RATIO:	1.91%
ANNUAL PORTFOLIO TURNOVER:	41%
BEST BENCHMARK:	Wilshire 4500
VOLATILITY:	10
SAME MANAGER SINCE:	1994
TOTAL ASSETS:	$4 billion
MEDIAN MARKET VALUE:	$9.3 billion
MINIMUM INITIAL INVESTMENT:	$10,000, $2,000

PHONE NUMBER: 888-884-2675
WEB SITE: www.firsthandfunds.com
TICKER SYMBOL: tvfqx

SPECIAL RISKS: When tech stocks fall, this fund will likely fall further. Landis keeps attracting more money into his funds because of their success. In a couple of years, that could jeopardize this fund, unless he hires enough gifted analysts.

INVESCO TECHNOLOGY

William Keithler has been a technology analyst and manager since 1982. "Things change in a heartbeat in this area, which is why I like it so much," he says. He has three analysts dedicated to the fund. "We focus on leadership companies," says Keithler—leadership *and* diversification. Few stocks represent more than 2% of the fund's assets. Keithler is bullish on wireless companies, and on companies helping to build the Internet's infrastructure, including fiber optics firms. He is not enthusiastic about most e-tailers and other consumer Internet companies. Keithler has almost doubled the fund's volatility since his arrival in 1999.

INVESTMENT STYLE: technology
THREE-YEAR RETURN: 47.9%
FIVE-YEAR RETURN: 38.41%
TEN-YEAR RETURN: 31.81%
ANNUAL EXPENSE RATIO: 1.2%
ANNUAL PORTFOLIO TURNOVER: 143%
BEST BENCHMARK: Wilshire 4500
VOLATILITY: 10
SAME MANAGER SINCE: 1999
TOTAL ASSETS: $4.9 billion
MEDIAN MARKET VALUE: $16 billion
MINIMUM INITIAL INVESTMENT: $1,000, $250
PHONE NUMBER: 800-525-8085
WEB SITE: www.invescofunds.com
TICKER SYMBOL: ftchx

SPECIAL RISKS: There's no place to hide during a sell-off like the one in the spring of 2000, when the technology-laden Nasdaq fell 37%. The fund had returned 47% for the year on March 10 and very soon thereafter plunged to –10%, that is, a 57% drop.

International Funds

T HESE FUNDS INVEST ABROAD. MOST PORTFOLIOS SHOULD contain at least one international fund, although currency fluctuations and political uncertainty often pose additional risks in investing overseas. Confining yourself to U.S. stock funds limits you to a little more than half the world's stocks. Also, foreign stock markets tend to hit peaks and troughs at different times than the U.S. market, although this is tending to be less the case as stock markets globalize. Investors who are getting closer to needing their money will want to trim their exposure to international funds.

ARTISAN INTERNATIONAL

San Francisco–based Mark Yockey has achieved great numbers with this fund and had similarly strong results running United International Growth from 1990 to 1996. Yockey likes companies with rapidly rising earnings. He and his two analysts spend about one-fifth of their time identifying countries to invest in and the rest examining companies in those nations, frequently in person. "We look for the best-run, fastest-growing companies," he says. While most of the fund is invested in developed countries, primarily in Europe, about 25% may be invested in emerging markets—that is, stocks in developing countries, mostly in Asia and Latin America.

INVESTMENT STYLE:	international
THREE-YEAR RETURN:	30.35%
FIVE-YEAR RETURN:	NA
TEN-YEAR RETURN:	NA
ANNUAL EXPENSE RATIO:	1.38%
ANNUAL PORTFOLIO TURNOVER:	79%
BEST BENCHMARK:	Morgan Stanley Europe Australasia and Far East
VOLATILITY:	7
SAME MANAGER SINCE:	1995
TOTAL ASSETS:	$3.7 billion
MEDIAN MARKET VALUE:	$11.2 billion
MINIMUM INITIAL INVESTMENT:	$1,000, $1,000
PHONE NUMBER:	800-344-1770
WEB SITE:	www.artisanfunds.com
TICKER SYMBOL:	artix

SPECIAL RISKS. This is a pedal-to-the-metal, growth-style fund. When telecommunications and other fast-growing companies are out of favor, expect it to swoon.

DEUTSCHE INTERNATIONAL EQUITY

While Artisan invests mostly in stocks of fast-growing companies, Deutsche pays more attention to price. Deutsche also devotes a bit more effort than Artisan to trying to determine which countries will do well. Michael Levy, who manages the fund along with Robert Reiner and Julie Wang, says that identifying which countries to invest in accounts for about a fourth of their stock-selection process. The purpose is "to figure out which countries have more of a tailwind than a headwind compared with other markets," says Levy. "It's used as a tiebreaker." If they're finding equally exciting opportunities, they'll go with companies in countries whose economies are doing better. Economic analysis is about half the job when picking stocks in emerging markets, in which the fund may invest no more than 15% of its assets. No matter how attractive an emerging-markets stock looks, "almost nothing will get us to invest if the economic environment is unfavorable," says Levy.

INVESTMENT STYLE:	international
THREE-YEAR RETURN:	10.82%
FIVE-YEAR RETURN:	15.41%
TEN-YEAR RETURN:	NA
ANNUAL EXPENSE RATIO:	1.5%
ANNUAL PORTFOLIO TURNOVER:	NA
BEST BENCHMARK:	Morgan Stanley Europe Australasia and Far East
VOLATILITY:	5
SAME MANAGER SINCE:	1994
TOTAL ASSETS:	$2.3 billion
MEDIAN MARKET VALUE:	$35 billion
MINIMUM INITIAL INVESTMENT:	$2,500, $500 for IRAs
PHONE NUMBER:	800-730-1313
WEB SITE:	www.deam-us.com
TICKER SYMBOL:	bteqx

SPECIAL RISKS: Levy declares, "This decade belongs to Europe." If he's wrong and the fund doesn't change course, it could be in for trouble.

Doing Good While Doing Well

SOCIALLY RESPONSIBLE FUNDS have been around for decades. But they have one, big problem: It's hard for people to agree on what's socially responsible.

Most socially responsible funds have a liberal bent. They generally avoid investing in companies that pollute the environment, are hostile to women's rights, or make weapons.

But an increasing number of socially responsible funds back a more conservative agenda. These funds typically oppose companies that have policies favoring homosexuals, that promote sex or violence in the media, or whose employees' health insurance policies cover abortions. Both right and left usually oppose companies involved in tobacco, alcohol and gambling.

In choosing funds for this book, we've emphasized funds with a liberal agenda, not because we favor that, but because these funds have longer track records, and there are far more of them.

Citizens Emerging Growth
(800-223-7010,
www.citizensfunds.com, waegx)
This tech-laden, aggressive-growth fund, which specializes in stocks of medium-size companies, is a contrast to the majority of socially responsible funds, which invest in stocks of large companies. Manager Richard Little has returned an annualized 39.4% over the past five years by buying firms and accelerating earnings.

Citizens Index
(800-223-7010,
www.citizensfunds.com, waidx)

This index fund has returned an annualized 26.1% over the past five years. It starts with Standard and Poor's 500-stock index, weeds out the half of the index that doesn't meet its social criteria, and adds about 150 "good" companies. Performance has been enhanced in recent years, because the resulting index emphasizes technology companies, which have had such a great run in the stock market.

Vanguard Calvert Social Index
(800-635-1511,
www.vanguard.com, vcsix)
This is another interesting index fund, a mostly large-company fund that's based on a socially responsible index, which was designed by the Calvert Group. Because it's so new (open since May 31, 2000), we wouldn't even mention this index fund, which is similar to Citizens, except for its low, 0.25% annual expense ratio.

Aquinas Equity Growth
(800-423-6369,
www.aquinasfunds.com, aqegx)
This fund promotes the investment guidelines of the National Conference of Catholic Bishops, which include opposition to contraceptive drugs. The fund takes a unique approach: This multi-manager fund buys stocks *before* looking for social blemishes. When it finds them, it lobbies the companies for change. The fund, which invests mainly in medium-size growth stocks, has returned an annualized 18.9% over the past three years and 21.8% over the past five years.

TWEEDY BROWNE GLOBAL VALUE

John Spears and brothers Christopher and William Browne are dyed-in-the-wool value investors, who delight in finding small and medium-size companies stuffed with cash or other valuable assets that other managers might overlook. (A company with far more assets than its stock-market value is usually a terrific buy.) They have been managing money in their unhurried, almost academic style since 1958 and have $19 million of their own money in this fund. Unique among the foreign funds listed here, Tweedy Browne hedges against all of its foreign currency exposure, so that a rise or fall in the dollar against other currencies has little effect on the portfolio's value. "We are stock pickers, not currency speculators," explains Spears. While currency gyrations tend to even out over time, currencies can be nearly as volatile as stocks over the short run. Thus, this fund is far less volatile than most foreign funds.

INVESTMENT STYLE:	international
THREE-YEAR RETURN:	14.34%
FIVE-YEAR RETURN:	18.57%
TEN-YEAR RETURN:	NA
ANNUAL EXPENSE RATIO:	1.41%
ANNUAL PORTFOLIO TURNOVER:	23%
BEST BENCHMARK:	Morgan Stanley Europe Australasia and Far East
VOLATILITY:	2
SAME MANAGER SINCE:	1993
TOTAL ASSETS:	$3.2 billion
MEDIAN MARKET VALUE:	$2.3 billion
MINIMUM INITIAL INVESTMENT:	$2,500, $500
PHONE NUMBER:	800-432-4789
WEB SITE:	www.tweedy.com
TICKER SYMBOL:	tbgvx

SPECIAL RISKS. Unlike the other foreign funds in this section, Tweedy, Browne is a global fund and typically invests 10% to 15% of its money in the U.S. (For more on global funds, see page 166.) Be aware of that when allocating your assets so that you don't end up with less invested in overseas stocks than you intended. Also, this is a conservative fund that won't keep pace with more aggressive funds in bull markets.

How to Pick Top Bond and Money-Market Funds

Low expenses are the key

E VER WISH YOU COULD STAY AT THE RITZ CARLTON and pay Days Inn prices? If so, you'll love buying bond funds. Being a cheapskate pays off in spades: You'll not only wind up with less expensive funds, but you'll usually get better-performing and lower-risk funds, too. Why? Because high expenses drag down bond funds' returns, and their managers must take greater chances if they hope to do well.

Expenses, of course, figure into the total returns of all kinds of funds. But a good stock-fund manager can often overcome the handicap of high expenses by skillful stock-picking. Not so with bond funds. A bond is a bond is a bond, and it's hard for a bond-fund manager to get an edge. As John Markese, president of the American Association of Individual Investors, puts it: "You're playing for a quarter of a point here, a sixteenth of a point there." Bond managers count their gains and losses in basis points—hundredths of a percentage point. Expense ratios, which often vary by one-half of one percentage point or more among bond funds, can overwhelm whatever value adroit management can add to a bond fund.

To test this premise, I lumped together all high-quality corporate-bond funds, mortgage-bond funds and government-bond funds, and then divided them into two categories: those with below-average expense ratios and those with above average-expense ratios. (The average was 1.01%.) As a group, the cheap-

er funds over the past one, three, five, ten, 15 and 20 years had:
- **higher total returns** than their more expensive brethren
- **higher dividend yields**
- **shorter maturities** in their portfolios (making them less sensitive to interest-rate fluctuations)
- **less month-to-month volatility.**

So, not only are these funds better-performing, they are also less risky. The same characteristics hold true when you look separately at the expense ratios of municipal-bond funds and high-yield, or junk-bond funds.

THE VANGUARD DIRT-CHEAP ADVANTAGE

What's more, dirt-cheap beats merely cheap. It turns out that funds in the cheaper half of cheap funds did better on all counts than their merely cheap counterparts. Many of the dirt-cheap bond funds (those that charge less than 0.69% of fund assets per year) are run by Vanguard. Vanguard is the lowest-cost provider of mutual funds. It's technically owned by its shareholders and doesn't try to turn a profit. As a result, it's hard to beat Vanguard when it comes to bonds, particularly municipal bonds.

Signposts of Quality

EXPENSES ARE AN IDEAL STARTING POINT FOR PICKING BOND funds. For most bond funds, the expense ratio should be no more than about 0.8%—just this side of dirt-cheap. Be especially frugal when looking at municipal-bond funds, which have lower yields than taxable funds. Conversely, you can tolerate higher expenses for junk-bond funds (or funds that contain a fair amount of junk), which can be nearly as different from one another as stock funds are. Here are other things to consider when you're shopping for a bond fund (all of which are listed for each fund discussed later in this chapter):

Total return. Don't fixate on the size of your monthly income check to the detriment of all else. The better number to know about a bond fund is its total return—the income yield plus (or minus) capital appreciation. Yield can be juiced up, but sometimes only by guaranteeing future declines in a fund's value. Total return is the bottom line.

Weighted average maturity. Make sure you compare apples with apples: Compare long-term funds with other long-term funds and short-term funds with other short-term funds. The most useful number to know is a fund's weighted average maturity, which essentially tells you how long the average bond holding in the fund has until its maturity date. A bond's maturity date is the date on which the issuing company or government agency is due to pay off all it owes on a bond. This date is set before bonds are sold—although often issuers are allowed to redeem bonds early. (A fund's maturity is "weighted," meaning bonds that make up a larger portion of the portfolio count for more than bonds that are a smaller part of the fund.) The higher a fund's weighted average maturity, the more long-term the fund is, and the more it will fluctuate in value as interest rates change. Other things being equal, long-term bond funds—those with high weighted average maturities—tend to be riskier than short-term bond funds.

Credit quality. A high-quality (or investment-grade) bond fund should hold mostly bonds rated BBB– or better by Standard & Poor's. The lower a bond's credit quality, the greater the risk that it will decline in value during periods of economic weakness, and the greater the risk that its issuer will default on interest payments. At the same time, low-credit-quality bonds tend to have higher yields and to be less sensitive to interest-rate changes. A fund's credit quality—the average quality of the bonds it holds—is also important when assessing its performance. Make sure to compare high-quality funds with other high-quality funds and low-quality funds with other low-quality funds.

Manager tenure. As with stock funds, a good past record isn't as meaningful if there's a new manager, so favor funds with experienced managers. Some top bond houses, such as Loomis Sayles and PIMCO, tend to hire top managers even for new funds.

Volatility. It's important to know how much a fund's performance bounces around from month to month. The lower a fund's volatility, the better it should hold up when rates rise (remember, bond yields always move in the opposite direction of bond prices—when bond prices fall, yields rise, and vice versa). For instance, a volatility score of 1 means that a taxable bond fund is less volatile than 90% of all taxable bond funds. For a muni fund, a score of 1 means it's less volatile than 90% of all tax-free bond funds.

Consistency. Even more so than with stock funds, you don't want a bond fund that tops the charts one year only to fall to the bottom the next. Bonds are the ballast of your portfolio. You want to hire a sure-handed skipper to manage your low-risk money.

Sales fees. It's difficult to justify paying a sales load for a bond fund. If you use a full-service broker and plan to hold your bonds for a long time, you'll likely do better buying and holding individual bonds if you have at least $50,000 to invest (see box on page 246). Among bond funds with loads, Bond Fund of America and FPA New Income are solid performers.

Bond Funds by Category

I'VE DIVIDED BOND FUNDS INTO SEVERAL BROAD CATEGORIES. Note that I haven't included all the varieties listed in Chapter 13. That's because many of the best bond funds tend to buy bonds from a number of different areas of the bond market, rather than confining themselves to one segment. Following are first-rate funds in several categories:

HIGH-GRADE CORPORATE BOND FUNDS

These mutual funds invest mainly in bonds of companies with high credit quality.

Harbor Bond

Through adept interest-rate calls and an unwillingness to go too far out on a limb, manager William Gross has built a consistently superior record over the past two decades. His dead-on forecast that rates would drop dramatically on long-term Treasuries in 2000 was just one example of his canny predictions. Harbor Bond reflects those skills and conservatism. Over the past three, five and ten years, it has delivered returns in the top 10% among its peers. Gross holds a lot of government bonds and mortgage-backed securities, and spices the portfolio with a few lower-quality bonds and foreign bonds.

THREE-YEAR RETURN: 5.68%
FIVE-YEAR RETURN: 7.27%
TEN-YEAR RETURN: 8.69%
ANNUAL EXPENSE RATIO: 0.65%
WEIGHTED AVERAGE MATURITY: 7.5 years

AVERAGE CREDIT QUALITY:	AAA
VOLATILITY:	7
SAME MANAGER SINCE:	1987
MINIMUM INITIAL INVESTMENT:	$2,000, $500 for IRAs
PHONE NUMBER:	800-422-1050
WEB SITE:	www.harborfunds.com
TICKER SYMBOL:	habdx

Loomis Sayles Bond

Sometimes called "the best bond picker in America," Dan Fuss has been managing bonds since the 1960s and still favors a slide rule over a computer for many calculations. His fund is a lot riskier than Harbor Bond, because Fuss buys longer-term bonds and tends to keep about a third of this fund in junk bonds. He ventures abroad, often finding attractive bonds in such locales as the Philippines. "We do a lot of strange things," Fuss says. Fortunately for shareholders, few of them fail. Even in periods of rising rates, such as 1994 and 1999, Loomis Sayles has managed to hold up relatively well.

THREE-YEAR RETURN:	4.56%
FIVE-YEAR RETURN:	NA
TEN-YEAR RETURN:	NA
ANNUAL EXPENSE RATIO:	1.00%
WEIGHTED AVERAGE MATURITY:	17.6 years
AVERAGE CREDIT QUALITY:	BBB
VOLATILITY:	10
SAME MANAGER SINCE:	1997
MINIMUM INITIAL INVESTMENT:	$5,000, $5,000
PHONE NUMBER:	800-633-3330
WEB SITE:	www.loomissayles.com
TICKER SYMBOL:	lsbrx

T. Rowe Price Spectrum Income

This fund of funds charges investors nothing beyond the costs of the underlying T. Rowe Price funds it invests in. It spreads its bets among seven other funds, including a high-quality corporate bond fund, a junk-bond fund, a money-market fund, a mortgage-backed fund, a foreign-bond fund, and even a high-yielding stock fund. The mix is adjusted periodically. The point of using different funds, says manager Ned Notzon, is that some are doing well when others are not. The method has worked: Spectrum Income has produced good returns with moderate risk.

THREE-YEAR RETURN:	4.54%
FIVE-YEAR RETURN:	7.07%
TEN-YEAR RETURN:	8.57%
ANNUAL EXPENSE RATIO:	0%
WEIGHTED AVERAGE MATURITY:	9.7 years
AVERAGE CREDIT QUALITY:	AA-
VOLATILITY:	7
SAME MANAGER SINCE:	1998
MINIMUM INITIAL INVESTMENT:	$2,500, $1,000
PHONE NUMBER:	800-638-5660
WEB SITE:	www.troweprice.com
TICKER SYMBOL:	rpsix

HIGH-YIELD CORPORATE BOND FUNDS

So-called junk-bond funds invest mostly in lower-quality bonds. While these funds can be nearly as volatile as some stock funds, in small helpings they not only provide high income but also help diversify your portfolio. You might consider putting about 25% of your bond money into junk-bond funds.

Fidelity Capital and Income

Fidelity is known for its stock funds but runs a pretty good bunch of bond funds, too. Fidelity Capital and Income, begun in 1977, has finished in the top 10% against other junk-bond funds over the past three, five, ten, 15 and 20 years—albeit with high volatility. David Glancy, who has managed the fund since January 1996, tries to buy lower-quality bonds when they are out of favor and slightly higher-quality (but still junk bonds) when they are popular. At this writing, junk bonds were in the midst of a three-year bear market. Returns had been meager in each of those years. Glancy was loading up on low-quality bonds. "The Federal Reserve will quit tightening at some point, we'll have the last default (of a company unable to pay off its bonds when they come due), and we'll rally hard," he predicted.

THREE-YEAR RETURN:	8.08%
FIVE-YEAR RETURN:	9.08%
TEN-YEAR RETURN:	12.68%
15-YEAR RETURN:	11.04%

ANNUAL EXPENSE RATIO:	0.82%
WEIGHTED AVERAGE MATURITY:	NA
AVERAGE CREDIT QUALITY:	B
VOLATILITY:	10
SAME MANAGER SINCE:	1996
MINIMUM INITIAL INVESTMENT:	$2,500, $500
PHONE NUMBER:	800-544-8888
WEB SITE:	www.fidelity.com
TICKER SYMBOL:	fagix

Northeast Investors Trust

Ernest Monrad has been investing in junk bonds since the 1960s, and his son Bruce joined him in 1993. Experience must count for something: This has been one of the best-performing junk-bond funds. The fund is not for the faint of heart, though. The Monrads often shop at the bottom of the junk-quality barrel, and they use leverage (borrowed money) to buy more bonds when they are bullish on junk bonds. They also hold some high-yielding stocks to flesh out their portfolio. In short: This is a risky bond fund, but one whose gambles have paid off handsomely.

THREE-YEAR RETURN:	2.63%
FIVE-YEAR RETURN:	7.87%
TEN-YEAR RETURN:	10.99%
15-YEAR RETURN:	10.19%
ANNUAL EXPENSE RATIO:	0.61%
WEIGHTED AVERAGE MATURITY:	7.1 years
AVERAGE CREDIT QUALITY:	B
VOLATILITY:	9
SAME MANAGER SINCE:	1960 (1993 for Bruce)
MINIMUM INITIAL INVESTMENT:	$1,000, $500
PHONE NUMBER:	800-225-6704
WEB SITE:	www.northeastinvestors.com
TICKER SYMBOL:	nthex

Mortgage Funds

These funds invest mainly in home mortgages. They are less pre-dictable than other bond funds, because they lag when rates fall (and homeowners refinance at lower rates), as well as when rates rise. But they also pay higher yields. The key is not to overdo mortgage-backed funds (about 25% of your bond portfolio is enough) and to stick to funds that keep it simple.

Vanguard GNMA
This fund gives you just what the label says: government-guaranteed mortgages backed by Ginnie Mae (the Government National Mortgage Association). Manager Paul Kaplan has worked on the fund since its inception in 1980 and took sole control in 1994. He doesn't stick his neck out very far on the direction of interest rates, but he buys high-yielding securities because he knows many shareholders depend on the fund's income. "I pay attention to yield," Kaplan says. The fund has produced top returns with low volatility.

THREE-YEAR RETURN:	5.36%
FIVE-YEAR RETURN:	6.62%
TEN-YEAR RETURN:	7.67%
ANNUAL EXPENSE RATIO:	0.30%
WEIGHTED AVERAGE MATURITY:	NA
AVERAGE CREDIT QUALITY:	AAA
VOLATILITY:	3
SAME MANAGER SINCE:	1994
MINIMUM INITIAL INVESTMENT:	$3,000, $1,000
PHONE NUMBER:	800-635-1511
WEB SITE:	www.vanguard.com
TICKER SYMBOL:	vfiix

SHORT-TERM BOND FUNDS
Funds with short weighted average maturities, say three years or less, can be a great place to stash money you plan to spend in a couple of years. You get higher income than you would in a money-market fund, and you incur little risk of loss if rates rise.

Strong Advantage and Strong Short-Term Bond
Both these funds use the same method to obtain relatively high yields with low volatility. The only difference is their weighted average maturities. Ultra-short-term Advantage, run by Jeffery Koch, keeps average maturity at a mere 0.7 years, while Short-Term Bond, run by Bradley Tank, keeps average maturity at around 2.5 years. To make up for their relatively high expense ratios, both these funds pick up extra yield by placing 20% or more of assets in junk bonds. In a weakening economy, some

bonds might face a risk of default.

THREE-YEAR RETURN:	5.43% (4.88%)
FIVE-YEAR RETURN:	5.98% (6.14%)
TEN-YEAR RETURN:	6.71% (7%)
ANNUAL EXPENSE RATIO:	0.7% (0.8%)
WEIGHTED AVERAGE MATURITY:	0.6 years (1.7 years)
AVERAGE CREDIT QUALITY:	A (BBB)
VOLATILITY:	1 (1)
SAME MANAGER SINCE:	1991 (1990)
MINIMUM INITIAL INVESTMENT:	$2,500, $250 ($2,500, $250)
PHONE NUMBER:	800-368-1030
WEB SITE:	www.strongfunds.com
TICKER SYMBOL:	stadx (sstbx)

USAA Short-Term Bond

This fund buys high-quality, short-term bonds, exposing investors to far less risk than either of the Strong funds. As with many USAA funds, expenses are higher than Vanguard's but lower than just about anybody else's. Add to that USAA's record for steady fund management—rarely topping the charts, but almost never providing unpleasant surprises—and you have a recipe for a good, solid short-term fund that will deliver more income than a money-market fund (this fund actually holds about one-third of assets in cash) with very little extra risk.

THREE-YEAR RETURN:	5.23%
FIVE-YEAR RETURN:	6.04%
TEN-YEAR RETURN:	NA%
ANNUAL EXPENSE RATIO:	0.5%
WEIGHTED AVERAGE MATURITY:	2.4 years
AVERAGE CREDIT QUALITY:	BBB
VOLATILITY:	1
SAME MANAGER SINCE:	1993
MINIMUM INITIAL INVESTMENT:	$3,000, $250
PHONE NUMBER:	800-382-8722
WEB SITE:	www.usaa.com
TICKER SYMBOL:	ussbx

Vanguard Short-Term Corporate

Like most Vanguard funds, this one is straightforward. Robert Auwaerter has produced results similar to Strong Short-Term

Bond's. Indeed, the weighted average maturity is similar, at 2.4 years. But this fund doesn't buy any junk bonds, and expenses are just 0.27%. You won't get quite the kick that you get from the Strong funds, but the risks are much lower.

THREE-YEAR RETURN:	5.34%
FIVE-YEAR RETURN:	5.90%
TEN-YEAR RETURN:	6.88%
15-YEAR RETURN:	7.59%
ANNUAL EXPENSE RATIO:	0.27%
WEIGHTED AVERAGE MATURITY:	2.4 years
AVERAGE CREDIT QUALITY:	A
VOLATILITY:	2
SAME MANAGER SINCE:	1984
MINIMUM INITIAL INVESTMENT:	$3,000, $1,000
PHONE NUMBER:	800-635-1511
WEB SITE:	www.vanguard.com
TICKER SYMBOL:	vfstx

MONEY-MARKET FUNDS

These funds hold bonds with less than six months until they mature. While their yields vary, they seek to maintain a stable share price of $1. That makes them an ideal place to park short-term savings—money you don't need in a bank checking account, but that you wouldn't want to put in a risky investment. Most money-market funds offer check-writing privileges.

Because money-market funds invest in only the shortest-term bonds, and because federal rules require them to invest almost all their assets in high-quality bonds, expenses are paramount in picking a money fund. Fund sponsors know this, so sometimes they hold "sales"—waiving expenses on a money-market fund while they build up assets and a good track record, and then slowly reinstating expenses. If you're prepared to move your money to another fund when a sale ends at a money-market fund, pick one that is waiving expenses. But if you write a lot of checks on money-markets, you'll need to be careful not to bounce a check while you're transferring your money.

Low expenses. The simpler way to shop for a money-market fund is to look for one that charges consistently low expenses and stick with it. Two good ones are *USAA Mutual Money Market* (800-531-8181, www.usaa.com) which charges 0.46%, and *Vanguard Money*

Money-Market Math

TO FIGURE YOUR taxable-equivalent yield on a muni money-market (or any muni fund) so you can compare it with the taxable yields of other funds, divide the yield by one minus your tax bracket. For instance, a 3% yield on a muni money-market, divided by 1 minus 31% (or .69), equals a 4.35% taxable-equivalent yield. That means a taxpayer in the 31% bracket would have to earn more than 4.34% on a taxable money-market to do better than in a 3% tax-exempt money-market.

Market Reserves Prime (800-635-1511, www.vanguard.com), which charges 0.33%.

Miscellaneous service charges. When you pick a money fund, check whether its sponsor assesses pesky little charges for, say, writing a check or more than a certain number of checks, or your balance falling below a certain amount, or even for making deposits or withdrawals. Also find out the minimum for which you can write a check on your money-market account, and whether the fund returns your checks or copies of them. Dreyfus Basic Money Market (800-645-6561, www.dreyfus.com), for instance, requires you to maintain a minimum balance of $10,000, and has a minimum check amount of $1,000. It also charges a $2 fee for every check if your balance is below $50,000 (other Dreyfus money-market funds have lower requirements).

Deep pockets. In the unlikely event that a money-market holds bonds that go into default, it helps to have your money invested with a well-capitalized company, such as Dreyfus, Fidelity, T. Rowe Price or Strong. Such companies have the financial strength to eat the loss, rather than forcing you to. If you're very concerned about your share price ever falling below a dollar, which is what could happen if a borrower defaults on some of a money-market's bonds, you can invest in a slightly lower-yielding Treasury-only money-market, such as Vanguard Treasury Money Market, which is virtually risk-free.

MUNICIPAL BOND FUNDS

These are exempt from federal income taxes and usually are good deals for anyone in the 28% tax bracket or higher. Funds that hold muni bonds issued in a single state are also exempt from that state's taxes, but generally charge higher expenses and limit your diversification. There's really no need to look beyond Vanguard for tax-exempt funds. Besides charging the lowest costs, around 0.2% annually, Vanguard has Ian MacKinnon. He has served capably as lead manager of these funds since 1981,

Bonds or Bond Funds?

IN TWO CIRCUMSTANCES, it's cheaper and sometimes better (though more work) to buy individual bonds rather than bond funds:
• if you're buying Treasury securities
• if you're investing more than $50,000 in municipal bonds and plan to hold them to maturity.

Individual municipal bonds

Buy individual munis only if you're fairly certain you'll hold them until maturity. Using an online or full-service broker, put together a "laddered" portfolio—one with staggered maturities, which will help insulate you against interest-rate fluctuations. You might, say, buy one bond maturing in roughly four years, one in eight years, one in 12 years and one in 16 years. Then, when the four-year bond matures, replace it with another 16-year bond, which returns your portfolio to the same maturities it had originally.

Purchase only low-risk, AA or AAA-rated bonds, and, to keep things simple, stick to general-obligation bonds, which are guaranteed by the taxing power of a city, county or state. Or buy insured bonds, which automatically are rated AAA. If possible, avoid bonds that can be called (redeemed early by their issuer).

Comparison shop among brokers for the best prices on specific bonds. With some bargaining you should be able to keep your commissions to no more than 1.5% of the bonds' price. You can sell these bonds before they mature, but if you do, your expenses will likely wind up higher than if you'd simply bought a muni fund. By purchasing high-quality individual munis and holding them to maturity, you'll probably earn as much as you would in a bond fund and keep your risks lower.

Treasury securities

Treasury securities are as safe as the U.S. government, so there's no need for the diversification or professional management you get in a mutual fund. You can buy Treasuries through a broker for about $50, or you can avoid commissions by buying them directly from the Bureau of the Public Debt (Division of Customer Services, Washington, DC 20239; www.publicdebt.treas.gov; 202-874-4000) or from any of the 36 Federal Reserve banks and branches across the country. (The regional banks and branches, listed in the blue government pages of your phone book, are usually easier to deal with than the Bureau of the Public Debt.) Buying Treasuries directly from the government almost always costs less than buying a government-bond fund. Also, if you need to sell a Treasury before maturity, the government charges just $34.

ensuring that they buy high-quality bonds and don't make overly aggressive interest rate bets. The results, over most time periods, are among the best of any muni funds.

Vanguard Intermediate-Term Tax-Exempt (800-635-1511; www.vanguard.com; VWITX) makes a good center-of-the-plate bond fund. It has a weighted average maturity of about six years, which means it won't get killed when rates rise, yet it produces generous income.

For the more aggressive part of your portfolio, consider *Vanguard Long-Term Tax-Exempt* or *Vanguard High-Yield Tax-Exempt*, both with average maturities of more than 10 years. (High Yield is not a junk-bond fund; its average credit quality is AA.)

For short-term money, *Vanguard Limited-Term Tax-Exempt*, with an average maturity of 2.8 years, and *Vanguard Short-Term Tax-Exempt*, with an average maturity of 1.2 years, are good choices.

Another bond fund worth considering is *Excelsior Long-Term Tax Exempt* (800-446-1012; www.excelsiorfunds.com; UMLTX). A top-performing fund—albeit one with high risks because of its recent 19.9-year weighted average maturity and its manager's attempts to guess the direction of interest rates—Excelsior has returned an annualized 2.57% over the past three years, 5.45% over the past five years, and 7.43% over the past ten years. Annual expenses are 0.76%. Manager Kenneth McAlley buys longer-term bonds when he thinks rates will fall; he buys shorter-term bonds and even raises the percentage of assets in cash when he thinks rates will rise. "The major risk to bond investors is rising interest rates," he notes. "If you're not aware of that, you're asleep at the watch."

On the other end of the risk spectrum, *Sit Tax-Free Income* (800-332-5580; www.sitfunds.com; SNTIX) is also worth a look. This fund is for the risk-averse investor looking for tax-free income. Its weighted average maturity is generally between 14 and 19 years, but that overstates its volatility because manager Michael Brilley hunts for high-yielding bonds with low sensitivity to changes in interest rates. Not surprisingly, the fund has held up well in bear markets. It returned 3.11% over the past three years and 5.25% over the past five years. Annual expenses are 0.71%. "We buy high-income, stable-value securities," Brilley says. "When you do that, you don't have to worry about interest-rate forecasting."

Key Points

- *Expenses are crucial in choosing bond funds and money-market funds.*
- *Vanguard's low expenses are hard to beat, but there are other good bond funds.*
- *While a fund's long-term record is important, so is its volatility, weighted average maturity and average credit quality.*
- *Compare bond funds with their peers.*
- *Some investors will do better with individual bonds than they will with bond funds.*

AFTERWORD

The DiBenedettos: Novices No More

P AUL AND NANCY DIBENEDETTO HAVEN'T APPEARED much in the book since the early chapters. Yet a lot has changed for them since I first knocked on their front door just before Christmas 1996. On October 12, 1997, Nancy gave birth to their second son, Andrew. As a result, the DiBenedettos are already salting even more money away for college—a move made easier since Nancy got a promotion at work, too. Instead of a recreation therapist at the National Rehabilitation Hospital, she's now a quality improvement specialist, working, among other things, to prepare the hospital for visits by hospital accrediting organizations. Paul Jr., now 6, and Andrew, now 4, are thriving in day care.

The DiBenedettos' investing plans are on track, helped by the soaring stock market of the late 1990s and unhindered by 2000's flat market through the summer's end. Paul is adding more each month to his 403(b) plan through his employer, the Arlington County, Va., school system. Nancy's retirement plan at work is funded entirely by her employer. For college money for their children, the DiBenedettos are investing $500 a month. They are dividing that money among just three funds recommended in this book: *Artisan International, Harbor Capital Appreciation* and *Selected American Shares*.

In putting together their portfolio, Paul and Nancy skipped

the funds that invest in stocks of small companies suggested in the "Investing for College" chapter. That's because they are investing in small-stock funds through Paul's 403(b) at work—which, of course, will go towards their retirement.

In essence, Paul and Nancy are building one portfolio that will finance both college and retirement—something I recommend in the book to keep your finances simpler. The only plan without a sales charge available through Paul's school system buys USAA funds. While the USAA funds don't have the sterling records of the funds recommended in Chapter 17, they are solid, low-cost funds. Paul is putting $200 a month into his retirement plan. As the couple's salaries grow, and especially after the children go off to college, they'll escalate their retirement investing.

The DiBenedettos also made another major investment since the first edition of this book: They traded their increasingly cramped condominium for a four-bedroom split level. "It's a nice house," says Paul. "We like it a lot. Nice neighbors, too." The couple also bought a new sports utility vehicle to accommodate their family. They temporarily reduced their retirement and college contributions to make the down payments, something most families find inevitable when they make major purchases. But the DiBenedettos, now that they have seen how their money can grow in the stock market, were quick to resume investing. And they've found that they can invest without having to deprive themselves. They have remained active skiers, visiting Vermont in 2000. They also spent a week at the beach, and enjoyed camping and canoeing with their children.

In the spring of 2000, technology stocks crumbled. Nancy admits that she was nervous, "but we rode it out." Being more knowledgeable than before about the stock market made investing easier—even during the sell-off, she says. She hardly needed to have worried. The couple's funds are well diversified, and the panic in tech stocks barely, and then only briefly, affected their net worth.

Why did the DiBenedettos delay investing until our conversations in 1996 and 1997? "The biggest barrier for us was procrastination," Paul says. Adds Nancy, "We were a plain and simple couple in terms of not investing a lot and trusting in the good old savings account. Taking that first leap into finally investing in something was definitely difficult." Indeed, the first step in investing is usually the hardest. Nancy's father, a retired Navy admiral, loves stocks. But she says the couple has discovered that funds are more their speed. "We don't have the time to find the stocks and track them. Instead, we trust in the funds to do it for us." While Nancy admits to still being a little intimidated by the numbers in the business section of the newspaper, Paul says he reads the fund listings and the business news more often than he used to. "Owning funds gives you more of a feeling of personal interest. It gives you a sense of ownership," Paul says. "It's a lot better than just putting money in a savings account. I feel comfortable with investing. We're in control of things."

I hope investing in mutual funds will do all those things for you, too—and help you make your financial dreams come true.

INDEX

Investing for retirement.
See Retirement planning
Investing styles
about, 173–175
definitions of stock size,
177–178
fads and, 175–176
four style types, 180–181
fund managers and,
181–183
growth *versus* value
considerations, 178–180
investors and, 181–183
large- and small-company
styles, 175–178
large-company growth
funds, 181
large-company value
funds, 181
making valid comparisons,
176–177
mini styles, 182
product mix and, 174–175
reducing a portfolio's
volatility, 177
shifting, 183
small-company growth
funds, 181
small-company value
funds, 181
stock funds, 64
Investment objectives, 64,
164–168
Investment pitfalls
all market funds, 131–132
bear market funds,
131–132
chasing performance,
124–126
delaying action, 129
historical perspective, 130
instinct and emotion and,
128
keeping funds failing to
keep up, 127–128
market timing, 122–124
momentum investing, 125

seeking perfection, 131
shorting stock funds,
133–134
single-industry sector
investing, 126–127
strategy and, 125–126
too many funds, 133
too much information,
129–130
waiting for stocks to fall,
121–122
IRAs. See Individual
retirement accounts

J

Janus Mercury fund, 68–69,
86, 214–215
Jellison, David, 226
Junk bonds, 169, 236,
239–242

K

Kaplan, Paul, 242
Keithler, William, 228
Keogh plans, 63
Kiplinger's Personal Finance,
195
Koch, Jeffrey, 242

L

Lammert, Warren, 214–215
Landis, Kevin, 228
Large-company funds
growth funds, 64, 204–205
investment styles, 175–178,
180–181
value funds, 64
Late retirement portfolios, 72

**Legg Mason Opportunity
fund,** 68, 70, 86, 221
Levy, Michael, 231
**Liberal funds/socially
responsible funds,** 232
Life expectancy
considerations in
retirement planning, 54
Lipper fund research, 107
Load and no-load funds,
6–7, 108, 118–119
See also Sales charges
and transaction fees
Long-term investing
average returns, 154–156
bear market, 158–159
combining stocks, bonds,
and cash, 156
historical perspective,
156–159
inflation and, 152–153
intermediate periods, 154
international examples, 157
long periods, 154
performance over time, 152
"performance snapshots,"
153–156
reward and risk over time,
153, 156–157
short periods, 154
stocks *versus* bonds *versus*
cash table, 155
Long-term-growth funds
about, 64, 165
profiles, 218–224
Loomis Sayles Bond, 69–70,
86–87, 90, 239

M

MacKinnon, Ian, 246–247
Magazines, mutual fund, 195
Managed funds
versus index funds, 38–42
tax-managed index
funds, 62